News for US

Citizen-Centered Journalism

Paula Lynn Ellis
The Poynter Institute
The Kettering Foundation

Paul S. Voakes
University of Colorado Boulder

Lori Bergen
University of Colorado Boulder

 cognella®
SAN DIEGO

Bassim Hamadeh, CEO and Publisher
Todd R. Armstrong, Publisher
Michelle Piehl, Senior Project Editor
Alia Bales, Production Editor
Abbie Goveia, Graphic Design Assistant
Trey Soto, Licensing Coordinator
Natalie Piccotti, Director of Marketing
Kassie Graves, Senior Vice President of Editorial
Jamie Giganti, Director of Academic Publishing

3970 Sorrento Valley Blvd., Ste. 500, San Diego, CA 9212

To OUR FRIEND DAVID HOLWERK, WHO ENCOURAGED US, CAJOLED US AND ultimately conferred his trademark "Wholly Adequate" stamp of high praise on the book he didn't live to hold in his hands. We are grateful to have had this journalist extraordinaire as an accomplice at the Kettering Foundation. (Feb. 5, 1947–Nov. 23, 2020)

WHOLLY
ADEQUATE

Brief Contents

Detailed Contents

Foreword

Neil Brown

President, The Poynter Institute for Media Studies

J OURNALISM JOB BOARDS ARE FULL OF OPPORTUNITIES FOR "AUDIENCE ENGAGE-ment" editors — the strategic multimedia minds who help news organizations grow their social media profiles and web traffic to connect their news content, advertising and brand with their viewers, readers and customers.

Over the past decade, audience editors have become as much a part of the newsroom as the reporters on the city hall or cops beat. That's not a lament. Engagement sits squarely at the intersection of relevance (useful journalism) and revenue (sustainability). Direct outreach to readers recognizes that in today's competitive media environment, we must constantly market our work rather than rely, high-mindedly, on the long-held belief that journalism is so obviously valuable that "if we build it, they will come."

To be clear, journalism remains as valuable as ever; independent, trustworthy information is absolutely essential to our democracy and civic life. But with the collapse of traditional business models that pay for journalism, the pursuit of new resources has led to a co-opting of the term "engagement." Rather than describe an intellectual, emotional and even lasting involvement — a *relationship* — with the citizens we serve, the term has become business-speak for the potential to glean dollars from readers and advertisers.

The day-to-day language of engagement is a litany of metrics, such as "time on site," "page views per session," or "visits per month." Again, no lament. The science of audience development is putting more eyes on our journalism than ever and reaching more people in more places and, yes, replenishing some of the dollars needed to produce it.

But what of a deeper engagement — the kind that speaks to a purpose beyond a customer transaction? Wouldn't the connection between journalists and citizens be of greater value and meaning if they were authentically engaged with each other on matters of importance to their communities?

In *News for US: Citizen-Centered Journalism*, three of America's leading journalist-scholars have offered a powerful and optimistic playbook for journalists to embrace new and adaptive thinking about *how* journalism can be an effective tool of democracy, rather than settle for the trope that it simply is.

Paula Ellis, Paul Voakes and Lori Bergen are eloquent on the stakes for both journalism and democracy, which are sorely being tested by tribalism, misinformation and an erosion of trust. Ellis, Voakes and Bergen have dedicated their professional lives to the belief that journalism's main purpose is to serve communities and help citizens participate in democracy. For decades they have practiced the craft, taught newcomers the ropes and challenged the world of journalism to hold-fast to high standards of ethics, accuracy and relevance.

In *News for US*, they give voice to next-level thinking. While an "audience-first" economic imperative has properly forced journalists to move beyond the generations-old attitude that "we're the experts, eat your peas," the authors show that journalism needs even deeper change if it is to strengthen democracy. It needs a new mindset.

Should we call it a "citizen-first" approach? The fascinating case studies in *News for US* reveal that a better description might be "journalist and citizen together."

Ellis, Voakes and Bergen champion "relational journalism" and their wonderfully accessible book explains the concept and offers specific skills training. They are unabashed in what they believe it will take: a professional realignment.

Rather than a patriarchal approach to representing the interests of the readers, relational journalists start their work in collaboration with them. KPCC, a major public radio station in Los Angeles, asked listeners to help put together its "Human Voter Guide," creating the questions for politicians, involving listeners in two-way follow ups and editing — all while bringing genuine journalistic rigor and polish to the work.

The leading statewide news organization in Alabama, AL.com, enlisted community members to join with their journalists and create a start-up of sorts within its own halls to tackle some of the thorniest local issues, including Confederate monuments and abortion rights. Citizens collaborated as the journalists employed fresh storytelling forms such as cartoon histories, video commentary and podcasts. Called "Reckon," the site and its related spinoffs dive as deep into issues as any Sunday paper exposé and have, themselves, become an expression of democracy in action.

Ellis, Voakes and Bergen make clear there will be fits and starts, but that a collaborative approach is taking root — and gaining results — in a number of news organizations. And that's what makes the timing of this book exciting and vital: relational journalism is poised to move beyond the beta phase.

The authority of this textbook emanates from individuals who have lived and breathed this cause for decades. Ellis has helped shape every corner of the journalism field. As an editor, publisher and strategist, there are few industry professionals who can match her record of driving editorial and revenue results, be it running a small community-oriented newspaper, a national Washington-based newsroom, or directing a large newspaper chain's pivot to the internet. For the past decade she has directed her boundless energies to the cause of democracy, journalism and citizenship.

Voakes' distinguished record as one of the leading journalism educators of the past generation speaks to an expertise across disciplines. He is an award-winning writer and has been honored extensively for teaching and writing that is relevant to students and professionals.

Bergen is the founding dean of the College of Media, Communication and Information at the University of Colorado Boulder. She has been a strong advocate for public service journalism and has spearheaded innovative partnerships such as a Milwaukee program that brought Marquette University together with a major neighborhood support organization and an online news service to cover the challenges faced by disadvantaged urban residents and identify solutions.

I am grateful to be able to lean on Ellis and Bergen, who both are trustees at the Poynter Institute for Media Studies. They not only are tireless advocates for quality journalism and the pro-democracy ideas put forth in this book, but they are also tremendous at horizon-watching. My belief in their findings is born of firsthand experience with their rigorous thinking and incredible decency.

Several weeks after the police killing of George Floyd, a Pulitzer Prize-winning reporter contacted Poynter with an idea. She had chronicled "what protesters want" while spending time with peaceful demonstrators on her city's streets. The newspaper had quoted police about what they saw from their own vantage about the marchers, the tension and at times the violence. Would it be possible, the reporter wondered, to convene the protesters, the police and perhaps some citizens for a sit-down? Maybe the dialogue would yield ideas for moving forward.

This reporter believed her story was the start of something, not the destination. She said the leaders of her news organization had no objection to bringing people together, but there just wasn't time or much of an apparatus to figure it out. The pandemic's ups and downs prompted everyone to table the project.

But I've got an idea. I'm sending them this book.

Preface

IN THE MIDST OF THE DISRUPTIONS AND DISTRUST THAT HAVE PLAGUED TRA-ditional media in recent years, and a degree of polarization rarely seen in American history, a new style of journalism is emerging. Dozens of news organizations, from corporate powerhouses to home-office startups, are reviving a classic role of American journalism: inspiring and enabling Americans to do the difficult, authentic and ultimately rewarding work of citizenship in a democratic society.

These journalists view their communities not as an audience or customers but as people trying to get common problems solved. They see themselves not as experts controlling the latest information but as participants in a vast ecology of information — and as partners, at times, with community members in the production of news and features. They see their facilitation of community dialogue as every bit as important as their actual posting of the story. This kind of journalism is so transparent, so inclusive and so committed to community-building that it has the potential to bring about a decline in trolling and "fake news" accusations.

This book is a first-ever guide to this new approach — one that enriches the skill set of the 21st-century journalist with the mindset of civic engagement. In this textbook, we explain the principles of citizen-centered journalism and apply them to the realities of news and feature reporting. Along the way, readers will meet leading innovators and experimenters in these new forms who will describe their challenges and offer their guidance.

The potential is here to revitalize American journalism — and in the process revitalize American democracy.

Journalists like those featured in this book are changing the way they relate to and interact with members of the public. Our term for this shift is "relational journalism." People once thought of as "the audience" are respected as capable citizens and, at times, as co-producers of useful, action-mobilizing information. In this new role, journalism is more facilitative. It promotes dialogue , deliberation and shared sense-making. It recognizes that because no one media outlet alone sets the public agenda, journalism must adapt its role and create unique value. It embraces the full participation of members of the public, all of whom have access to a host of media distribution platforms.

Now is the time for this book. Its central ideas, once inchoate and theoretical, are beginning to take shape in pioneering news outlets across the nation and world. Articles and essays on this phenomenon have appeared from time to time, but this is the first comprehensive, book-length treatment, and the first to weave the concepts of relational journalism with its emerging practices. Our research methods have blended academic scholarship with case studies that highlight practical innovations to produce a comprehensive look at the emergence of this fundamental shift in the journalistic mindset. At a time when journalism is struggling in so many ways, this book offers a way forward. Our hope is that it will inspire further exploration by both students and professionals.

The book is the product of the decades-long personal journeys of its three authors.

Over the course of her four-decade media career, Paula Ellis repeatedly returned to one motivating question: How could journalism better serve democracy in communities and across the nation? As a Knight Ridder Washington bureau editor in 1988, Ellis helped supervise the presidential campaign coverage and got a first-hand look at the widening gap between the interests of the professional political class and the concerns of everyday Americans. This election also proved pivotal for journalism when editors across the country began to recognize that their reporting didn't adequately address their readers' concerns or include their voices. Thus was the public journalism movement born. During this period, Ellis, then managing editor of *The State* in Columbia, South Carolina, and a proponent of new, more inclusive approaches, heard an admonition from Kettering Foundation's David Mathews that would guide her career: The public was not apathetic; it had been squeezed out of the public square and now needed pathways to participation. This, and the onset of the internet age, inspired a career of inquiry and innovation. As a journalist, Ellis was a reporter, editor, publisher and ultimately a vice president of Knight Ridder. After the sale of Knight Ridder, Ellis joined the Knight Foundation as a vice president focused on transformational change in journalism and communities. In 2013, her pursuit of answers to that one simple question led Ellis to the Kettering Foundation where, as a senior associate, she collaborates with program officers and the foundation's extensive network of civic innovators to explore how to make democracy work as it should. Kettering is a place of serendipity — a lucky space designed so that people of like mind can meet sort-of, by chance. That's exactly how this textbook came about. We three authors buddied up thanks to Kettering.

Ellis and her colleagues at Kettering had been hosting learning exchanges with media innovators, and separately with journalism educators, to explore how their work — doing journalism and teaching it — could be reimagined to better serve democracy.

Lori Bergen, a journalism educator and administrator, was a regular participant in these exchanges. As incoming president of the Association for Education in Journalism and Mass Communication (AEJMC) in 2015, she worked with Paula Ellis, David Holwerk and other Kettering Foundation staff to develop a presidential initiative dedicated to the promotion of research and teaching that advanced journalism's role in civic engagement. The initiative included a special call for research on developing pedagogy and curriculum for journalism education that could help journalists support the work of citizens in a democracy and to define and address their shared public problems.

Paul Voakes was an editorial writer for the San Jose *Mercury News* when Knight-Ridder owned the paper and when the company began experimenting with public-journalism projects. He then became a professor of journalism, first at Indiana University and then the University of Colorado, and for the last 25 years he has continued to explore the viability of public journalism in a fast-changing media environment — both in his teaching and in his research. As president of AEJMC in 2016–17, he continued the organization's focus, initiated by Lori Bergen, on applied research into innovations in citizen-centered journalism.

After several animated conversations at AEJMC conferences and Kettering meetings, the three of us realized that our field urgently needed a textbook for relational journalism — one that encompassed both its theory and its practice. For the next two years, writing this book became our shared mission, and our passion.

Theory Meets Practice

This is a reporting textbook that takes the unusual step of presenting a new conceptual framework to deepen students' understanding of the book's innovative reporting practices.

Part I lays the conceptual foundation for what we will refer to as relational journalism for the 21st century. In Chapter 1, we explore the basic relationship between democracy and journalism. We examine the changes of the last 25 years that have profoundly altered the role of journalism in society, not the least of which is the replacement of the exclusive institution of professional journalism with a complex, decentralized information ecosystem that includes all manner of digital communicators. Unlike other journalism texts, we outline the ways in which studies in psychology, technology, sociology and other fields have merged to provide new understandings of networked communities — and the basis of hope for greater levels of citizenship in the future. By understanding networked communities, students can better understand journalism's role in networked communication.

Chapter 2 takes us to the theoretical heart of the book: a deeper dive into relational journalism. We explore the literature on media's *facilitative* role, which calls upon journalists to assist in any way plausible the work of citizens in a democracy. By building relationships with citizens and among citizens, journalists begin to practice relational journalism — and in the process begin to build civic capacity in the communities they cover. By turning away from "extractive" or "transactional" journalism, in which the journalist's relationship with citizens lasts only as long as it takes to get the story (or maybe just a good quote), journalists have a chance at recovering that elusive asset known as trust.

In Chapter 3, we take an important historical detour to explore the roots of this book's theme — roots that were set down in the 1990s under the banner of public journalism, or civic journalism. The chapter gives current trends in relational journalism some valuable context (we have found that most students and young journalists are unaware of the public journalism movement.) Rather than just summarizing public journalism's controversy in the 1990s, we analyze what was learned and in what forms it has re-emerged in recent years.

In Chapter 4, we confront that tricky 21st-century question of "Who is a journalist?" We explain a shift (in thinking about "journalist") from a state of employment to a set of attitudes and behaviors that advance a community's need for information and for problem-solving capacity. Rather than the usual contrast of "citizen journalist" with "professional journalist," we present a continuum of collaborative relationships by which more authentic journalism is being done.

The remainder of the book brings Part I's new ideas to life. In Part II, we distill from the theories and concepts of Part I what we call the Five Principles of Relational Journalism. To help with real-world applications of these principles, we have peppered the chapters in Part II with case studies. Based on our own professional and academic experience, we developed a list of innovative news organizations that seemed to be practicing some aspect of relational journalism. For these case studies, we conducted in-depth interviews with leaders of 19 news entities between July 2018 and June 2019. Eight of the case studies involved physical observation of journalists in their workplaces and interviews with several journalists at each site. For the remaining 11 news organizations, we conducted Zoom video interviews with the editorial leaders. The authors have been informally researching the emergence of citizen-centered journalism for more than a decade; this book also is informed by the dozens of innovative news organizations we have worked with over the years.

We introduce each principle more fully in Chapter 5, but here is a preview:

Journalism Is in Itself an Essential Democratic Practice

Chapter 6 will introduce the myriad ways in which journalists are coming to realize that they can do more than simply supply information that may produce informed voters. Here we get our first examples of how journalists are doing that. We introduce journalists from Your Voice Ohio, a collaboration of 53 news organizations in and around Ohio that shares coverage of issues identified as important by citizens in community discussions; Solutions Journalism Network, a New York-based nonprofit that is developing and spreading the practice of going beyond the reporting of problems, to seeking solutions as well; New Jersey News Commons, which facilitates collaboration among news outlets in New Jersey, most pointedly among small, local outlets; and Zócalo, a Los Angeles-based nonprofit that works to connect people from diverse backgrounds to ideas and to each other, largely by organizing events.

Journalists and Citizens Are Collaborators

In Chapter 7 we show that many of the innovative news organizations we observed are succeeding by blending the best in professionals' and citizens' work. Professional journalists are trained in specific skills, but we consider also what collaborating citizens can bring as well. We feature journalists from Hearken, a media platform and consulting group that advocates for story development that begins with — not ends with — feedback from the public; WBEZ's "Curious City," the first radio program to adopt Hearken's principles; City Bureau, a nonprofit news outlet in Chicago that trains and pays residents to gather local news with new, citizen-centered approaches; KALW in Oakland, which has turned to the Maynard Institute's "Voices" program to train residents from underserved neighborhoods to tell the stories of their communities; and GroundSource, a mobile engagement platform that helps journalists listen more carefully to members of the communities they serve.

Journalists Facilitate the Work of Citizens

Beyond informing voters with comprehensive reports and analyses, journalism serves democracy more deeply by helping to build the "civic capacity" of a community. Here we present a skill set, with exemplars, that is unlikely to appear in any other journalism text: listening for "shared values" among community members that are not immediately obvious; facilitating dialogue among people who think they are mired in intense disagreement; helping people identify the "common good" beyond an immediate problem. We describe the work of AL.com in Birmingham, Alabama, which hopes to regain the public's trust by working together with community members to identify, discuss and solve the state's most complex public problems; Spaceship Media, which has pioneered "dialog journalism" to bridge different perspectives among citizens and reduce polarization; *The Tennessean*, Nashville's leading newspaper, whose editorial-pages staff invokes creative approaches like book clubs to engage residents in discussions aimed at solving the region's difficult problems; and the *Times Record News* of Wichita Falls, Texas, which led the search for solutions to the city's chronic water shortage.

Relational Journalism Updates Time-Honored Traditions

As we searched for innovative ways to better serve democratic practice, we realized we simply cannot jettison those practices and principles that have made journalism the positive force it has been since the founding of the American republic. These include truth-seeking and accuracy; fairness and the battle against bias; independence; investigative journalism's "watchdog" role; accountability; and a consistent sense of what is newsworthy. But in Chapter 9, we suggest a "refresh" so that the traditions are still relevant and meaningful in today's fast-changing media environment. We offer case studies of KPCC, the Murrow Award-winning radio station in Pasadena, California, which experiments with its relationship with the public with projects like Unheard LA, a series of public events where the speakers are ordinary citizens with extraordinary stories; Storyful, a company that uses proprietary technology to quickly verify (or debunk) possibly newsworthy content from a variety of social-media sources; and Milwaukee's Neighborhood News Service, a nonprofit, hyper-local news outlet that was founded to report on city neighborhoods the mainstream media had long ignored or, worse yet, portrayed only in a negative light.

Journalism Must Follow New Paths to Financial Sustainability

Is journalism dying? The rapid decline of print media's business model doesn't signal the end of journalism itself. In Chapter 10 we examine a few promising strategies for sustainability. We don't pretend to offer business instruction in this book, which after all is about a new approach to the doing of journalism. But today's business innovations and the ethos of relational journalism are not unrelated. We feature such exemplars as *The Texas Tribune*, a nonpartisan public affairs outlet whose monetary support comes from a balance of members, corporate underwriters, donors, foundations and funds generated by live events; The Membership Puzzle Project and *The Correspondent*, parts of a network of projects based at New York University whose premise is that a news organization can be more accurate and more engaged in its communities if it invites collaborations with knowledgeable nonjournalist members — who also pay an annual membership fee; and 100 Days in Appalachia, one of a growing number of new partnerships between regional media outlets and university journalism programs (in this case, West Virginia University).

The book concludes with "A Challenge to Future Journalists," Chapter 11. Here we explain our optimism for journalism's future at a time when pessimism abounds. We summarize the book's instructional goals in the form of a skill set and a mindset — culled from our interviews with the journalists featured throughout the book. We conclude on a hopeful tone, based in part on recent research on Generation Z. Today's young people, especially in the context of the "emerging citizen," are more aware than other generations of the community-building potential of networked digital communication — the form in which today's and tomorrow's journalism will excel.

A Text for Advanced Reporting

We hope that this book will find its way to working journalists, students and scholars of public communication, and anyone else concerned about the future of journalism and democracy, but it is intended primarily to help teach courses that focus on advanced (upper division or master's level), innovative techniques of reporting. To be clear, this is not intended as a replacement for more basic texts on writing and reporting news and features. At this level, students are already familiar with the fundamental skills of information-gathering and interviewing, writing for public audiences, multiple (media) forms of delivering public information, and the role of journalism in American society. Also at this level, students often do reporting in communities beyond the campus environs, for example covering local government, public safety, education and other "beats" common to local newsgathering. For this kind of course, our book will contribute to the basic outcomes — proficiencies in community newsgathering — but through the use of ideas and methods that are starkly different from those of traditional approaches. For example, most students at this level have little experience in (or, initially, little taste for) approaching bureaucrats and elected officials for their stories. This book will teach an approach of accessibility, whereby the reporter learns to work in partnership with "ordinary" citizens, not just community elites and official documents. The coproduction of useful, citizen-mobilizing information will seem not such a daunting task as the production of comprehensive, authoritative analyses, which advanced reporting courses traditionally expect of their students.

Journalism majors today present a blend of those who wish to pursue traditional (mainstream public-affairs) journalism, those who are seeking specialty fields such as sports, entertainment or style journalism, those who prefer advocacy journalism and those who wish to develop their skills in writing, research or presentation on multiple media platforms for use in other communication work. Their greatest obstacle to mastering course content, we contend, is that they struggle to see the relevance of reporting the official proceedings of government institutions using the standard practices of the last 60 years. They intuitively see their news audience as young people like themselves, and they see a disconnect between what they are required to produce in the course and what their contemporaries value as useful, new, public information. By having students begin the process with their attention focused on the interests and informational needs of community members (not just public institutions and public officials), this book will make doing local journalism seem more immediately accessible.

Likewise, advanced reporting courses over the last 20 years have witnessed a fuller incursion of social media. This book will show students how to harness the energy of social media into public discourse that will mobilize and empower community members to "commit acts of citizenship and journalism" that have the potential to improve community conditions. In so doing, the book can help future reporters make the connections between the priorities and concerns of citizens and the policy-making that occurs in the seats of community power.

Specifically, we offer hands-on applications at the conclusion of each chapter. In Part I, each chapter includes "keywords" as part of a running glossary of important concepts and discussion questions to hone critical thinking about these new concepts. The exercises at the conclusion of each chapter in Part II enable students and readers to try their hand at the actual techniques — either on their own, with classmates or coworkers or with the guidance of an instructor.

The organizing concept for the book is to explicate the five principles of relational journalism — and then to apply the principles to the doing of local journalism, with illustrative help from numerous case studies. What's different here from most reporting texts' examples "from the field" is that we present them within a unified and consistent framework: the five principles explicated in the first half of the book. Our hope is that when young reporters and editors form a deeper understanding of journalism's unmet potential to make democracies stronger, their powerful new skill set will be informed and inspired by a powerful new mindset.

Acknowledgments

We are deeply indebted to the Kettering Foundation, not only for its intellectual guidance as we formed the principles that guide this book, but also for the enthusiasm with which the foundation's leadership and program officers encourage stronger democratic practices. In particular, we wish to thank Kettering CEO and President David Mathews; John Dedrick, executive vice and senior operating officer; program officers David Holwerk, Paloma Dallas, Derek Barker and Nick Felts; and Collette McDonough, archivist and library manager. We owe a special thanks to Dallas for generously sharing her knowledge and insights and for her patience and friendship.

The most colorful portions of the book — the case studies in Part II — would have been impossible to write without the generous cooperation we received from our hosts in the eight site visits:

- At AL.com in Birmingham, Kelly Scott, editor and vice president of content; and Michelle Holmes, former vice president of Alabama Media Group

- At City Bureau in Chicago, Harry Backlund, executive director of operations, and Darryl Holliday, co-founder and executive director of design and innovation

- At Curious City in Chicago, Alexandra Salomon, editor

- At Hearken in Chicago, Jennifer Brandel, co-founder and senior vice president

- At KPCC in Pasadena, Ashley Alvarado, director of community engagement

- At *The Texas Tribune* in Austin, Emily Ramshaw, former editor-in-chief

- At Your Voice Ohio, in Dayton, Doug Oplinger, project manager

- At 100 Days in Appalachia, in Morgantown, West Virginia, Maryanne Reed, provost and former dean, and Professor Dana Coester, Reed College of Media, West Virginia University

We are also extremely grateful to the many other sources for the book's case studies, who took time to discuss their journalism with us via Zoom or telephone: Cheryl Carpenter, a faculty member at the Poynter Institute; Sara Catania, director of journalism school partnerships for the Solutions Journalism Network; Emily Gologoski, research director at the Membership Puzzle Project; Andrew Haeg, founder and CEO, GroundSource; Keith Hammonds, president of the Solutions Journalism Network; Jesse Hardman, founder of the Listening Post Collective; Chris Horne, founder and publisher, *The Devil Strip*, Akron; Kelly Jones, senior journalist, Storyful; Doug Livingston, reporter, *Akron Beacon Journal*; Joe Mathews, California editor, Zócalo Public Square; Sharon McGowan, founding editor-in-chief, *Milwaukee Neighborhood News*; Andrew Meyer, news director, WKSU, Kent, Ohio; Stefanie Murray, director of the New Jersey News Commons; Eve Pearlman, chief executive officer, Spaceship Media; David Plazas, opinion engagement editor, *The Tennessean*; Andrew Rockway, program director, The Jefferson Center; Gregory Rodriguez, founder and former publisher, Zócalo Public Square; Linda Shaw, West Coast regional manager, Solutions Journalism Network; Rick Thames, executive in residence, Knight School of Communication, Queens University, Charlotte, North Carolina; Ben Trefny, news director, KALW, Oakland; and Deanna Watson, editor, *The Times Record News*, Wichita Falls, Texas.

We wish to thank the six academic colleagues who reviewed an early draft of the book and who provided a wealth of insights and helpful recommendations: Charles N. Davis, dean of the Henry W. Grady College of Journalism and Mass Communication, University of Georgia; Donica Mensing, Vail M. Pittman associate dean and professor at the Reynolds School of Journalism, University of Nevada, Reno; Sue Robinson, Helen Firstbrook Franklin professor of journalism at the University of Wisconsin-Madison; Jack Rosenberry, professor of media and communication at St. John Fisher College; David M. Ryfe, director and professor at the School of Journalism and Mass Communication, University of Iowa; and Tom Warhover, associate professor at the University of Missouri School of Journalism.

We also extend our deepest thanks to Todd R. Armstrong, Cognella's publisher for communication, journalism and media studies, Michelle Piehl, senior project editor, and Alia Bales, our production editor. Todd's astute guidance and his enthusiasm for this project, right from Day One, kept us on track and helped our workflow better than we could have hoped. Michelle has been a steady presence behind the scenes, asking great questions and attending to detail with amazing aplomb. Alia led us through the final stages of the project with great efficiency and patience.

Paula Ellis wishes to thank her husband, Gary Galloway, for listening to these ideas as they evolved over the years and encouraging her to the finish line.

Paul Voakes wishes to thank his wife, Barbara Voakes, whose patience with this process, and whose "outsider" insights, proved invaluable.

Lori Bergen is grateful to CU Boulder colleague Errol Hughes, who helped to coordinate many of the Zoom interviews the authors conducted for this text, and she thanks her husband, Charles Mangano, for patience and pasta with broccoli and sun-dried tomatoes.

Relational Journalism

Y OU CAN PRACTICALLY SEE THE NERVES BOUNDING AROUND THE ROOM.
Nine speakers are preparing to step onto a spotlighted stage, one by one, to read a story they've written about some unusually interesting part of their life in Southern California. They are the "storytellers" in this season's "Unheard LA," another innovative project at Pasadena's nonprofit public radio station KPCC.

The station hosts a handful of events each year in which residents — carefully selected and coached by KPCC staff — read their five-minute stories in a packed theater and before a live radio audience. They are not professional writers, and most of them have never spoken to a large audience before.

Their stories are as varied as their backgrounds. Jonathan describes his first night as an Uber driver. Will describes his adventures in online dating after suddenly finding himself single. Sean, who is disabled, describes his escape as a teenager from abusive caregivers. Pat describes the day she literally brushed shoulders with Robert Kennedy — the same day he was assassinated. Pickle describes his first performance in Drag Queen Story Hour at a local library.

Is this journalism? Ashley Alvarado, KPCC's director of public engagement, and Jon Cohn, the show's managing producer, reply with an emphatic "yes." That's also the reply of the three authors of this book. We hope to demonstrate in the following 11 chapters that new forms of journalism, including experiments like "Unheard LA," are improving the quality of journalism and, in the process, the quality of democratic practices among the citizens of the United States.

Since the invention of internet browsers in the early 1990s, the practice of journalism has been undergoing a dramatic transformation. The rate of technological change, business disruption and innovation is dizzying. Through it all, though, one trend has held steady: the public is taking on roles once performed exclusively by professional journalists. In this noisy, newly contested ecosystem of producers, certain questions persist: Who is a journalist? What do they do? What should they do?

At the same time, increased polarization, heightened partisanship and growing distrust alert us to the troubles democracy faces. The speed and complexity of today's public challenges have outpaced and overmatched our democratic practices and institutions. Trust in most major institutions has declined, as has citizens' faith in elites and professionals. Government can't easily fix the deep-seated, ongoing social problems that plague local communities. The times call for a better way to harness the wisdom of a diverse people. Should journalists be concerned about these failings of democracy? Do they have a role to play in addressing them?

In this book, we suggest the answers are yes and yes. And we explore a new role that journalism can play in the 21st century. This new approach rests on the belief that an actively engaged public is essential to democracy. It argues that democracy is the work of citizens and that a reimagined journalism should support their work. Our purpose here is to equip young journalists with new, sophisticated additions to their *skill set* for reporting, and to introduce them to a journalistic *mindset* that is taking an increasingly important place in today's journalism.

Here is how we'll get there:

Part I: The Relational Mindset

Our name for this new mindset is relational journalism, and Part I of the book lays the conceptual foundation for the more specific practices of relational journalism presented in Part II. In Chapter 1, we examine the basic relationship between democracy and journalism, a theme we return to several times in subsequent chapters. Even 200 years ago, some Americans — and one extremely influential visitor to America — saw journalism as a particularly valuable form of "association" that was critical to the success of a young democracy. But tectonic shifts have occurred. We'll explore the recent changes that have profoundly altered the role of journalism in society, not the least of which is the replacement of the exclusive institution of professional journalism with a complex information ecosystem that includes all manner of digital communicators. We'll also explore what it means to be an "emerging citizen" in a time of networked digital communication. Is it possible for journalism to assist these "emerging citizens" in their quest to solve problems "for the public good?"

Chapter 2 presents the conceptual core of the book. We'll explore what it means to be a citizen in a democracy going through turbulent times. It's much, much more than occasionally voting. In pondering how journalism in the 21st century can facilitate the work of citizens, we dive deeply into relational journalism, the approach that strives to build relationships between journalists and citizens and among citizens themselves. It requires from journalists a long-term commitment to the communities they cover, an ability to cope with differences, high levels of transparency and an ability to listen to and meet citizens' informational needs. It embraces the full participation of members of the public, most of whom have access to a host of media distribution platforms themselves. It's new, and it's difficult, but its potential for the future of journalism is great.

In Chapter 3, we discover the roots of relational journalism in a movement in the 1990s known as public journalism, or civic journalism. We'll discuss why this citizen-centered period of experimentation never gained broad acceptance in the profession. We'll analyze what was learned from that movement, what principles have survived and evolved and what innovative news organizations have been doing lately to improve on those early principles.

In Chapter 4, we confront that tricky 21st-century question of "Who is a journalist?" We'll explore the ways in which the First Amendment has expanded its reach from protecting just publishers and their professional employees to include, in recent years, anyone "committing acts of journalism." Some of today's most authentic and interesting journalism is done not by highly trained professionals but collaborations involving those professionals and various kinds of nonprofessionals committing various acts of journalism. In fact, we present a continuum of citizen-journalist collaboration that offers the best of both worlds.

Part II: The Relational Skill Set

The first four chapters of our book introduce quite a few new ideas, inspired by some lofty goals for journalism and American democracy. The remainder of the book brings these ideas to life. Each chapter will feature numerous case studies, where you'll meet creative young journalists experimenting in various aspects of relational journalism. For these case studies, in 2018 and 2019 we conducted in-depth interviews with leaders of 19 news entities; eight of these involved physical observation of journalists in their workplaces and interviews with several journalists at each site.

In Part II, we transform the theories and concepts of Part I into what we call the Five Principles of Relational Journalism. Here's a preview of each:

Journalism Is in Itself an Essential Democratic Practice

Because the work of public communication has now become a blend of the professional and the volunteer, and the huge corporation and the tiny non-profit, freedom of the press belongs to every citizen as never before. But great freedom does indeed come with great responsibility, and we believe that anyone who steps into the arena of public communication must abide by certain fact-based, trust-building practices. For us, the heart of journalistic responsibility lies in journalism's facilitative role in a democracy. Chapter 6 will introduce the myriad ways in which journalists are coming to realize that they can be facilitators for citizen action — not just suppliers of material that may produce informed voters. They are willing to swallow some 20th-century competitive pride, willing to expand their reporting range to include all kinds of different citizens — not just the power holders — and willing to be transparent about what they do not know and what help they need.

Journalists and Citizens Are Collaborators

Thanks to technological developments of the early 21st century, anyone who wants to share new, truthful information for the purpose of serving the public good is now able to "commit an act of journalism." In Chapter 7 we explain that many of the successful, innovative news organizations we observed are succeeding by blending the best in professionals' and citizens' work. Professional journalists are good writers; good photographers and videographers; diggers of reliable information; sleuths for verifying or debunking suspicious claims; good curators of what is generally known so far about a given trend, issue or controversy; and good at navigating bureaucracies and halls of power (and the people who work in them). But we'll consider what collaborating citizens can bring as well: lived experience in the issue at hand; honest, transparent opinions; expertise on the subtle social networks and relationships that define a neighborhood or community and the ability to identify community resources that may not be visible from City Hall.

Journalists Facilitate the Work of Citizens

Beyond informing voters with comprehensive reports and analyses, journalism serves democracy more deeply by helping to build the "civic capacity" of a community. As we describe in Part I, civic capacity develops when citizens begin to feel they have the understanding and the strategies to solve shared problems and effect positive change. To do this, they first need to identify shared problems and then discover the shared values that will enable a group to see its way to a solution to the shared problem. They need to be aware of that elusive goal known as "the common good," or "the public good." They need to know how to listen to people with whom they think they disagree — sometimes listen to people they think they dislike. That all may seem far afield from the doing of journalism, but in Chapter 8 we will meet journalists who are discovering the spots where journalists can contribute to these capacity-building activities.

Relational Journalism Updates Time-Honored Traditions

As we searched for innovative ways to better serve democratic practice, we realized we simply cannot jettison those practices and principles that have made journalism the positive force it has been since the founding of the American republic. These include truth-seeking and accuracy; fairness and the battle against bias; independence; investigative journalism's "watchdog" role; accountability; and a consistent sense of what is newsworthy. But in Chapter 9, with each of these time-honored elements of journalism, we'll suggest they be refreshed so that the traditions are still relevant and meaningful in a fast-changing media environment. As one example, accuracy, in today's newsgathering, now requires journalists to be able to spot fakes on social media — impostor accounts, doctored photos and the like. We'll show how some of the most creative innovators in journalism, including radio station KPCC in Pasadena, are still careful to uphold the worthiest of journalism's time-honored traditions.

Journalism Must Follow New Paths to Financial Sustainability

Is journalism dying? Chapter 10 represents your authors' attempt to answer that question during this time of lightning-fast change with limited visibility into the future. Print news may be fading, but that doesn't signal the end of journalism itself. At this stage it is far too early to know what combination of strategies will sustain journalism, but in Chapter 10 we'll take a look at a few that offer promise. We don't pretend to offer business analysis or business strategies in this book, which after all is about a new approach to doing journalism. But the business and the ethos of journalism are not unrelated. A new approach to journalism, a citizen-centered approach, has the potential to attract trust in new ways, leading to new audiences and new revenue streams.

The book concludes with "A Challenge to Future Journalists," Chapter 11. Here we explain our optimism for journalism's future at a time when pessimism abounds. For starters, young people are especially well equipped to deal with these challenges. Research shows that Generation Z has a reform-minded attitude and DIY approach to problem-solving that is likely to allow them to see the "broken" nature of 20th-century journalism as an opportunity. Young people, especially in the context of the "emerging citizen," are also aware of the community-building potential of networked digital communication — the form in which today's and tomorrow's journalism will excel.

We're not advocating that journalists abandon all the worthy types of journalism being done today. Think of this book as adding a new dimension to what's gone on before. It's ultimately a mindset that will inspire everything journalists do, whether it's the environment, City Hall, local schools, sports, food or travel. Journalism is more productive and more promising for communities when the thinking of citizens is the first thought rather than the afterthought.

Now back to the question of whether KPPC's "Unheard LA" program qualifies as journalism. By Chapter 11, we hope you will see that KPCC embodies most, if not all, of the innovative principles featured in the book. Alvarado explained that a news organization focused on citizen engagement is constantly searching for ways to attract new listeners and forge bonds between the station and its community — even if that means sometimes turning the mic over to nonjournalists.

"These are stories that a radio audience would otherwise never hear," she said, "but they are as authentic in their depiction of L.A. life as any standard piece of journalism would be."

Cohn adds that the professional reporters at KPCC know how to utilize public officials and experts for their stories, but the NPR culture tends to be homogeneous. "Authentic, diverse experience counts too," Cohn says, as he thinks about how a station can represent a community. "LA is one of the most diverse places in the world, and people of all kinds of backgrounds want to see and hear themselves represented on air."

Alvarado resists the notion that "Unheard LA" is an indulgence in amateur radio. She, Cohn and other staff members coach the writers until their pieces are clear and tight. During dress rehearsal, they provide notes after each speaker's reading. In the end, Alvarado says, journalism has always been enhanced by good writing. "The well-crafted narrative — whether spoken, written or told in video or photos — is always more effective than an FAQ treatment or a list."

"Of course it's journalism," Cohn says. "It's long-form journalism at its best."

We offer here a few modest disclosures. In highlighting 19 innovative news operations over the course of the book, we want to acknowledge that they represent only a small fraction of the growing number of innovators in citizen-centered journalism. Our case studies do represent the best of the ideas we're presenting, but in 2020 promising startups were rocketing onto the scene at a rate of at least one per month. Chapter 1 provides a more comprehensive listing of engagement-focused news organizations, but again: No list in this realm can be truly exhaustive. In a similar vein, we must acknowledge that as we write the book in 2020, we are taking a snapshot of this genre of journalism at this time. If one thing is certain, the genre will have changed already by the time our readers pick up this volume. In both of these limitations, however, we take hope that we have described here a set of principles that is only beginning to blossom into successful, pervasive practice.

We suggest these principles and practices mindful that they represent an emergent phenomenon. The principles are, by necessity, under development. But *now is the time* for journalists, and journalism students, to consider this new approach. The book's central ideas, once inchoate and theoretical, are beginning to take shape in pioneering news outlets across the nation and world. We see this book as a guide that is generative, catalyzing doers and thinkers who want to see democracy thrive, with a strong assist from journalism.

PART I

The Relational Mindset

CHAPTER 1

Journalism for a New Age

JOURNALISTS HAVE ALWAYS AIMED TO SERVE DEMOCRACY, A ROLE DEEMED SO essential that it is protected by the First Amendment of the U.S. Constitution. But how they do this has changed markedly over the decades.

Breakthroughs in technology, societal shifts and fluid interpretations of what democracy requires of its citizens have forced journalists to reimagine their role at critical junctures.

This is such a time. The transformation of journalism is well underway.

In times like these, when the journalism industry is being fundamentally restructured, rules collapse. When they do, it's time to shed old ideas, examine longstanding routines and imagine anew. As the dominance of so-called "legacy" media fades, it is being replaced by a dizzying ecosystem of internet-based media outlets.

Amid today's news industry chaos, heightened ideological conflict and eroded public trust comes opportunity — a chance for journalists to reassert the mission-critical role they can and must play in a democracy. Innovative journalists across the country are trying to do just that. Creativity and entrepreneurship are flourishing, particularly at the local level in communities across America.

In this book, we'll explore the shifts taking place. And we'll introduce you to some entrepreneurs who are inventing new ways journalism can move beyond its traditional role of raising awareness about public problems to a more active role in encouraging people to participate in solving them.

Underlying these shifts is the profound belief that in a democracy, **citizens** hold the sovereign power and that only through their sustained participation will it thrive.

What then can journalists do to encourage and support the democratic work citizens must do to solve shared public problems and shape the emergent future?

Democracy is much more than a system of governance, contested elections and faceless institutions. It is a way of life, a culture shaped and strengthened by the every-day actions of people. It relies on a shared vision of the common good and the norms and practices that support it. What then can journalists do to nurture a healthy and inclusive culture of democracy?

Our answer is relational journalism, an emerging approach to journalism that places the interests of the public at the center of all it does. Relational journalism recognizes that journalism is a service, not a consumer product. Journalism is in service to a democratic people and facilitates their efforts to evolve a shared vision and to solve problems. And it is done best in close partnership with the people. By more fully embracing this mission to serve, we believe, journalism can reassert its legitimacy as a public good and close the gap between what it provides and what a self-governing people need.

This new relational approach is a practical response to the urgent call of the times. It captures the creativity of today, builds on recent advances in technology and incorporates an enhanced understanding of social networks.

To set the stage for the book's deeper dive into the theory and practice of relational journalism, let's examine some of society's megatrends that are helping to steer the course of these changes.

"Relational" is a term that incorporates:

- A greater understanding of the essential role networks play as the basic architecture of nature, technology, society and communications.

- An increased understanding of the relationship between community connectedness and social, emotional and economic well-being. Often this is called social capital, as distinguished from financial capital, but every bit as valuable.

- A recognition that decades of focus on individualism have jeopardized our sense of belonging and connection to one another, making it easier to disrespect the "other."

- A greater understanding of how people make sense of things by interacting with each other individually or in groups. And a recognition that collaboration among people from diverse backgrounds propels invention, supplanting earlier myths about the superiority of the lone genius.

- The recognition that when media moved from a one-to-many broadcast model to one-to-one communication, networks of relationships became more visible as did their importance in the distribution of news.

The People's Democracy

At this point, you may be wondering what any of this has to do with democracy. That's our point exactly. Democracy is a political system, but it is much more than that. It is a social system designed by the people for the people, supported by institutions, norms and practices that evolve over time as circumstances change and new knowledge emerges.

So, first things first. Let's take a closer look at what it means to be a democracy as we begin to think about the essential role journalism can play in this new era.

Our definition of democracy is one that demands the full participation of everyone and recognizes that too many people have felt (or have been) excluded. The word "democracy" is derived from two Greek roots, "demos" (the people) and "kratos" (power) (Ober, 2008). In a democracy, the sovereign power rests in the hands of the people, not a monarch. In our republic, the people rule through their chosen representatives. But electing them is not all there is to **citizenship**, as we will see.

Democracy as Associations

In communities that thrive, residents have a sense of belonging to a place, an ideal, and people they care about. They feel seen and heard. Even in the face of consumcrism and other pressures toward individualism and isolation, people are naturally drawn to associate with others for existential and practical reasons.

This "spirit of association" was recognized as distinctly American and democratic in the 19th century by Alexis de Tocqueville, who visited the United States when its democracy was still young. He wrote eloquently about the many private voluntary associations he discovered, calling this freedom to associate "the mother science" that explained how society functioned and how complex problems might be solved.

In his classic account of why democracy was succeeding in the United States, de Tocqueville identified the newspaper as a type of association that brings individuals together for common action because through it, they speak to one another (Tocqueville, 2002). "A newspaper not only has the effect of suggesting the same design to many men; it furnishes them the means of executing in common the designs they themselves had already conceived ... " (Tocqueville, 2002, p. 493). "There exists, therefore, a necessary relation between associations and newspapers; newspapers make associations, and associations make newspapers" (p. 494).

Journalism from its earliest days has been an agent of connection and community building. It connects people to one another. It helps them identify common interests and concerns. It helps them find resources to solve problems. It enables people to exchange views and learn continuously together.

This give-and-take is fundamental to democracy, which the social philosopher John Dewey described as a process of community learning that is social and experiential.

"Wherever there is a conjoint activity whose consequences are appreciated as good by all singular persons who take part in it," Dewey wrote, "and where the realization of the good is such as to effect an energetic desire and effort to sustain it in being just because it is a good shared by all, there is in so far a community. The clear consciousness of a communal life, in all its implications, constitutes the idea of democracy" (Dewey, 1954, p. 149).

Journalists might then be seen as builders of democratic communities, fostering connections among people and between people and institutions. Through these networks of relationships, journalism provides a platform for the cocreation of public knowledge and action.

No matter how the modes of production and distribution have changed over the decades, journalism's essential function is to serve citizens by connecting them and supporting their associational work, as Tocqueville observed in his heralded examination of republican democracy in America.

In a complex democratic society like ours, citizens elect representatives to carry out the day-to-day work of governing and hold those politicians accountable through a system of regular elections. But a successful democracy requires much more of its citizens than going to the polls every few years. For democracy to truly flourish, citizens must also do the more difficult work of identifying and solving common problems on their own, for the benefit of the common good in a community. Known as the **republican theory of citizenship**, this approach values participation in deliberation and decision-making, holding public office and working with others to create a better society. It focuses less on the formal institutions of government and more on citizen identity, agency and the processes they use to exercise judgment (Stanford University, 2006).

Similarly, adherents to the **participatory theory of democracy** believe members of the public should participate directly in collective decision-making rather than delegating it to elites. A step removed from direct democracy, participatory democracy calls for active citizen involvement in deliberation and participation in civic life. If the public appears apathetic, adherents argue, it is because citizens have few meaningful opportunities to participate beyond monitoring their elected representatives and government (Barber, 1984).

Journalism can play an important role here by highlighting opportunities for citizens to participate, explaining the processes for participation and telling stories that focus on people taking action as individuals or in groups. It is difficult for people to see their essential place in democracy if journalists view the republic exclusively through an institutional lens.

What do we mean by "citizen"? In this book, our emphasis is on the full participation of all persons in an array of shared democratic practices. We recognize that in today's hyperpolarized identity politics, the meaning of the term "citizen" is hotly contested. While some favor its narrow use as a legal term for subjects of a nation or state, we prefer a more inclusive interpretation that recognizes all the people who live in a community and have the potential to work for its betterment. The term "citizen," for us, suggests actions and responsibilities, not legal status or cultural identity.

"Good" Public Work

Helping people practice democracy more fully requires journalists to broaden their view and see people — all people — as principal actors.

Journalism plays an essential role in helping society manage the inherent tensions between the private and public realms and between the interests of individuals and the community. For this reason, it is known as a mediating institution, meant to provide a bridge from one perspective to another so that mutual understanding can be found. It can help people transcend the misconceptions between "I" and the "other" that lead to unproductive conflict and polarization. News reporting also can clarify the distinction between what individuals may want for their own benefit and what the public wants in the interest of society as a whole.

When journalism does not reflect the experience and perspectives of a diverse citizenry, it fails to serve democracy.

Often, journalism is referred to as a calling, a vocation that is purpose-driven and a way of life. And journalists who specialize in the coverage of politics and public affairs assert they are essential to democracy not just as providers of information but as agents of understanding.

For all the above reasons, journalism is known as "**good work**." It has a broad mission of service and a guiding set of ideals. In their influential book *Good Work: When Excellence and Ethics Meet* (Gardner et al., 2001), a renowned team of social scientists examined journalism and other professions to identify "good work" and how to do it in difficult times. The authors explored the tensions between the ideals of journalism and the threats to the business that already were underway in 2001. They raised prescient questions about how the internet might threaten the mission and ideals of journalism. To continue doing "good work," they said, journalists, when facing pressures, must hold tight to their mission and ideals. They gain control of their work when "they call forth inner moral codes that help them resist illegitimate pressures and remain focused on the truth-seeking mission" (Gardner et al., 2001, p. 180).

Journalism also can be thought of as "public work" in that it supports the work of the public. "Public work" is a framework for thinking about participatory democracy that recognizes the capacity of diverse citizens to build political communities together. Harry C. Boyte, architect of this approach and a veteran of movement building, asserts that doing "**public work**" requires a paradigm shift "from the dominant views and practices of politics as warfare, citizens as consumers and democracy as centered on government" (Boyte, 2019.) Journalists perform "public work" when they enable the public's ability to participate and when they share examples of people doing so.

Journalists support the work of citizens when they help shape a public narrative about how people create a democratic way of life. Building on the public narrative concept first developed by the legendary civil rights activist and community organizer Marshall Ganz, Boyte suggests that journalists, like other professionals, should "see themselves as citizens" rather than as people dealing with citizens. "It is a new frontier of media as a space for public narrative-building" (Boyte, 2017, p. 86).

The Networked Public Sphere

The "good work" and "public work" of journalism is there to ensure the free flow of the information that provides oxygen to the public sphere, a conceptual space in which Jürgen Habermas theorized people would gather as a public to identify and address public needs (Habermas, 1991). The public sphere does not exist as a physical location, as Habermas originally envisioned it. Rather, it exists between and among people who are trying to figure out what they think and what they might realistically do. Communication then is central to the process. And our methods for communicating with one another have evolved over time, driven by technological advancements.

Today's media ecosystem is much more complex than it was when Habermas introduced the concept of a public sphere. Thanks in large part to the advent of the internet, media is a system of multilayered communication **network**s through which information and disinformation can spread rapidly from one node to another. It is polycentric, with no central hub. These are relational structures that can be thought of as networks of interrelationships. They value connectedness and mimic neural networks by being able to identify how objects are related to each other.

The networks can be easily accessed by anyone who has something to say, unmediated by any central authority that might impose traditional journalistic standards of truth, verification and minimizing harm. Thus, mainstream media's influence over public access to information, known as its gatekeeping function, has eroded, as has its ability to set the public agenda.

In this diffuse, ever-changing system of systems, journalism is in a war for attention. Information is abundant, perhaps overabundant, and people have more sources to choose from than ever before. Some might argue that when newspaper and television monopolies reigned, people had no choice but to bump into information about a public issue. Now, amid the abundance, it can be difficult to make sense of politics and government. Political scientists worry that many aren't even trying. These "low-information voters" aren't interested in thinking things through and rely on cognitive shortcuts (Fording & Schram, 2016) such as political and cultural identity.

While those who study civil society worry about the decline of traditional journalism and newspapers as a mediating institution, innovative journalists see opportunities to enhance journalism's ability to serve democracy. The emergence of new technology and media platforms, the transition from mass-to-one to one-to-one communication, and advances in understanding the transformative power of networks have kindled the imaginations of journalists who are deeply committed to preserving and expanding participation in the public sphere.

Relational Networks

As they invent new ways for journalism to connect people and encourage their participation in the public sphere, the innovators we visited place great value on the age-old maxim that relationships matter. Relationships matter at every unit of analysis: individual, group, community, national and global. Relationships within, between and among networks are powerful because they are the ways ideas and actions spread and scale. In a highly distributed, nonlinear set of processes, relationships provide the glue that a healthy network needs to thrive and grow. Social movements, for example, are action networks that can begin with individuals, spread to groups and scale up to span the nation or world. In the political realm, the Tea Party movement and Arab Spring uprisings of the early 2010s are examples, followed later by social movements such as #BlackLivesMatter, #MeToo and the student-led March for Our Lives campaign against gun violence. This process of scaling up through networks is what it means for something to "go viral," propagating like a virus.

This simple, seemingly obvious, realization about the importance of relationships has transformative powers. Hal Saunders, an experienced diplomat who drafted the historic Camp David peace accords in 1978, discovered this when he upended traditional diplomatic processes by introducing his relational paradigm (Saunders, 2005). It focuses not on the machinery of government and politics but on citizen interactions sustained over time. "Its value lies in its being seen as a whole — an overall relationship." Through these interactions "people create a shared context in which they interact — a world of their own. They create it together — often without talking about it; neither could create it alone; one cannot see it; but it is valued in its own right, and it shapes action. It is the essence of relationship" (Saunders, p. 67). Many refer to this space, as does Saunders, as "the space between." It is a generative space in which people co-create knowledge.

Peace, Saunders believed, could emerge from these networks of relationships that allow for conflict mediation, resolution and the shared understanding on which community is built.

This sense of connection and relatedness is known as **social capital**. Sociologists distinguish between two types of social capital: bonding and bridging. Bonding capital refers to connections within groups of people who have many similarities like family and friends. Bridging capital connects people across groups by providing a bridge between them. Journalism can serve as an agent of both.

Social media, and the communication networks through which it rushes, support the formation of both types of social capital. The creation of bonding capital is at work on cable television stations such as Fox News and MSNBC. Each tries to build a loyal audience by orienting its coverage to reinforce the attitudes and beliefs of its viewers. This propensity to associate with "my" group is known as the tribal mind. The internet, which shattered mass-market barriers to entry, enabled the creation of these niche online outlets. For them, it is essential to maintain tight bonds with their users because they have traded mass reach for narrower, intensely loyal users. In contrast, bridging capital can be seen at work in news reports that include multiple perspectives, encourage learning about differences and promote understanding between groups in the interest of finding common cause.

Informed by a growing understanding of how social media networks work, journalists who recognize their jobs as building community, not audience, are focused on the urgent need to build bridging capital. They believe it's their job to help citizens bridge across divides of race, class, gender, religion or politics to reduce the hyperpartisanship and polarization that have hijacked our politics and threaten our ability to solve shared problems.

Network theorists understand that relationships can be thick or thin and that information is spread most quickly through connectors who have weak ties with large numbers of people. Networks are the highly adaptive, relational structures that provide a bridge between chaos and the status quo. It is through networks that change happens.

Community capacity is built on these relational networks (Safford, 2009), which undergird all intentional networks no matter their scale. In his groundbreaking examination of two economically challenged cities, Allentown, Pennsylvania, and

Youngstown, Ohio, Safford found that what mattered most for recovery and resilience was the quality of relationships and the networks that built the context for cooperation between people and groups. The diversity of the networks was key to success.

"Small world" networks of connections and relationships may only be composed of neighboring elements, but they scale by joining other networks (Buchanan, 2002). This is the idea behind the notion that we all are within only six degrees of separation from each other. The concept is at work when the algorithms behind Facebook and LinkedIn, for example, recommend friends of friends with whom you can connect.

Also critical to understanding networks is to recognize that everything has value and holds that value only in relationship to something or someone else (Christakis & Fowler, 2009).

Now, with a more complete understanding of the architecture and behavior of networks in both the physical and virtual worlds, journalists are gaining new insights about how information and news could support community learning and change. Media scholar John Wihbey (2019) offers a framework for thinking about this new role for a new era. He suggests journalists think of their role as fostering "networks of recognition," a term he coined to describe the process by which "... citizens become aware of and reflect on their common ties and concerns — and thereby to sustain collaborative, interpretive activity." Wihbey, echoing Dewey, believes that the goal of journalism "is to produce knowledge of how citizens are connected to the world" (p. 14).

"The debate over journalism's future is increasingly not necessarily a matter of engaging (populist) versus informing (elitist). Journalism in the era of expansive digital connectivity has the potential to create a kind of 'virtuous circle' involving journalism and democratic citizenship fueled and framed by knowledge" (Wihbey, 2019, p. 142).

This growing understanding of network effects coincides with significant advances in brain research and the emergence of the field of positive psychology, a strengths-based approach to individual and community well-being that focuses on wellness not illness and assets not deficits. At the same time, health practitioners, network theorists and others are continuing to evolve their understanding of social contagions, the process by which ideas, attitudes and behaviors spread rapidly through groups. This is what is meant when things "go viral." Combined, this new knowledge about human behavior and social media networks suggest powerful avenues for rethinking decades-old approaches to news that emphasized conflict, deficits and problems. Many of today's innovators recognize the critical role optimism plays in catalyzing individuals and communities to face today's challenges with hopes of a brighter future. Increasingly, journalists recognize a need to share examples of solutions, identify assets and frame complex problems as adaptive challenges for which there is no easy, technical fix.

Entrepreneurial Citizens

As entrepreneurial journalists explore new ways to serve democracy, a frustrated public is becoming more self-reliant and collaborative because they have lost trust in institutions and expertise. This decline in trust is in part due to a growing recognition that institutions and their leaders can't manage or "fix" complex, adaptive problems with technical solutions that are easy to identify and implement.

At the same time, a DIY (Do-It-Yourself) attitude of can-do-ism has taken hold in the new economy that rewards entrepreneurialism over industrial-age efficiency. The information era continues to usher out legacy institutions, diminishing them with software and internet inventions. It has ushered in the age of participation and more self-organizing enabled by social media communication networks. As part of these tremendous shifts still unfolding, hierarchies of all types are falling. This is particularly true in the knowledge economies where the widespread availability of information has democratized access to it and increased the value of experiential ways of knowing, once undervalued as not scientific or rational.

More than 50 years into the digital age, today's news is produced, distributed and consumed within digital networks. Journalism seeks to engage citizens both as producers and consumers, in networks that often mix public and private communication with their personal and civic interests.

Media scholar Paul Mihailidis (2014, 2018) has conducted exhaustive studies of digital communications in the context of civic engagement and American youth, which makes his work particularly valuable for this book. Like many observers, Mihailidis sees an environment in which the news media are no longer a system of one-way communication of polished, expertly vetted information that is consumed by citizens. Instead, technology has irreversibly blurred the distinction between the media consumer and the media producer. Mobile platforms are ever-present and highly accessible; anyone, not just a trained journalist, can share information; that sharing can spread across the globe virtually instantaneously. Mostly, however, the sharing is done to other members of social networks — a curious hybrid of private and public communication.

Mihailidis describes the "emerging citizen" in this digital world, based on historian Michael Schudson's conception (1998) of the "monitorial citizen." Schudson sees a different citizen from that of the 20th century, who was regularly informed about public affairs by a daily reading and viewing of mass-media content. In the digital age, the citizen is more likely to "monitor" the news and become involved only on issues they feel moved to engage with. Whereas 20th-century citizenship was defined by "duties" such as voting, paying taxes and entering military service, the monitorial citizens are known for their "engagement," that is, their carefully selected activities in the public sphere and their sharing of information and opinions in digital networks. Their citizenship depends heavily on the information they receive and share, but Mihailidis points out that digital news is vulnerable to misinformation uncritically passed along, and by social media companies' tendencies to create algorithms that provide only information that conforms with the user's previous reading. That creates filter bubbles and echo chambers that stand dangerously in the way of true community-building.

Mihailidis's antidote to the antidemocracy effects of digital communications is to build up media literacy in the emerging citizen. By "media-literate," Mihailidis means a citizen who can curate (aggregate, organize and interpret responsibly before sharing in networks); critique (apply critical thinking skills to evaluate what's being received); contribute (share only the most reliable or useful of what you've received); collaborate (find a common cause with others and then find a role to help with that cause); and create (produce fresh ideas, but more often repurpose others' ideas in fresh and creative new ways). In this way, Mihailidis believes, young citizens can utilize their advanced skills on social media to connect with others in ways that can empower citizens and effect social change. Journalism is uniquely positioned to welcome these "emerging citizens" into media environments that focus on public information for the public good.

Young people become "active agents in the process of meaning making" through their use of technologies to manipulate and remix reality, and perform such acts in networked space," writes Mihailidis, quoting media scholar Mark Deuze. "These activities, embedded in networks that mix the personal and public, enact a form of cultural citizenship where cultural production and consumption of personal and civic, private and public, occur in the networked public (Mihailidis, 2019, pp. 31–32).

More than Rational

As we've seen, the networked world in which journalists operate today is profoundly different from the late 20th century's "golden age" of professionalism when a stable set of practices and principles were evolved and spread to ensure quality. To help guide working journalists and nurture the public's trust, professional organizations and news outlets developed codes of ethics commonly meant to assure the free flow of information that is accurate, fair and thorough.

This professionalization actually began back in the 1910s, when universities started offering degrees in journalism and teaching a fact-based, "objective" approach to reporting (Daly, 2018). Many of the new practices were themselves rooted in Enlightenment Era ideals that rested on the belief that if members of the public had factual information, they would make rational choices. Walter Lippmann, one of the country's most renowned journalists and public intellectuals, was an early proponent of this role for journalism, but he grew skeptical that the 20th-century American citizen could fulfill those Enlightenment ideals. People were simply too busy with their jobs and families to keep up with politics or complex public policies, Lippmann wrote. He urged the development of an expert class in society, which would explain complex issues to journalists, who would pass the information on to their readers. The citizens themselves would be spectators; aside from an occasional vote, they had no real role to play in civic life (Schudson, 1998). Lippmann's critique of modern democracy drew criticism – but hardly a groundswell of outrage. His most prominent opponent on the matter was none other than the philosopher John Dewey, who argued that the public hadn't failed democracy; it had temporarily lost its way. Dewey believed that ordinary people are capable of making their own decisions, not just in their private lives but on public matters as well. Given the chance, Dewey wrote, citizens are actually very good at working through difficult public problems (Rosen, 1999).

Self-governing citizens do need accurate information. In today's elaborate web of social media networks, rapid information sharing and increased polarization, it's become increasingly difficult to parse true from false. That's problem enough. But citizens need more than accurate information to tackle the increasingly complex public problems faced by a more pluralistic society at a time of declining trust in institutions and expertise.

As they explore ways to meet the public's changing needs, journalism innovators aren't abandoning the value Enlightenment thinkers placed on facts, truth and reason. However, they are learning from the significant strides cognitive scientists have made in understanding that rational thought is not the only factor in decision-making. Emotion and social relationships also govern how individuals make sense of the world.

Public issues have become more ideologically charged, thanks in part to the freedom of expression internet technologies have unleashed. Sophisticated purveyors of propaganda, misinformation and disinformation have instant, unmediated access to the public. Their tactics incorporate a deep understanding of the "tribal brain" and methods for triggering it. To cope with ambiguity and complexity, people often rely on familiar cognitive shortcuts. These shortcuts can take many forms that plug into our existing conceptual frames. These frames, sometimes referred to as mental models, are unconscious structures created so that it is easier to make sense of overwhelming amounts of information. Reality isn't only shaped by the literal meanings of things or by facts alone. It also is shaped by symbolic thought, the stuff of story, metaphor, symbols and conceptual frames. This deeper understanding of how symbolic thought shapes reality has led to an explosion of story wars. To persuade others, rival factions believe they must control the narrative. In other words, they must produce a conceptual narrative that reduces complexity and provides shortcuts to decision-making.

In the ever-evolving, networked ecosystems of news and information, once clear distinctions between fact and opinion, serious news and entertainment and truth and advocacy are eroding. Members of the public, once only consumers of news and information, today also are content creators and distributors.

Amid this cacophony, journalism is fighting for oxygen, relevance and its public purpose.

A Shift in Professional Mindset

Across the country we see a profound shift taking place led by journalists who embrace the ideals of participatory democracy and are questioning once-sacrosanct norms in an effort to better align their work with the needs of the public. To some journalists, the shift is seen as a threat to their professional identity. But many of its supporters see professionalism as part of the problem, arguing that it has distanced journalists from citizens and contributed to declining trust in the institution of journalism.

This professional realignment suggests that to be more useful for citizens trying to govern themselves in a democracy, journalists should alter their stance from objective and distant to caring and connected — and accountable for increasing the community's capacity to solve problems and seize opportunities.

Seen this way, citizens, not institutions, are the driving force of democracy. No longer are readers, viewers or listeners considered to be an audience to whom a content product is delivered. No longer do journalists see themselves as working for an inchoate public and claim to be exclusively protected by First Amendment freedoms. Instead, journalists embrace the value of working "with" community members.

Journalists with this mindset take a relational stance. They recognize that they are co-creators of news and knowledge who work with members of the public. Through their work, they also aim to foster relationships between people so that they together can solve wickedly complex problems. Journalists would continue to be fair-minded and factual in reporting, but they also would place a premium on finding ways to inspire and support people as they go about the everyday work of citizens constructing their shared future. It is less institutional and more grassroots to journalism.

Innovation at the Community Level

Most of this civic-oriented experimentation and innovation in journalism is taking root at the local level. That's partly because innovation starts small, often at the hands of rebels, and on the margins of large, existing systems that resist change. Gradually the changes spread, and only after the once-taboo notions become the norm is it possible to look back to understand what factors aligned to create the tipping point. In the midst of it, things look chaotic because systems change is a messy, perplexing, and at times murky process.

It may also be true that innovation at the local level is exploding because in communities — neighborhoods, towns and cities — residents can more easily connect with people and events that enhance their sense of belonging. In this case, scale matters: small scale.

When public problems seem distant and impossibly difficult to solve, it's easier to fall for oversimplifications and caricatures. But when the problems are local, recognizable and involve people you may even know, neither glibness nor avoidance work as readily.

As Dewey said: "Democracy must begin at home, and its home is in the neighborly community" (1954, p. 213).

Understood as a network of relationships, communities look quite different than when viewed only as an amalgamation of governmental and other institutions, businesses, civic organizations and churches. Community network structures can differ dramatically. Sean Safford (2009) vividly describes this when explaining why Allentown, Pennsylvania, could rebound from economic disruptions and Youngstown, Ohio, could not. He and others who study community change have shown that the structures of local networked relationships — economic, political and civic — can account for the differences. "Action is shaped by social embeddedness and in turn recursively influences social structure itself" (Safford, p. 33).

Because it is increasingly distributed through social and peer-to-peer networks, community news and information flows also differ in quality and efficacy.

In communities, information is constantly flowing through official networks and self-organized ones, all of which have expanded reach, thanks to the power of the internet as a communications platform. Community network structures, and therefore news and information flows, can differ dramatically in this web of one-to-one communication, renewing concerns about equitable access to information and participation in public affairs.

For professional journalists, the end of one-way, mass-media distribution and the forced reliance on these varied communication networks has profoundly altered traditional journalism's once preeminent position as the trusted source for the information self-governing citizens need in a democracy.

Local government agencies that once depended on the media to get their message out today provide information to citizens directly. Nitty-gritty information about such things as road closures, school lunch menus and where to vote, once the exclusive domain of local news outlets, is widely distributed by government officials and redistributed by citizens using the internet or through a growing industry of civic technology apps. Official and unofficial views about matters of public policy also flow through these communication networks.

In this open, decentralized communication ecosystem, some of journalism's agenda-setting authority has eroded. Once seen as custodians of the public sphere in the era of mass media, journalists provided a common set of information to citizens so that they could use it to make individual and collective judgments about what ought to be done. Today, however, Habermas's public sphere is more accurately conceptualized as a multiplexity of networks with nodes of social interactions between people and groups that may or may not produce civic interaction or forge collective identities.

At times it looks like a dysfunctional public sphere and media system. And still, public problems persist. Not only do community problems persist; they are becoming more complex, highly adaptive and unresponsive to technical solutions. These are known as "wicked problems" because of their confounding, multivariate nature. Solutions to these social and political challenges rely on public judgment — not a judgment driven by algorithms, the "wisdom of the crowd" or the ability of one group to manipulate or prevail over another. Public judgment is a deliberative process by which citizens identify and discuss a shared concern, explore options for addressing it and, after weighing the benefits and risks, choose a path forward. It is consistent with the republican theory of citizenship, which emphasizes working with others to solve democratic problems. This process of coming to public judgment emphasizes deliberation and dialogue to produce the unique type of shared knowledge that people create only by talking to one another (Yankelovich, 1991).

Journalists commonly held the belief that their role primarily was to provide information and perspective about a public issue — contaminated drinking water, failing schools, crime or homelessness as examples. After that, it was up to community institutions, civic groups or citizens to do as they chose with the information, and journalists would track their progress.

In today's hyper-partisan, polarized world, journalists across the country are questioning this once clear line between providing information and activating the public. Seeking a better way for journalism to support democracy in communities, they are partnering with a wide array of local groups to explore novel approaches.

These experimenters are sifting through long-standing habits of thought and practice to reexamine their role and establish new routines that incorporate modern understandings about human behavior, community dynamics and technology.

Aided by these new understandings emerging from disparate fields — technology, network theory, psychology, community organizing, conflict resolution and other social sciences — journalists are experimenting with fundamental changes in mindset and craft while holding tight to the core values that distinguish them as practitioners of "good work" done for societal benefit. They are learning more about the drivers of community well-being, the role of networks in collective learning and social change, and the impact of strengths-based approaches emerging from the field

BOX 1.1 The Changing News Ecosystem

Michele McLellan, a digital news consultant who has followed the growth of digital and nonprofit news outlets for more than a decade, is a trusted, oft-quoted source on this ever-changing arena of news startups.

McLellan developed "Michele's List" as a fellow at the Reynolds Journalism Institute in 2009–10. The list bearing her name is considered the most comprehensive source for such information. In addition, she is responsible for the INN (Institute for Nonprofit News) Index.

These links provide information about the scope and vitality of these digital native news outlets.

Michele's List is a database of nearly 500 independent digital news startups in the United States and Canada: http://www.micheleslist.org/

INN Index is the most comprehensive study of nonprofit news in the United States: https://inn.org/innindex/

Here is the membership list of the Institute for Nonprofit News: https://inn.org/members/

of positive psychology. Increasingly, they are recognizing the critical role optimism plays in catalyzing individuals and communities to face today's challenges and exert control over their future. To support citizens in their work, they are sharing examples of solutions, identifying community assets and framing complex problems as adaptive challenges that require public judgment because there is no clear right or wrong answer and no easy, technical fix.

It's difficult to keep track of the exploding number of local news outlets coming and going across the country. There is no one source for this information. Online news startups, for example, can be formed as part of an existing media company or as standalone nonprofits or for-profits. There are different trade groups with different tracking methods for each.

Because of definitional problems, it's even more difficult to categorize their areas of focus. What does it mean to have a civic focus or to emphasize civic engagement? Is civic-oriented news the entire focus of the outlet, a large portion of it, or one smaller aspect?

The purer the focus, the smaller the number. As with the daily newspaper, online media companies recognize they need to offer customers a buffet of topic choices to attract and hold their interests.

Digital news consultant Michele McLellan, who has followed these developments closely from the outset, said there has been an explosion of digital-only news media nonprofits devoted mostly to the news in the public interest and for-profits serving small local communities (McLellan, personal correspondence, November 6, 2019, April 19, 2020). Numbering in the hundreds, these outlets "tend to put more effort than traditional media into engaging with their communities." This is especially true of the 200-plus nonprofit news organizations in the United States, about half of which cover a local community or a state. McLellan, citing the INN (Institute for

Nonprofit News) Index 2019, said that virtually every nonprofit news organization conducts one or more engagement activities.

Led and staffed by veterans of "legacy" media organizations and a fresh breed of digital natives, these news organizations share a similar impulse to help make democracy work for its citizens, but their approaches vary significantly. Over time, as the big shift takes place, their ideas will evolve and, like recombinant DNA, help shape the still-emerging media landscape.

Social media theorist Clay Shirky has written extensively about how the internet, like technologies that came before it, is changing media and society:

> When ecosystems change and inflexible institutions collapse, their members disperse, abandoning old beliefs, trying new things, making their living in different ways than they used to. It's easy to see the ways in which collapse to simplicity wrecks the glories of old. But there is one compensating advantage for the people who escape the old system: when the ecosystem stops rewarding complexity, it is the people who figure out how to work simply in the present, rather than the people who mastered the complexities of the past, who get to say what happens in the future. (Shirky, 2010)

In the pages that follow, you'll meet some of the journalists who are escaping the old system to reimagine how journalism can work with the public to fulfill the promise of a government "of the people, by the people, for the people."

Consider this a guide to their work, meant to inspire yours.

KEYWORDS

Citizens: The people who live in a community or country and are willing to be responsible for its governance.

Citizenship: The active participation of people in governing themselves through deliberation and decision-making on shared, public issues.

Good Work: Work that connects your values with your actions, for the benefit of society as a whole.

Network: An interconnected, interactive group or system that consists of nodes and hubs.

Participatory Theory of Democracy: The theory that advocates for direct participation in collective decision-making — to the extent possible — rather than delegating public decisions exclusively to elites or representatives.

Public Work: The act of collaborating with others on work that has a public purpose and impact.

Republican Theory of Citizenship: The theory that citizenship relies on the active participation of citizens in processes of self-governance such as deliberation, decision-making and holding public office. It emphasizes political agency to ensure that people are citizens, not subjects.

Social Capital: The reciprocal benefits produced by social relationships and a community's network of relationships. There are two types: bonding (connections within a group) and bridging (connections between groups).

QUESTIONS FOR DISCUSSION

1. How did you think about democracy and citizenship prior to reading this chapter? What is the same or different?

2. How are citizens represented in the media you consume? Select a recent news report to analyze. What are "ordinary citizens" shown to be doing? How are they portrayed? Is it clear in the story that citizens play a central role in a healthy democracy? If citizens are not represented in the story, how could they be?

3. As you think about the news you rely on, through what networks does it flow to you? Trace the specific path of the news, from its origins, through networks, to you.

CHAPTER 2

Relational Journalism
A Deeper Dive

T HE FIRST CHAPTER SUGGESTED THAT A CONFLUENCE OF CHANGES IN American society in the last 25 years has created an opportunity for profound change in the way that citizens exercise their democratic rights and in the way journalists can be a part of that opportunity. In this chapter we take a few deep breaths, and a few steps back, to explore why a society like ours needs journalism, in the hope that understanding the role of journalism in a democratic society will clarify the importance of our book's theme: **relational journalism**.

A vibrant, successful democracy requires more of citizens than going to the polls every few years. For democracy to truly flourish, citizens must also do the more difficult work of identifying — and then solving — common problems on their own, for the benefit of the common good in a community. This is the basis of what we referred to as "participatory democracy" in Chapter 1. In this way, citizens influence their elected officials and help them become more effective at governing. As David Mathews, president and CEO of the Kettering Foundation, a pro-democracy research foundation, has said many times, "For a democracy to be strong and resilient, citizens have to be producers, not just consumers" (Mathews, 2014, p. 141). But again, this work is difficult. Citizens need help. This is where the news media come in. By helping citizens engage in important **democratic practices**, we believe a struggling system of journalism and a struggling democracy can help save each other.

Democracy Needs Journalism

In their book *Normative Theories of the Media*, five world-renowned media scholars — Clifford Christians, Theodore Glasser, Denis McQuail, Kaarle Nordenstreng and Robert A. White — dissected the many possible functions news media can play in societies around the world in the 21st century. In a representative democracy like ours, they identified a handful of essential duties (Christians et al., 2009) similar to those developed over the years by several other media scholars (see for example Blumler & Gurevitch, 1995; Weaver et al., 2007; Knight Commission, 2019).

At the most basic level, democratic society needs journalism to:

- Discover, collect and select reliable information. Every person discovers new facts every day, but any community needs persons dedicated to the task of selecting and collecting those bits of new information that are most important to many in the community.

- Transform that learned information into accounts we call "news." This is what distinguishes massive amounts of data from journalism. Information becomes digestible when it is transformed into an appealing narrative.

- Publish the accounts to a wide audience. If the news is learned by only a small faction within a community, how does that serve democracy?

In fact, these three basic tasks of journalism point to an essential factor in the relationship between democracy and journalism: *In order to cast informed votes or solve shared problems, citizens need a shared set of reliable facts.* Few groups in American society are as trained or as motivated to provide that shared set of reliable facts as journalists.

It doesn't stop there. Journalism has a deeper, more nuanced set of duties than the basics listed above. Borrowing again from the scholars cited above, today's democracies also need journalism to:

- Provide context for the news. This is where journalism lends meaning to the cascade of updated information that pervades today's media system, every hour of every day.

- Provide ongoing surveillance of the society's environments — from the economic and political to the physical and social.

- Provide analysis and commentary, and provide spaces for citizens to offer their own commentary.

- Help citizens understand others whose experiences are different from their own.

- Act as a check, or "watchdog," on powerful people and institutions, to guard against their abuses of that power.

- Investigate claims to distinguish verifiable facts from unfounded rumor.

Freedom, with Responsibility

Christians and his colleagues used the term "normative" in their book's title to signify that these theories suggest the norms that "ought to" direct journalistic behavior and policies, and citizens' support for them. But in the United States, citizens and journalists must also acknowledge a powerful, explicit and legal expectation of journalism: The "ought to" is backed up by a strong "shall." That's the freedom of the press guaranteed in the U.S. Constitution's First Amendment.

Judges, legal scholars and media scholars have spent decades attempting to interpret that short clause "Congress shall make no law ... abridging the freedom of speech, or of the press." When we think about how journalism might best serve our democratic culture, a paradox emerges immediately: If we take "freedom of the press" seriously, doesn't that mean the media are constitutionally "free" to reject any and all roles any of us might want to prescribe for them? In a literal sense, the answer is yes. And because journalism is essentially a private-sector industry, shouldn't its managers be free to create whatever product maximizes profit, regardless of any beneficial "social role" we might prefer the media play? Again, yes. We see this every day: Media content frequently includes harmful, erroneous, salacious, or even danger-inciting words and images, but the First Amendment protects them from censorship or punishment.

And yet we must wonder: If that's all citizens should expect of the media, why did the authors of the Bill of Rights insist on including the inalienable right of freedom for the press — the only private-sector enterprise so protected in the entire Constitution?

Shortly after World War II, this conundrum was addressed by the Hutchins Commission, more formally known as the U.S. Commission on Freedom of the Press (1947). American leaders, inside and outside government, had grown concerned about the recent, sensationalistic behavior of the mass media. The commission attempted, for the first time, to assign certain responsibilities to the media, for the greater benefit of American society. The duties were hardly surprising:

1. Provide a full and reliable account of daily events

2. Provide a forum for a free exchange of comment and criticism

3. Keep opinion separate from fact

4. Provide a picture of contemporary American society that is "representative"

Note, however, that there was no attempt — and in the ensuing 70 years there has been none — to mandate these duties by law. Still, the Hutchins Commission's implication was clear: If the media expects to have its freedom protected by the American government, it ought to provide something important in return. At the very least, the media ought to *serve the public interest* (such as in the ways the Hutchins Commission enumerated). Does such a bold demand threaten media freedom? Again, in the last 70 years, journalists by and large have appeared to be perfectly fine with the notion that their work should somehow serve the public good. As Christians et al. stated (2009), American journalists' work "has always seemed to include strong elements of altruism alongside self-interest" (p. 135).

News Media's Roles in a Democracy

Just how should the media serve the public interest in exchange for their sturdy freedom from censorship or punishment? This brings us back to the normative theories of the media. We start with the tasks and duties listed above. And what Christians and his colleagues discovered in *Normative Theories* was that these journalistic tasks and duties can be applied for different purposes, in different cultures, and with different goals. They identified four distinct roles for media in democracies: one in which the media collect and distribute information about current events (and the most common role for American mainstream journalism for more than a century); one in which the media align with the government's messaging (usually in a young democracy) for the sake of national security; one in which the media join the opposition to the ruling government; and one in which journalism does what it can to help citizens improve the public life.

Christians et al. call this last role the **"facilitative role."** It celebrates journalism that promotes not only the basic democratic practices like voting but also inclusiveness, pluralism and a "collective purpose" in which citizens search for the common good. This is the role that forms the basis for relational journalism. Christians et al. note that the facilitative role "has a constant, though implicit, presence" (p. 176) in the way most media scholars think about the roles of the media in a democracy.

In this respect, the purpose of our book is to make the implicit *explicit*.

The Important (and Difficult) Work of Citizens

"How can *we* come together to build the kind of community we want?"

That's the simple question that best sums up the work of citizens in a democracy, according to the Kettering Foundation's Mathews (p. 141). The answer to that question, in the minds of Mathews and many other democratic theorists, invokes the difficult process of **deliberation**.

We normally think of a citizen's democratic action as voting for candidates or proposals on a ballot, or sometimes even campaigning for a candidate or proposal. This requires minimal participation, in view of all that government does. And few indeed would argue that democracy is succeeding under the current situation with minimal citizen participation. As we saw in Chapter 1, the level of citizens' trust in institutions, including their government and their elected politicians, is alarmingly low. One way to restore power to citizens, in ways that help restore their trust in their government, is to enable people to take a more active and direct role in seeking the public good.

That's a tall order. For starters, as Mathews writes, citizens are too often on the sidelines. Many people don't see their concerns being addressed by those in power. When they do see problems being addressed, they feel they have little voice in the debate unless they have vast amounts of funding to influence the outcome. On top of that, the issues are often discussed (in public forums and in the news media) in ways that promote polarization — a battle between two extreme positions — with little patience for complicated facts, let alone ideas in the middle. This leads to decisions being made not only in haste but influenced more by emotion and ideology than by information and logic. Even when citizens do get involved, their efforts often are scattered in so many different directions that they are ineffective overall, and citizens then have little desire to stay engaged with the process. Worst of all, citizens today tend not to trust governmental institutions — and the feeling is mutual. Major institutions doubt that citizens are capable or responsible. There's little wonder that effective citizen engagement is so rare.

So what kind of democratic practice would overcome these obstacles? Citizen deliberation is at the heart of any democracy. Deliberation is not just people meeting, discussing or debating an issue. Deliberation is the process by which citizens weigh options together to determine what should be done about a shared problem. When there are no clear right or wrong answers to problems, citizens must exercise judgment, and deliberation is a process for doing so.

Aristotle was the first theorist to defend this process, arguing that "ordinary citizens debating and deciding together can reach a better decision than can experts acting alone" (Gutmann & Thompson, 2004, p, 8). Deliberation rests on the principle that "citizens owe one another justifications for the laws they collectively impose on one another" (Gutmann & Thompson, 126).

These deliberative exchanges between and among citizens can happen in formal settings or as part of ongoing everyday talk. Harvard political scientist Jane Mansbridge sees a continuum of settings for deliberation, with everyday talk involving two or three people on the informal end and policy formation by elected officials on the formal end (Mansbridge, 2012). But deliberation occurs anywhere along the spectrum, and Mansbridge warns that everyday talk should never be ignored by anyone wishing to understand deliberation. After all, how do problems often surface for public deliberation in the first place? Residents talk about what concerns them; they do so on a coffee break, in emails or at the grocery store. As Mathews writes (2014), everyday talk will sometimes sound like complaining, or like looking for someone to blame, but it often includes talk about what action should be taken to solve a problem. And that's where the process of deliberation takes off.

The Kettering Foundation has identified six democratic practices that fuel community life and enable citizens to work together effectively (Mathews, 2014). They also serve as a guide to understanding how citizens deliberate. When they deliberate, citizens:

- Identify and define a problem
- Identify the important values that underlie the problem, and importantly those values a community has in common
- Consider different courses of action — based on information that everyone can agree is reliable — and weigh alternatives against those important values
- Identify community resources — not just government funds — that can support action
- Come to a **public judgment** — a decision or action reached after considering the trade-offs and likely consequences
- Commit to organizing themselves for follow-up and longer-term continuity

Strengthening this process matters, Mathews argues, because if citizens' views can coalesce like this, they have more power. As a result, citizens are better equipped to take action and their voices are more easily heard in the halls of government. When officials give more credence to citizens' voices, they in turn earn more legitimacy from citizens.

As we said, as important as the work of citizenry is, it's difficult. Most adults have work and family to attend to — and have limited time and energy to devote to policy formation. This, we believe, is where journalism has significant, and unmet, potential.

Truly Facilitative News Media in the 21st Century

Despite — or perhaps because of — the disruptions that have upended the news business in the early 21st century, journalism is extremely well positioned to help democratic practice, even as it helps itself. If journalists can frame the democratic process as a conversation in which, as Christians et al. have written, "citizens engage one another on both practical matters and social vision" (p. 159), they could turn an audience's attention away from conflicts, gossip and scandal and toward shared problems whose solutions could raise the quality of community life. And because journalism is already doing the work of disseminating information to large audiences quickly, only a tweak is required to emphasize the information — verified, reliable, unbiased — that will help citizens with their deliberation on a particular issue.

That's a good start, but there is much more that journalism can do to facilitate citizen success. Like many institutions in American society, journalism has too often been seduced by elitism — the ease of expertise and punditry to explain issues and problems. Paradoxically, the journalists, pundits and experts often have no personal experience in the issue they're analyzing. Citizens quite often do. A truly facilitative journalism will not just listen to everyday citizens whenever they happen to have the microphone but actively seek out the experiences and "everyday talk" of those folks and grant them legitimacy alongside the expert analysts and political advocates.

In fact, journalists have no choice in the matter. Thanks to "Web 2.0," that is, the developments that enabled the internet interactivity we call social media, ordinary folks have been publicly sharing their experiences for more than a decade. If anything, there is *too much* authentic experience available on social media. Media scholar Jeff Jarvis (2014) sees a fundamental shift in the outlook of today's facilitative journalism. For 200 years, journalism followed a dynamic of the few not only disseminating information to the many but basically controlling that flow — selecting what is "news" every day and thereby setting the agenda for citizens' public consumption and discussion. But because of the explosion of grassroots media startups, from neighborhood newsletters to the advocacy platforms of national interest groups, the traditional news media no longer enjoy that control. Journalism, Jarvis writes, is best thought of as a flow of information that has many, many sources. And professional journalists are participants in that flow. They are usually excellent writers trained in fact-gathering techniques, but they are nonetheless participants alongside thousands and thousands of others disseminating information (and sometimes inaccuracies — "misinformation" — or intentional falsehoods — "disinformation").

To the extent that mainstream journalism still commands the respect of large audiences in the communities they serve, its journalists can serve democratic practice by serving as curators. Just as curators in libraries, museums or art galleries will select and authenticate the work of others and add context to that work, professional journalists have the skill to pluck out the useful information from an otherwise chaotic cacophony on the internet. If journalistic curators can organize information that serves the purpose of shared, verified information that citizens need as they begin to deliberate, journalism will indeed be facilitating the democratic process.

Another fact of today's networked, interactive world comes into play as we think about democratic deliberation. In the past, the "public sphere" in which citizens gathered was always a physical space. Today, the sphere can more easily become available as a virtual space. Citizens can do the work of deliberation from their homes or offices, for example, via videoconferencing. As media scholars Jack Rosenberry and Burton St. John point out (2010), if a citizen-centered news organization wanted to help improve the public life in its community, it could easily build a web-based platform, well stocked with reliable facts and context, in which citizens could deliberate on an issue that the journalists, having already listened to citizens' concerns, have researched. The deliberative process can be moderated by journalists so that the group stays focused on seeking the public good and steers clear of trolling, polarizing positions or tangents. In later chapters we'll see examples of this kind of work already under way.

In fact, Ethan Zuckerman, a media scholar at MIT, has listed seven ways in which social media alone can facilitate democratic deliberation (Zuckerman, 2018). For all its downside risks and attributes, social media can also:

- Inform citizens in ways mainstream media cannot
- Amplify important voices and issues that mainstream media may not be aware of
- Provide a tool for connections and solidarity among citizens
- Serve as a space for citizens' debate and deliberation
- Serve as a space for citizens' mobilization to action
- Provide a tool to show a diversity of perspectives
- Role-model behaviors for how a community can be governed democratically

A facilitative role for media in the 21st century, then, is complex, but that complexity gives it great potential for positive change. Deliberation studies have shown that relationship-building is a reliable precursor to collective problem solving — as is shared access to reliable information. Journalism has the potential to contribute in both regards.

Relational Journalism — Facilitative Media at Work

The second half of this book will explore in detail the practical aspects of the media's facilitative role in a democracy, but it may be useful here to outline the conceptual parameters. What are the major tasks by which media can help build **civic capacity,** that is, the capacity for citizens to succeed in building community and affecting public policy? Overlaying the new *skill set* that journalists must develop to do facilitative journalism is a new *mindset* — a bundle of attitudes and values that propel citizen-centered journalism. Our term for this mindset is relational journalism.

This term is derived from relational communication, which the Oxford University Press's Dictionary of Media and Communication (Oxford University Press, 2016) defines as communication in which the primary focus is the development of an ongoing relationship between the participants. Deliberation studies have shown that relationship-building is a reliable precursor to collective problem solving — as is shared access to reliable information. Journalism has the potential to contribute in both regards.

Communication scholars Gerard Hauser and Chantal Benoit-Barne imagined the benefits of relational communication in a journalistic context in a 2002 essay in which they urged journalists to explore the "vast associational network in which most citizens experience democratic participation and deliberation" (Hauser & Benoit-Barne, 2002, p. 266). They argued that when journalists join citizens in an ongoing process of public participation, public trust in media will, over time, rise. Jan Schaffer, executive director of J-Lab, a nonprofit catalyst for journalism innovation, wrote in 2015 about "Journalism as Relationship-Building," after spending time with the students in the Social Journalism program at CUNY, whose curriculum emphasizes journalism's role in helping communities solve shared problems (Schaffer, 2015). She observed that this new kind of journalism is investing a great deal at the beginning of the reporting process, that is, in listening to citizens' concerns, as distinct from the traditional "audience engagement" that measures page visits and reader comments, at the end of the process.

More recently, scholars and educators have begun to use the term "relational journalism" more commonly to describe an approach to journalism that helps communities help themselves. The Agora Journalism Center at the University of Oregon organized a project called "Find Common Ground" in which journalism innovators in North America and Europe shared best practices on engaging citizens in difficult conversations that sometimes crossed political or cultural differences, in order to solve shared public problems. The result was Agora's "Report on Supporting the Practice of Relational Journalism" (Agora, 2019). And in 2020, a research team at the University of Wisconsin, led by communication scholar Megan Zahay, interviewed and studied the online work of 42 working journalists and found ample evidence that relational journalism had found its way into the daily practice of some (but certainly not all) professional journalists (Zahay et al., 2020). They found that relational journalism was slow and gradual work, compared to the fast turnarounds of traditional reporting, because of the time it takes to build mutual understandings between journalists and everyday people. But the payoff for journalism is worth the effort, they concluded, as it can restore people's trust in the media: "When journalists understand their work as the facilitation of public deliberation, community belonging and democratic participation, that orientation transforms to one of connection and immersion, where trust in journalism emerges from ongoing interpersonal relationships" (p. 5).

Our own research for this book underscored these earlier conclusions with more specific examples of this kind of news work, which is occurring with greater frequency around the country. Based on our own first-hand observations of this new mindset, here are the key attributes of relational journalism.

Commitment to the Long Term

The vast majority of commercial journalism in recent decades is characterized by what we call "extractive journalism," where the journalist views each source as an opportunity for extraction or exploitation and then moves on to the next story or project. "I just need a good quote from the opposition" epitomizes the extractive attitude, whereby that one encounter between source and writer will probably enhance the appeal of one article — and the journalist expects never to encounter that source again. Even if the quote accurately represents the source's point of view, that source is likely to feel exploited by a process that essentially has only fleeting interest in the source's deeper experience. Now imagine, by contrast, a journalism that is committed to a deeper understanding of citizens' experiences. This will require an open-ended commitment to stay with those involved in an issue or problem for as long as it persists. But the payoff seems apparent: Citizens who see their voices listened to over time will not only feel empowered; they will also give the news workers who keep returning to listen to them a good deal more respect than the "extractive" journalist is likely to have.

One of the abiding elements of this kind of commitment is a deep degree of listening by the journalist. Linda Miller, a longtime newspaper and public-radio journalist who was among the first adopters of relational journalism practices, honed "deep listening" practices as director of engagement at Minnesota-based American Public Media. As one example, when APM was planning a series of stories on financial planning, it invited middle-aged, single women to discuss what "financial security" meant to them. The results were in stark contrast to what certified financial planners had identified. Events like these, she told us, are acts of trust-building, and they contribute to the next building block of relational journalism, connecting citizens to one another.

Working with Citizens in Deliberation

If we return briefly to the process of citizens' deliberation described above, we can see how journalism may play a role. Citizens first engage in a process the Kettering Foundation (2011) calls "**naming**": they identify and define a problem, especially a problem that reflects what's most valuable to them. When citizens name a community problem in their own terms, rather than using the language of experts, they can see how the problem affects them and more readily participate in finding solutions. After it is named in a "public" way, accessible to all, comes the work of identifying options and anticipating the consequences of each. This step is known as "**framing**" the issue, that is, setting up a framework for considering various options to solve the "named" problem. Framing should ensure that all options are considered fairly and that the tensions between these options are known. Then begins the difficult job of "working through" the disagreements and weighing the necessary trade-offs. Often called "choicework," this process enables people to move forward on collective action even if they aren't in complete agreement.

Journalists who listen to citizens — not to get one quote but to deeply understand citizens' concerns — can publish, post or broadcast the situation the citizens have named and framed as a community issue. Citizens then identify underlying values and discover which values they all hold in common; journalists can help to do that, in a cohesive and public way. Citizens then must have reliable information that's as free as possible from bias; again, this is what journalists are trained to provide. Eventually citizens deliberating must come to a public judgment — a decision or array of actions that seem likely to enhance the greater good of a community. Even here journalists can contribute without becoming advocates for one policy over others. The Solutions Journalism Network, for example, trains journalists to research solutions one community has found for a particular problem, in ways that citizens in a different community, with a similar problem, might learn and be inspired by. Instead of urging a particular solution, the journalists report on what has worked elsewhere. And finally, citizens in deliberation commit to "collective learning" to stay committed and organized for the long term. Journalism again is organized to archive — for easy retrieval — the information from past weeks, months and years regarding important issues.

If journalists help citizens deliberate in any of these ways, none of that work will necessarily result in a story the next day or week. But with the mindset of relational journalism, this behind-the-scenes work will virtually guarantee more comprehensive and accurate reporting, which will garner more respect and engagement from news audiences. More importantly, it will establish the news media as a factor in the revitalization of democratic practice.

Advocates for greater citizen engagement — as alternatives to, say, the leadership of well-heeled interest groups or politicians — don't always specify who initiates this valuable deliberative process. Mathews (2014) trusts that ordinary citizens will rise into leadership roles as needed, once they become aware that they have something to contribute. Citizen-leaders, he writes, "are leaders because they know how to interact with fellow citizens; they know how to listen" (p. 125). Journalists, by training, also know how to listen, and to connect with citizens.

Sharing the Work of Journalism with Citizens

As we noted above, no one group owns or controls the dissemination of new information, as the journalism profession did in the 20th century. That doesn't mean journalism is dying, though — far from it. What it does mean is that journalists must adjust to new ways of working with the citizens formerly known as "the audience." Again, here is where relational journalism can contribute. News websites can easily construct platforms for virtual dialogue, conversation, debate — all of those dynamics that can eventually lead to deliberation. They can use the legitimacy of the news organization to guide the conversation toward common values and solutions, and away from language that divides communities.

Sharing journalistic tasks with citizens is nothing new, but it has often meant simply inviting citizens to offer "tips" for future stories and to provide feedback on previously posted or published work. Today we see an entire range of citizen collaboration. A pioneer in this area was Linda Miller, who at APM launched the ground-breaking Public Insight Network in 2009. It brought members of the public into the process of making news, as expert consultants or sources on specific topics, and opened journalists to the idea of getting help in their fact-finding. City Bureau, a nonprofit news organization in Chicago, trains citizens to do public-affairs reporting, and the newly minted journalists cover neighborhood government issues that mainstream news organizations no longer have the resources to cover. Also in Chicago, "The Curious City" series at WBEZ radio selects questions submitted by listeners and then invites whoever submitted the selected question to collaborate with the reporter on the story that will answer that question.

New Levels of Transparency

For the last few decades, journalism has heard more calls for greater transparency. In fact, media ethicists McBride and Rosenstiel (2014) identified transparency as one of the three overarching principles that define ethical journalism (the other two being "truth" and "community"). But with the new mindset of relational journalism, transparency must involve more than publishing more, and more honest, corrections after mistakes have occurred. The Knight Commission (2019) urged the adoption of "radical transparency," which calls upon editors to draw back the curtain that has traditionally cloaked the process of reporting. This could include publishing links to the primary sources reporters used in researching a story; explanations as to why a certain story was pursued and why another issue was not pursued for a story; separation of commentary from factual reporting and clear labeling as to which is which; and explanation as to why some sources were named and others allowed to remain "anonymous." The most radical news organizations in this area (and we'll meet a few of them in later chapters) proactively invite citizens to partake in every stage of the newsgathering process.

New Levels of Diversity and Inclusion

If the facilitative role turns its attention to everyday citizens, and the issues defined by them, it is by necessity increasing the diversity of its work. If by diversity we mean an array of different experiences and different points of view — especially including experiences and points of view that have historically been overlooked — then relational journalism seems ideal for expanding diversity. Again, consider the traditional alternative to the facilitative role: journalists relying almost exclusively on experts and officials (administrators or politicians) for the public-affairs information. If a citizen with no particular clout was included, it was often for the purpose of illustrating a theme established by the expert or official. When journalism displays a world constructed by those holding the greatest power, they may be staying close to important, official actions, but they are also exacerbating the divide that already exists between citizens and the institutions that control so much of their lives. Add to that a media fascination with the vanities and scandals of those at the highest levels of power, and it's no wonder ordinary citizens can at times feel alienated from the world they see in the media.

To regain the trust of citizens, news must become more relevant to more citizens. Linda Miller said that the practices of relational journalism almost always lead to greater sensitivity to subjects and sources, which cannot help but expand diversity. That, in turn, cannot help but broaden the scope, and enhance the authenticity, of the journalism. As one example, Miller said that at APM she encouraged reporters to pretest questions with members of underrepresented communities before beginning to interview subjects in those communities.

This, then, is the bird's-eye view of what journalism looks like when it takes its facilitative role seriously in a contemporary democracy. We hasten to emphasize that relational journalism must *not* be viewed as a replacement for the journalism that occurs today in most news organizations. News outlets, especially those reporting breaking news, must still cover election results, sports scores, school board decisions, park openings, business openings, road construction, and all the myriad activities that comprise community life in America. Relational journalism involves the recalibration of the journalists' mindset so that their attention turns more quickly and more often to questions of what citizens need to know *in order to succeed at the work of citizenship*. Not every story can be the result of behind-the-scenes journalistic assistance to citizen deliberation, or the result of collaborations with citizens as co-producers. But over the long term, with new levels of transparency and inclusiveness, and obvious commitments to the long-term success of a community, journalists are finding new levels of citizen trust in what they're doing. And trust, as several media managers will point out in Part II of the book, is a key component of financial sustainability for any news organization.

Relational journalism looks difficult, and ambitious, to be sure. Some might question whether it's worth the effort. But when pollsters have been finding over the last several decades that only 20 to 30 percent of Americans have much trust in the news media, why would anyone want to sustain the same old approach? What is there to lose in a new approach that's based on solidly democratic principles?

Media's problems are mainly discussed at the national level, but this book's level of analysis is nearly always at the local level. Why? The local level is usually where reform occurs.

The Kettering Foundation's Mathews has stated many times that change in democratic practice is bred, first and always, at the local level. This is where journalists and citizens together can see that a new approach has brought about a real change in public life or policy. Other localities read or hear about what was done, and can replicate that success at their own, manageable, local level. Eventually a network of communities has developed, all sharing in what seems to be working. As Mathews says, "Change can and does radiate out" (Mathews, 2014, p. 98).

The news-media industry is undergoing massive upheaval as the third decade of this century begins. Certain forms of delivery are disappearing, to be sure, but that doesn't doom the future of journalism itself. As media scholar Dan Kennedy has written, "Journalism will survive and thrive — even if it looks very different from the newspapers of decades past, less arrogant, more willing to listen and take part in a conversation with their communities, more willing to 'be' part of their communities" (Kennedy 2013, p. 152).

KEYWORDS

Civic capacity: The extent to which a person or community can participate effectively in the political decision-making process.

Deliberation: The process by which citizens make decisions that lead to problem-solving actions.

Democratic practices: Ways that citizens can work together to address shared problems. The Kettering Foundation has identified six of them. They are: naming issues in terms of what is most important; framing issues so that a range of actions are considered; making decisions deliberately; identifying resources; organizing actions in a complementary fashion and learning collectively from what has occurred.

Facilitative role: A role for news media in a democracy that seeks to help improve the quality of public life. It celebrates journalism that promotes not only democratic practices but also inclusiveness, pluralism and a "collective purpose" in which citizens search for the common good.

Framing: The presentation of different options for dealing with a problem, once that problem has been publicly "named," in order to build a framework for decision making.

Naming: The process by which someone — a political group, an official, a research team, the news media or even one citizen — defines a public problem. This is one of the early stages of democratic deliberation.

Public judgment: The point at which people hold steady views that indicate that they are knowledgeable about an issue and accept the risks, costs and trade-offs involved in the actions they take. The term was coined by public opinion analyst Daniel Yankelovich.

Relational journalism: Journalism whose primary focus is the development of an ongoing relationship with the community it serves. It involves a set of approaches that aim not only to restore people's trust in news media but also to increase citizens' power in the democratic process.

QUESTIONS FOR DISCUSSION

1. This chapter's conclusion cautions that relational journalism should be considered a complement to, not a replacement for, traditional (mainstream) approaches to journalism. What do you consider to be the aspects of traditional journalism that are most compatible with relational journalism? Least compatible?

2. Many traditionally oriented journalists told Megan Zahay's research team that the best path to restoring trust in the news media was to double down on the classic dedication to distributing reliable, accurate, objective news reports — and not getting involved with the sources or communities they covered. Yet this approach, pervasive over the last 80 years, has not stopped the erosion of trust in the media. Why do you think so few Americans trust their news media?

3. Of the five elements of relational journalism described near the end of this chapter, which one do you suppose would be most difficult for today's journalism profession to achieve? Why? Which element do you see as most easily within reach? Why?

CHAPTER 3

Relational Journalism's Roots and Shoots

RELATIONAL JOURNALISM EMERGED AS AN IMPORTANT NEW PHENOMENON in the late 2010s, but its roots extend fairly deep. To understand the origins and context of relational journalism, we reach back to **public journalism,** a movement in the 1990s where, for the first time in the history of American journalism, journalists gave members of the public a role in the identification and development of news. They recognized a disconnect between journalism and the public, and they sensed that the disconnect's growth would be detrimental not only to the news industry but also to civic life in America. Public journalism was where we saw the beginning of the shift in the journalistic mindset that we see accelerating now. Many of public journalism's experiments from the 1990s comprise the foundation of what innovators are doing today.

The Emergence of Public Journalism

Public journalism was an important, though short-lived, experiment that challenged journalists to consciously involve the public in democratic processes. The innovators, who experimented with new ways to engage people in journalism and public life, were responding to early signals from the public that neither journalism nor public institutions were serving their interests well.

Proponents of public journalism argued that reporting the news the way it had always been done wasn't good enough. They wondered how news might be different if citizens helped to identify issues and frame the questions asked. They suggested that news organizations experiment with ways to help the public understand a community problem more fully, discuss their views with others and engage in solving it.

At the time, even seemingly simple tweaks to longstanding reporting practices were considered at best unorthodox and at worse heretical.

This movement, from the early 1990s to early 2000s, was variously called public journalism or **civic journalism**. Its emergence coincided with two similar movements that influenced it. In response to heightened concerns about individualism as a threat to the nation's fabric, communitarianism, a social and political philosophy that emphasizes community and the common good, was gaining in popularity. Also underway was a national civic renewal movement that emphasized the role of ordinary citizens as producers of public goods.

Finding ways to inspire citizens to engage in public work in their communities was a central tenet of the public journalism effort, but it did not have one clearly articulated theory. Instead it was defined primarily by its practices and practitioners.

Since that time, the public's dissatisfaction with all institutions has grown, and trust in the media has plummeted. The business models for print and broadcast journalism have been thoroughly disrupted by digital technologies. Amid this disruption and chaos in journalism, white spaces of opportunity have now opened up and sparked one of the greatest periods of invention since Johannes Gutenberg introduced movable type and the printing press. Today's innovators are trying to harness the potential of these ever-changing digital "printing presses" born of the information era. They are looking for ways to use emerging technologies and new media platforms to provide journalism that will better serve the needs of citizens in a democracy. Some of this DNA can be traced back to the early ideas that energized the public journalism movement.

Who Was Doing It?

Many histories of the public journalism movement peg its beginning to dissatisfaction with the 1988 presidential election campaign coverage. But it likely was birthed earlier that year in Columbus, Georgia, when *The Ledger-Enquirer* reported on citizens' major concerns and the progress they would like to see. When government failed to respond and the "Beyond 2000" report on a citizen's agenda languished, editor Jack Swift, with help from the Kettering Foundation, organized deliberative gatherings in his backyard, at a local mall and elsewhere. At *The Wichita Eagle* in Kansas, executive editor Davis "Buzz" Merritt was enthusiastically exploring how to better cover elections and public affairs. In 1992, the *Eagle* published "The People Project: Solving It

Ourselves," using public journalism techniques to report on community issues. The newspapers Swift and Merritt led were among the 32 owned by Knight Ridder, whose CEO, James K. Batten, encouraged the experiments and helped spread the ideas.

Public scholars Jay Rosen at New York University and James Carey at Columbia University joined the effort by sharing academic insights, constructing theoretical models and providing practical support. The Kettering Foundation shared its expertise in public deliberation and community politics.

Major reporting projects began appearing across the country, with *The Virginian-Pilot* and *The Ledger-Star* in Norfolk, Virginia, *The Wichita Eagle*, *The State* in Columbia, South Carolina, and *The Charlotte Observer* playing early leadership roles. Most of the newspapers began experimenting with public journalism ideas by launching special projects about knotty social problems and policy options or about elections. Often the news organizations applied what they had learned in one project to others and, over time, made some of the practices part of their daily reporting routines. *The Spokesman-Review* in Spokane, Washington, offers one such example. After five years of experimenting, the newspaper produced a handbook on how it had incorporated civic journalism practices into its daily routines. In a December 1997 letter to newspaper colleagues across the country, editor Chris Peck shared what his team had learned about "techniques and practices that have led to great stories, helped develop some new beats, and most of all have strengthened the ties between the newspaper and the communities we serve" (Peck, 1997). At the outset of this letter, Peck acknowledges that civic journalism is not widely understood or respected. "When some editors hear the words 'civic journalism' their muscles tighten, and veins begin to pop out. Our experience in Spokane with civic journalism has had a much different effect."

Peck said civic journalism approaches led the newspaper to:

- Encourage readers to host a neighborhood meeting to discuss key community issues and share their discussion notes. The newspaper provided pizza.

- Abandon the traditional editorial page staff structure and redirect the focus by creating an interactive editor to bring more voices and reader-written commentaries into the opinion pages.

- Incorporate civic journalism techniques into enterprise reporting, including coverage of the antigovernment and white separatist movements in the Pacific Northwest.

The Central Tension

The public journalism movement brought to light a fundamental conflict among journalists about the role they should play in a democracy. Central to the dispute was an argument about objectivity, a longstanding principle that journalists should adhere to the facts and be neutral and detached. Public journalists thought it could create an unnecessary distance between them and community members. Traditionalists countered that this stance assured fairness.

Davis "Buzz" Merritt, former executive editor of Knight Ridder's *Wichita Eagle* in Kansas, and Leonard Downie Jr., former executive editor of *The Washington Post*, were stalwarts of the debate during this period and their published remarks typify the polarity. Merritt said he used the term "public journalism" because "it embodied the dual ideas of journalism as accepting its role in, and obligations to, public life, and because newspapers adopting it would be public, that is to say, open about their intentions" (Merritt, 2005, p. 202).

Downie, however, wrote, "Most civic journalism blurs a line we'd prefer remain bright and clear: the line that separates journalists, who are constitutionally protected observers of the world around them, from the people they are often observing, those who hold power in the community. Newspapers as deliberate community boosters make us uncomfortable" (Downie & Kaiser, 2002, p. 98). Merritt would reply (1995) that the "professional" detachment Downie advocated actually undermined journalism's claim to authority, because journalists, when obsessed with the "objectivity" of robotically giving equal space to both sides of any controversy, seemed not to care about actual outcomes. "Moving beyond aloofness means vigorously pursuing ... all of the possibilities of resolution of problems," Merritt wrote. "It does not mean trying to determine outcomes, but it does mean accepting the obligation to help the process of public life determine the outcomes" (p. 116). The debate, at times highly nuanced and often rancorous, raged for more than a decade among journalists and at professional conferences. Notably, mid-sized and smaller newspapers more closely connected to their communities were generally more willing to reconsider their role and embrace public journalism than were their regional and national counterparts.

Characteristics

Here are some of the ways in which journalists were shifting their roles and changing their professional routines (Lambeth et al., 1998). They would:

- Listen systematically to the stories and ideas of citizens, even while protecting the freedom to choose what to cover.

- Examine alternative ways to frame stories on important community issues.

- Choose frames that stand the best chance to stimulate citizen deliberation and build public understanding of issues.

- Take the initiative to report on major public problems in a way that advances public knowledge of possible solutions and the values served by alternative courses of action.

- Pay continuing and systematic attention to how well and how credibly it is communicating with the public.

In Practice: *The Charlotte Observer*

The Charlotte Observer was among the first news organizations to experiment with many of the approaches that would come to be known as civic or public journalism. Disappointed with coverage of the 1988 presidential election and that of a racially charged U.S. Senate race in 1990, *Observer* editors reoriented coverage of the 1992 campaign cycle to focus on the interests of citizens. Journalists at the *Observer* then began to apply what they learned to state and local political coverage and to reporting about complex community problems.

To cover the 1992 election campaign, the *Observer* eschewed tradition and shifted its focus to the public. The newspaper asked the public to identify issues that mattered to them and framed their coverage from the citizens' perspective rather than chronicling agendas advanced by the campaigns. Encouraged by its then-owner, Knight Ridder, to find ways to be more relevant, the *Observer* partnered with the Poynter Institute for Media Studies to pioneer reporting methods that might be more useful to the public and increase their levels of engagement. The first step was to survey residents in the newspaper's coverage area. It identified six areas of citizen concern on which reporters would focus. Rather than reporting on campaign tactics, horse-race polls and political fisticuffs, the *Observer* organized its coverage around this "Citizens Agenda." Journalists explored solutions to the issues and pressed candidates to address them. Political candidates weren't happy because "they thought they were losing their voice," said Rick Thames, former executive editor of the *Observer*. Journalists across the country criticized the effort, fearing that the news organization was compromising its independence. But the public seemed to appreciate the change and said so in calls and letters, according to Thames, who believes "the voter should be the boss" (Thames, personal interview, March 26, 2019).

What began as an experiment to change the way elections are reported evolved into a shifting mindset that generated new reporting practices and produced novel efforts to engage people in public life. In 1994 the *Observer* undertook an ambitious and gutsy reporting project that explored the increase in violent crimes in central-city neighborhoods. "Taking Back Our Neighborhoods: The People's Agenda" was designed to engage the entire city in understanding the root causes of increased crime violence and to address them.

Cheryl Carpenter, a former top editor who led the project, said that the earlier election coverage converted her to the ideals of public journalism and the power of putting the interests of citizens above all others. Carpenter and team wanted to figure out new ways to treat people living in the troubled neighborhoods as "every-day experts." Not only would people see themselves in the problem, but the reporting also could help them see themselves as part of the solution. "Anytime you let people see the power they can have; it becomes a clarion call for them to act" (Carpenter, personal interview, March 26, 2019).

The *Observer* produced rigorous database reporting, known in these early days as "computer-assisted reporting," which included the first geo-mapping of crime, provided backgrounders that explained the history of how things had evolved and used observational reporting practices. It conducted survey research and reported on possible solutions while carefully avoiding any appearance of advocacy. It also hosted forums and joined with radio and television partners to spread the reporting and engage the community. Journalists, however, weren't automatically trusted in many communities. To help them, the *Observer* hired a "community coordinator" with media experience and local credibility to organize neighborhood meetings with residents. This had never been done before and was criticized within the newsroom and the profession at large. The move was labeled "pandering" by some and seen as a risk to the journalists' position as independent, objective observers.

Carpenter vividly recalls being personally assailed by other journalists at the time. But she and her colleagues were onto something important back then, the implications of which would become more obvious over time.

Thames recalls that the neighborhood meetings were "amazing to watch" because "it was journalism unfolding in front of you."

Here are some observations she shared with her team about what they learned from the "Neighborhoods" reporting project (Carpenter, 1995):

- Interaction distinguishes your project but doesn't make it. You must supply readers with information to draw their best reactions. For the discussions to be truly meaningful, readers must be armed with information. You must dispel myths, confirm numbers, examine data, question policies and explore history.

- Be prepared for your success. You hope that your stories provoke people into some action or outrage. But are you ready to listen and to acknowledge them?

- Get closer, but realize it carries responsibilities. When you ask readers to share their opinions and solutions, they naturally develop expectations that you'll listen intently, and maybe even agree with them. Keep talking to readers about what you're doing and what you're trying to achieve. Tell them how your story is shaping up and how your readers fit in it. Keep stating your goals.

- As a reporting and editing team, talk often at the beginning. Repeat your goals among yourselves. You'll find you're paying more attention to the problems than to the solutions. You'll find yourselves resenting that you have to write stories of hope when you see so much chaos. But the stories of role models help distinguish and balance your project.

- Solutions reporting is more difficult than you can imagine. That's because it's about the art of the possible. Local officials might think small about solutions because they are thinking of their resources and their turf. You must think big.

- Your primary responsibility: Dissect these daunting and incomprehensible issues to their most practical end. Create convenient paths for readers to act and interact.

As we will see in Part II, many of today's innovators have come to similar realizations and are building journalistic enterprises around these insights.

What Was Learned?

In a 2016 piece for Poynter.org, Roy Peter Clark, former dean and senior scholar of the Poynter Institute, revisited the public journalism movement and wondered how the presidential campaign coverage might be better if public journalism's core findings were incorporated (Clark, 2016). Here is what was learned:

- Readers can be partners as well as customers.
- Exploring solutions is as important to readers as exposing problems.
- Allegiance of journalists to a distant, detached "objectivity" often comes at a price of community understanding and engagement.
- Political coverage should be about what's important to citizens, not just what's important to politicians or the press.
- News organizations can change; so, too, can the forms of journalism.
- Erosion of citizens and news readership are linked; to revive one, you need to revive both.

Building on What Was Learned

Today's media landscape is ripe with innovation and experimentation that aim to make news more available, relevant and useful to a more diverse citizenry. Many of the ideas being tested seek to solve problems that journalists earlier had only begun to identify. Those early experimenters and today's innovators share a common concern: How can journalism be more useful to citizens doing the work of democracy, from choosing their elected representatives to working together to solve public problems?

As outlined in Chapter 1, the context in which this question is being asked and answered has shifted dramatically over the intervening two decades. The new knowledge about networks, community building and positive psychology, for example, informs the work of today's innovators. Rapidly changing technology has opened new frontiers of possibility and peril. And in the face of declining trust and industry tumult, the case for experimentation and change seems more apparent and urgent than it did when advocates of public or civic journalism were proselytizing.

Let's take a look at some of the more prominent genres that have emerged, recognizing that these approaches are continuously under development. Today's innovators have adopted the tools of agile development and iteration. They experiment, reflect and adapt as they learn from the marketplace.

Each can trace a piece of its ancestry to the ideals of public or civic journalism, and each comprises a variation of what we call relational journalism. Each approach offers its own nuanced understanding of how journalism contributes to the root causes of polarization, disengagement and the lack of trust that imperils democracy. Each, however, requires that journalists first recognize the impact their work has on the body politic and take responsibility for it.

That so many journalists are ready, willing and able to do this represents a significant shift in the zeitgeist.

Constructive Journalism

This approach to news emphasizes reporting on solutions to problems by exploring what's possible, what's inspiring and what's working. *It borrows heavily from the field of positive psychology to reframe how journalists approach their work in an effort to more fully inform the public. It is future-oriented. The role of the journalist is to "facilitate," not "judge or police" (Haagerup, 2017). The journalistic stance is to be critical but constructive, not negative, as well as caring, not detached.

Pioneered in Scandinavia around 2007, this orientation continues to gain traction among journalists who think that by not focusing exclusively on conflict and negativity, they can provide the public with a more complete and accurate view of what's going on. Constructive news aims to offer the public a way out, hope, inspiration, call to action, education and perspective (Haagerup, 2017). Rather than reporting only on what has happened in the past, practitioners emphasize that news should help people create the future. This future-orientation is a key characteristic that guides many of the changes in journalistic routines.

It explores such questions as "What Now?" and "How?" to generate more constructive, solutions-oriented answers. It focuses on the root causes of complex issues and includes the perspectives and interpretations of those who are involved and affected. It surfaces emerging ideas, solutions and trends. It engages people by fostering "thoughtful conversation, collaboration and consensus building," and "illuminates how not only those in power are having/can have an impact" (Constructive Journalism Project, 2015). A news report fashioned as a **constructive journalism** piece would have the following characteristics: critical, objective and balanced; tackling important issues facing society, not trivial; calm in its tone and does not give in to scandals and outrage; bridging, not polarizing; forward-looking and future-oriented; nuanced and contextualized; based on facts; and facilitating well informed debate around solutions to well documented problems (Haagerup, 2017).

It is not promoting a specific agenda, crossing the line between journalism and politics; uncritical or naïve; promoting heroes, governments or civil society organizations; obscuring critical viewpoints; activism in any shape or form; dumbed-down, trivial or happy news; giving in to false equivalence/balance proposing solutions to problems or advocating one solution over another; or over-simplifying complex problems or solutions to complex problems. Journalists in the constructive news movement, like other solution-oriented journalists, continue to find evidence that the articles they produce are shared more on social media and engaged with for longer than are traditional reports.

As the distribution of news moves more to social platforms and moves at greater speeds, the role all media play in shaping perceptions is expanding. And the gaps between what people believe to be true and what is factually supported appear to be more pronounced. Constructive journalism recognizes that it plays a vital role as a filter between reality and the perception of reality.

Because workplace cultures help share the mindset of those who work in them, constructive news proponents suggest that newsrooms themselves must be transformed. It regards negativity, cynicism, conflict and drama as illnesses that infect the news as well as the people who produce and consume it. This relationship between organizational culture and the product it creates is well documented in studies of business management. Long before the rise of constructive journalism, a jarring 2001 study about newsroom cultures in the United States found that they were defensive, negative, self-protective and similar to military and hospital cultures (Nesbitt & Glaspie, 2004). After the report, leadership groups like the Associated Press Managing Editors began discussing how to create more "constructive" cultures.

Solutions Journalism

The name says it all. **Solutions journalism** focuses on reporting about how people are responding to problems.

The Solutions Journalism Network began in 2013 with an emphasis on educating journalists about the value of reporting on what works. Its work has expanded greatly since then as has its reach and impact. The best early examples of the emergent solutions approach were found in the Fixes blog in the Opinionator section of *The New York Times* where David Bornstein began examining why certain solutions to complex social problems worked, partly so that others might try them.

Today, these complex, persistent public problems are commonly referred to as "wicked problems" for which there is no technical solution. Homelessness, poverty, water shortages and childhood education are examples of these difficult, shared public problems that in a democracy citizens must engage and act on. The methods and practices of journalism weren't well suited to tackling complex problems either.

Bornstein, Fixes co-author Tina Rosenberg and Courtney Martin founded Solutions Journalism as a network they hoped would tilt the emphasis of journalism from what's broken and corrupt to what might work. The focus on negativity and failure, they said in a 2015 annual report, "undermines public discourse, it stunts citizenship, and it doesn't even succeed very well at its core functions: providing society with the information it needs to self-govern and self-correct" (Bornstein et al., 2015, p. 2).

What's missing, they argued, was a sense that solutions are possible.

"We seek to rebalance the news, so that every day people are exposed to stories that help them understand problems and challenges, and stories that show potential ways to respond," according to the mission statement of the nonprofit Solutions Journalism Network. In addition to changing community narratives, Solutions Journalism seeks to "catalyze activities that connect solutions reporting to constructive, de-polarizing public conversations" (Solutions Journalism Network, 2020, Who We Are /Mission page).

The nonprofit organization was founded to evolve its solutions-oriented approach, train and connect journalists who use it, support work in communities and partner with educators interested in teaching the reporting and public engagement approaches.

The organization says it has trained more than 10,000 journalists and worked with 160 news organizations, nine communities and 17 journalism schools to evolve and spread the approach.

If their ideas were to catch fire, leaders of the Solutions Journalism Network understood they would need to fight for legitimacy in a profession that had consistently rejected anything that sounded like feel-good news that lacked the type of hard-hitting, objective reporting rigor found in investigative reporting. From the outset, they emphasized that reporting done by the Solutions Journalism Network was rigorous and evidence based. Those who worried the effort lacked journalistic substance were reassured by the involvement and leadership of Rosenberg, a journalist who won a Pulitzer Prize for General Nonfiction.

Shortly after it was founded, the Solutions Journalism Network worked with *The Seattle Times*, already known as an innovator in the industry, to create the Education Lab to explore the complex challenges of public education, share solutions and engage with readers. Linda Shaw, the newspaper's Ed Lab leader, who now works for the Solutions Journalism Network, recalls how skeptical fellow journalists were about the solutions focus. But the concerns faded when colleagues saw the quality of the reporting and the increased interest from residents who attended the issue-oriented public events the newspaper hosted. We'll return to learn more from *The Seattle Times* in Chapter 6.

Dialogue Journalism

Dialogue journalism is founded on the bedrock belief that for democracy to succeed, people need to talk with one another to understand differing perspectives and work things through.

In this approach, the journalist's role shifts dramatically to that of a facilitator who actively supports and encourages people engaging with complex community challenges for which there is no right or wrong technical solution. To solve these "wicked problems," people must deliberate with one another to arrive at possible solutions.

"People think differently than journalists," said Jeremy Hay, who with Eve Pearlman founded Spaceship Media, where dialogue journalism was born. "There's a movement toward slow news for a reason." Members of the public need time, exposure to the ideas of others, verified facts and the opportunity to talk things through as they try to figure out what to do. "People want time to assess, think, connect and learn. They are not driven by the same impulse that many journalists are to create copy quickly," Pearlman said. People want to be treated as whole people, "not just avatars of particular political positions or views" (J. Hay & E. Pearlman, personal interview, June 25, 2018).

Spaceship Media has been working since 2016 to better align the interests of the public and journalists by developing and advocating for dialogue journalism, which it believes is essential to the machinery of democracy. The organization's mission is to "reduce polarization, build communities and restore trust in journalism."

To better assist the public, Spaceship Media asks journalists to examine their work carefully, at every step of the process, and reimagine it. "We honor a slower pace and host conversations that take place over weeks or months so that people have an opportunity to think, reflect, absorb and understand," Pearlman said. Dialogue Journalism values authenticity, not objectivity. To be authentic a journalist must "go in with an open heart" and "be as broad as possible in your pursuit of truth." "Journalists are driven by curiosity but also are driven to certainty in their desire to make meaning," said Pearlman. Dialogue helps journalists explore more issues more broadly and with greater nuance.

Dialogue journalism is intended to go directly to the heart of the issues that divide people. It surfaces the points of conflict, not to report a two-sided duel, but to enlarge the conversation. Attitudinally, it asks that journalists seek first to understand, then to be understood. Listening and community are at the center of every dialogue journalism process, said Pearlman, Spaceship's chief executive officer. Practitioners always are thinking about being of service and creating connections between people, she explained.

Spaceship Media, working with other media organizations that host the dialogues, has designed and facilitated conversations about guns, the achievement gap in education, immigration, race, electoral politics and other highly polarizing topics. This is a method for creating, moderating, nurturing and sustaining conversations between groups of people whose views are at odds. In Chapter 8 we'll learn more about these innovative journalistic methods.

Each of these three approaches to journalism unabashedly aims to help citizens in a democracy work together to solve shared public problems. They ask that journalists play a constructive role in community life; that journalists adopt a solutions orientation to pressing problems; and that journalists recognize dialogue as an essential democratic practice that can bridge divides, allowing common ground to emerge.

These three are part of a much larger and growing field that has emerged carrying some public journalism DNA. The field includes restorative narrative, peace journalism, developmental journalism, engaged journalism and social journalism. Restorative narrative, for example, accepts that journalists can help or hurt individuals and communities dealing with tragedy and trauma. Mindful that the narrative choices they make have impact, they deepen their reporting and explore the processes of healing, growth and resilience that accompany tragedy. This strengths-based approach, which incorporates insights from positive psychology, helps move stories and communities from despair to possibility. Curtiss Clark, editor of *The Newton* (Conn.) *Bee* in 2012 when a gunman killed 20 children and six adults at Sandy Hook Elementary School, encouraged this new way of thinking. He challenged himself and others to shift journalism from reporting exclusively on what happened to what's possible. "We need to extract ourselves from the sticky amber that freezes things in time" and highlight "acts of benevolence," he said (Aviv, 2013). Images and Voices of Hope, a nonprofit that had long advocated for a strengths-based approach to news, heeded Clark's call and created the genre of restorative narratives, recognizing journalism's larger role in attending to the well-being of a community.

How journalists identify and report on conflict goes to the heart of the definition of news. Like Spaceship, those who practice peace journalism make choices about how to frame conflicts in constructive ways that promote understanding, dialogue and solutions. Peace journalists choose their approaches with the intention of promoting nonviolent solutions. The Center for Global Peace Journalism at Park University is a good resource for this genre of reporting (Park, 2020). It outlines 10 core principles that include giving voice to voiceless and countering narratives that promote stereotypes and misconceptions.

Developmental journalism takes the mission to be inclusive, constructive and solutions-oriented one step farther. It is explicit in its desire to contribute "positively" to the development of the country in which it works. Interpretations of how to do this vary greatly and thus are hotly contested largely because of differences in how to apply principles of objectivity when dealing with governments. While developmental journalism is primarily practiced in the coverage of emerging countries, its influences can be seen in reporting about deeply challenged communities in the United States and elsewhere. The Listening Post Collective, which is featured in Chapter 8, incorporates some of its traits. Persistent, ongoing coverage of deeply rooted complex problems is common to all developmental journalism approaches.

As renewed interest in the ideas of public journalism has accelerated, professional groups and universities have introduced new terms to describe the styles of journalism they are developing together. Engaged journalism values connecting with community members, listening to them and collaborating with them in hopes that these connections will build trust. Social journalism recognizes the transformative effect the internet has had on journalism and communication. First introduced at the City University of New York's Craig Newmark Graduate School of Journalism, it builds on many of public journalism's impulses but enlarges the ideas, recognizing the unique opportunities the internet created for professionals and readers to join forces. As with other reform efforts, it aims to increase trust and recognizes that journalism is a service to people, not a product. It too emphasizes listening and building relationships.

Did Public Journalism Work? Can It?

Did the reforms that grew out of the first wave of public journalism have an impact? It all depends. Advocates of public journalism rightly sensed that their practices at the time were misaligned with the public. They couldn't clearly identify or articulate the disconnect but embraced experimentation as the way to find out.

Journalism at the time was not an entrepreneurial business. Rather, it was a stable profession with a resolute set of practices enshrined in its ethics codes. Practices of agile development and iteration were not the norm. The media outlets had few competitors. News and information were not as ubiquitous as they are today, and everyday citizens couldn't create and distribute content.

The reformers' inability to describe the problems they were trying to solve with precision left them open to criticism from those who feared professional standards were being breached.

In many ways, today's innovators are picking up where the public journalism pioneers left off. They are trying to answer similar questions to those raised more than 30 years ago. But how can we know if changes in journalism practice can improve public life when there are so many confounding factors and no clear causal relationships?

Philip Meyer (Lambeth et al., 1998) offered some short- and long-term indicators when asked to evaluate the effects of public journalism. As short-term indicators, he suggested:

- *Public knowledge*: Do more people know who the candidates are and specific details about the issues?

- *Political participation*: Measure voting and other forms of participation ranging from volunteering for campaigns to displaying bumper stickers.

- *Ideological consistency*: Do people have more coherent, self-consistent views than those who look at fragmented information in isolation?

- *Attitude strength*: Stronger attitudes are a sign of progress in developing public judgment.

- *Willingness to accept the consequences*: Does the holder of an opinion accept the implied consequences?

As longer-term indicators to determine if public journalism was successful, Meyer suggested looking at community ties, levels of trust between people and trust in institutions.

Both the short-term and long-term indicators ought to serve equally well, in the not-too-distant future, when media scholars evaluate the impact of relational journalism on the health of journalism and the health of the community.

KEYWORDS

Constructive journalism: Reporting that rejects traditional negative and conflict-based frames for news and, drawing on the concepts of positive psychology, focuses on the potential for constructive solutions.

Dialogue journalism: A set of practices to engage a wide-variety of people in often difficult conversations about polarizing public issues with the goal of bridging divides. Journalists supply facts and information to the discussion and often report stories about them, but the dialogue itself is the primary journalistic product.

Public journalism, or civic journalism: A reform movement of the '90s aimed at making news more relevant and useful to the public by going beyond providing information to encouraging participation in democratic life.

Solutions journalism: Reporting that focuses on helping people understand a shared public problem and offers solutions with a goal of spurring public discourse and citizen action.

QUESTIONS FOR DISCUSSION

1. Ever since the early days of public journalism, its critics have worried that engaged, citizen-centered reporting sacrifices objectivity, which in turn sacrifices public trust and credibility in the news media. Do you agree or disagree? Why?

2. Take another look at Philip Meyer's criteria for evaluating the impact of public journalism. From what you've read in this chapter about today's new "descendants" of public journalism, do you think they are having greater positive impact than the public journalists of the 1990s had? Explain.

3. If public journalism had been introduced 10 or 15 years later, after the advent of social media, do you think it would have enjoyed more, or less, initial success as a journalistic form? Why?

CHAPTER 4

Who Is a Journalist?

I F EVER THERE WERE AN OCCUPATION IN THE UNITED STATES SUFFERING A long-term identity crisis, "journalist" would be it. For almost the entire 20th century, journalists, the companies that employed them, and the universities that educated them strived to establish journalism as a profession. Increasingly, those in the journalistic work force had benefited from specialized education, they joined professional organizations, they fought for privileges within the legal system, and they saw themselves as providing widespread service to American democracy. Their work thus very much resembled a profession.

Then came the 21st century, and, much like their industry as a whole, professional journalists' dominance in the field came tumbling down. Today, most people's notion of "journalist" is quite different even from 20 years earlier. In the citizen-centered journalism we envision in this book, our notion of "journalist" is remarkably different.

In the early 1900s, as American intellectual leaders began to appreciate the virtues of the scientific method in everyday life, the idea of a disciplined set of procedures and values, together defining an occupation, began to take hold. Not only did physicians and attorneys consider themselves professionals, but now so too could accountants, architects, teachers, stockbrokers and workers in several other specialized fields — including, by the 1910s, journalists. Journalism education had already become part of curricula in dozens of universities, and in 1923 the American Society of Newspaper Editors adopted the nation's first code of ethics for professional journalists. For the next 80 years, the financial growth of the news industry, aided from time to time by U.S. Supreme Court decisions affirming the constitutional right of a free press, assured the prestige of professional journalism.

What's a professional journalist like? Since the early 1980s, media scholars David Weaver and G. Cleveland Wilhoit (2007) have paid close attention to that question by leading teams of researchers in surveys of thousands of working journalists across the country, tracking their characteristics and attitudes. They observed a consistent set of values and societal roles that the surveyed journalists supported. Most journalists have felt that their role of analyzing complex problems for the American people was extremely important, as is their role of "watchdog," whereby journalists investigate claims by those in power as a counterbalance to possible deception or abuse by government leaders. They also adhered to the idea of journalists "getting information to the public quickly" and reaching the "widest possible audience" with their work.

What do professional journalists look like? The fourth and most recent of these studies was conducted in 2013, and as with earlier versions, the researchers described a workforce that is like the U.S. population it serves — sort of. It's an older workforce than the U.S. civilian labor force — 56 percent are 45 years or older, compared to 44 percent for the general labor force. There are fewer women in journalism — 37.5 percent female versus 47 percent in the U.S. labor force. Journalists are more likely than Americans overall to be white — 92 percent, compared to 63 percent in the U.S. population (Weaver et al., 2018). They tend to be much better educated than Americans in general, with 92 percent having at least a bachelor's degree compared to 35 percent of the U.S. civilian labor force.

Does it matter that certain professionals are different from the clients they serve? Weaver and colleagues addressed that concern in their third report: "For many occupations, these differences would be considered of little interest or relevance, but not so for journalists, where these characteristics are assumed to be correlated with interests and perspectives that are reflected in news coverage" (Weaver et al., 2007, p. 240). In other words, journalists, to be successful, must be attuned to the needs and interests of their audience. But these demographic differences, especially the difference in education levels, raise the question, they wrote, "of whether journalists are elites" (p. 242).

This misalignment between professionals working in institutions and the public is a danger to democracy that political theorist Albert Dzur argues can and must be remedied. And in many professions, he finds evidence that innovators are adopting practices of **"democratic professionalism"** (Dzur, 2018). Like many of the innovators featured in this book, "democratic professionals" do their professional work democratically.

What does that mean? What distinguishes democratic professionalism, Dzur explains, is a commitment to working closely with the public by co-creating knowledge, sharing decision-making rights and serving as an intermediary between citizens and institutions. Rather than using their skills and expertise as they see fit for the good of others, democratic professionals aim to "understand the world of the patient, the offender, the client, the student, and the citizen on their terms — and then work collaboratively on common problems" (p. 15).

It is precisely the journalists' 100-year campaign toward professionalism, and the elite status that professionalism implies, that has sometimes become a problem, especially in the context of citizen-centered journalism. As the Weaver et al. research strongly suggests, traditional journalists for 100 years have proudly identified with a role that is vital to democratic function: supplying the facts people need, to succeed as informed citizens. Few would argue the importance of that service to democracy. But is that all journalism can do to help the democratic process? Consider the process behind that traditional news product. Elite journalists, whose primary contacts are elites in government and industry, using their sophisticated "insider" knowledge of how systems work, naturally develop a confidence that they enjoy, exclusively, the intelligence of the day. Journalists are members of the profession that tells citizens what they need to know. In Chapter 6, we'll see how Your Voice Ohio has worked to address the disconnect between Ohio journalists and residents (especially in rural Ohio).

Jennifer Brandel, founder of the innovative service Hearken (whose work we'll explore in Chapter 7), puts it this way: "The way that we make decisions is as old as the printing press. We still gather a small group of people (finite inputs) in a closed room to make decisions on what the rest of the public deserves to know. And we make the product in isolation and present it to the public once we're finished and move on to the next product. No feedback or improvements along the way" (Brandel, 2019).

Dzur suggests that to rebuild institutions, including in his own domain of higher education, professionals must undertake "active listening" and participatory innovation. "We care about democracy, and we are troubled by the sneaky ways our own habits, norms, practices, and social structures on and off campus, block and disable it" (Dzur, 2018, pp. 71–72).

If this initial elitism suggests a gap between journalists and the citizens they serve, then recent economic demands on the production of journalism have widened the gap. With the recent retrenchment of financial resources (which we'll explore in detail in Chapter 10), news organizations are having to produce more content in less time, with less staff. The result is what we referred to in Chapter 2 as "extractive journalism." This is where the journalist views each source merely as an opportunity for extraction or exploitation and then moves on to the next story or project.

The other important commercial imperative is to maximize audience appeal, in order to attract advertisers. Publishers have known for centuries that sensationalism attracts an audience, but the presence of lurid gossip persists as the economic pressure has increased. Even the "watchdog" role to expose government wrongdoing has been distorted at times into a focus on politicians' personal misbehaviors rather than systemic problems. The long-term result of this kind of reporting, media scholar James Carey asserted (1995, p. 393), is to turn citizens into "alienated spectators" of the messy squabbles of celebrities they feel no connection to.

How often do professional journalists contact citizens? A survey by the Pew Research Center in late 2018 suggested that 21 percent — about one in every five Americans — have ever spoken with or been interviewed by a journalist. The percentages were only slightly higher for citizens who were white, wealthy, well-educated and older adults. The most significant finding was that the overall percentage declined from 26 to 21 percent in just the two years since the previous Pew survey (Pew, 2019). Journalists, as a whole, do not mix and mingle among the citizens they theoretically serve.

The increased pressure on journalists to become more extractive has proven to be only the beginning of the erosion of the traditional journalist's exclusive power.

Along Comes Citizen Journalism

Media critic A. J. Liebling famously observed 60 years ago that "Freedom of the press is guaranteed only to those who own one" (Liebling, 1960, p. 109). He was referring, of course, to the exclusive nature of publishing in the mid-20th century. In the middle of the first decade of the 21st century, that would change forever. With the advent of interactive, networked communication, and the explosion of social media networks that soon followed, everyone with an internet connection now owned the equivalent of a "printing press." Thus was "citizen journalism" born.

Citizen journalists are people with no ties to news-media organizations "who utilize the convenience and low cost of social computing technologies by publishing their own content" (Miller, 2019). Actually, citizen journalists have contributed news and opinion since before the days of the American republic. "Pamphleteers" — citizens with observations on public affairs in colonial America — would leave a few copies of their essays in various locales. More recently, citizens with recording equipment have contributed, sometimes significantly. On Nov. 22, 1963, Abraham Zapruder documented the assassination of President John F. Kennedy with his movie camera and sold the film to *Life* magazine. In 1991, George Holliday contacted Los Angeles television station KTLA to sell the eight minutes of footage he had taken of LAPD officers beating Rodney King (Belair-Gagnon & Anderson, 2015). In both instances, the citizens' contributions helped define the way Americans have understood those events ever since.

The distribution of the citizen-produced content was ultimately in the hands of the mainstream mass media. In the 21st century, however, the citizen producer has a direct line of communication with millions of internet users, often instantaneously. The "media," the institution that historically has "mediated" news and other content produced for mass consumption, can be bypassed. Kenneth Neil Cukier, a commentator for *The Economist*, compares citizen journalism to the advent of literacy. Society's elites held tremendous power when only they could read and write. But when citizens became literate, the change threatened the elites. "But it empowered individuals, and led to a far better world," Cukier wrote. "The new literacy from digital media will do the same, even as it creates new problems" (Cukier, quoted in Glaser, 2006).

Has internet-fueled citizen journalism created a "far better world"? Many media critics certainly greeted it with enthusiasm in the early 2000s. On virtually any topic we're likely to see in the news, "the audience collectively knows more about it than one reporter alone can," wrote Mark Glaser (2006). In fact, citizen journalism was welcomed in some circles as a truly democratizing force for American communication. After glorifying the nation's accommodation for a "marketplace of ideas" for the previous 100 years, the internet seemed to have delivered just such a marketplace. After all, when thousands are now producing information on a given situation instead of half a dozen reporters, the content is inevitably more diverse, more comprehensive and more nuanced. The phenomena of "crowd-sourcing" and "wiki" content, with nonprofessional observers contributing bits of information to a collective whole, were seen to be improving veracity as well. The "crowd," theoretically at least, would be quick to root out inaccuracies or deliberate misinformation.

The answer to this chapter's big "Who" question, with the emergence of citizen journalism, seemed to be "We are all journalists." With citizen journalism's momentum and presumed advantages, what could go wrong? Plenty, as it turned out.

Even well-intentioned, pro-democracy, pro-citizen citizen journalists are still volunteers without training in the gathering of reliable information or the writing of clear, concise, accurate, appealing stories. With increasing frequency, citizen-journalism reports on public-affairs topics became random and episodic when citizens deserved regular, consistent coverage of important issues.

Media critic Alex Warren (2017) blamed the internet's expectation of immediate gratification for many of the problems with citizen journalism. It takes hard work, and often a long time, to verify rumors, conduct interviews and review the research on a topic. But this is standard operating procedure for professional journalism. Without these standards of performance, Warren wrote, "citizen journalism has become citizen speculation" (Warren, 2017). In the aftermath of the 2013 Boston

Marathon bombings, for example, citizen journalists were eager to pass along unverified rumors as fact, resulting in several accusations that severely damaged reputations. "Without the editorial expectations or legal consequences involved in working for a traditional news outlet," Warren wrote, "citizen journalists ran riot with the truth" (Warren, 2017).

Good journalism, we believe, is rooted in a commitment to make public life go well, that is, a commitment to the common good. The internet, Warren wrote, too often has come to reward immediacy and appealing narratives, which in turn produce the brass ring of internet success, "shareability." If the classic ethical values of journalism, such as an abiding commitment to discover truth, minimization of harm to news subjects and avoidance of undue influence, are shoved aside by drive for shareability at all costs, then journalism is not serving citizens the way it should.

All of this assumes good faith on the part of the citizen journalist. What if the "journalist" sees citizen journalism as a means of mass deceit? To many observers, the 2016 presidential campaign ushered in a new, ugly phase of citizen journalism in the United States, with all manner of misinformation and disinformation being broadly shared. The trouble with sensational misinformation is that it spreads on the internet fast; the needed corrections can't possibly compete with the speed and breadth of the original's dissemination. Trained journalists, arguably the persons best qualified to emphasize facts and context, and to debunk false rumors and innuendo, are themselves under attack — by a network of influential trolls who have exploited the early promise of citizen journalism.

So the question of "Who Is a Journalist" has become considerably more complicated, thanks to the arrival of citizen journalism. And the question has become more confusing still — thanks to the inevitable intervention of the legal system.

The Law and the "Journalist"

Of all the sectors of the U.S. economy, of all the possible occupations in the workforce, only one is explicitly protected in the U.S. Constitution: journalism. One of the five freedoms protected under the First Amendment (along with the freedoms of speech, religion, the right to assemble peaceably and petition the government) is freedom of the press. Like much of the Constitution, the framers' concise language has left plenty of room for interpretation. And "freedom of the press" has had its share of divergent interpretations over the years.

No longer is our "Who Is a Journalist?" conundrum a matter of political science, social advocacy or media ethics. Because the judicial system is charged with interpreting and then enforcing the provisions of the Constitution, our question is also a matter of law. And ever since the dawn of the internet age, the courts have been struggling mightily to discern just who should be protected in those moments when journalists' First Amendment rights are under threat.

Several other nations have systems of licensure for journalists, so the answer there is simple: A journalist is someone with a journalist's license, much like a license to practice medicine. But most legal scholars and jurists through the years have agreed that "freedom of the press" precludes any sort of licensing system in the United States. That would violate both the spirit and the language of the First Amendment. It would create too dangerous an opportunity for the government to grant licenses only to those journalists who voiced support for the party in power or the person currently in the White House, for example.

In many legal areas, the "expressive" rights of citizens and news media are bound together — and protected — regardless of whether "journalism" is involved. But in a few areas of legal dispute, the courts have had to distinguish between journalists and citizens. In recent years, the courts have struggled. The most common legal arena for this struggle is known as **"reporter's privilege."** It is important for this chapter's question because reporter's privilege is the place in which the legal system has most conscientiously attempted to define "journalist." This privilege is a "conditional" right of journalists to refuse to reveal certain information, such as notes taken in strict confidence or the identities of anonymous sources, to the courts or to law enforcement. Most judges over the last 70 years, as well as the many state legislatures that have passed "shield" laws granting journalists similar protections, have agreed that investigative journalism is so important to the well-being of the country that journalists should receive that extra layer of protection for their work. But to grant journalists that privilege or shield, the courts must define "journalist." Until fairly recently, when journalism was confined to the efforts of trained professionals working full time for media companies, the definition was simple. Even though both the U.S. Congress and the U.S. Supreme Court have yet to take up shield laws or reporter's privilege at a national level, most state-level courts and legislatures for years shared a consensus that a journalist is an editorial employee of a newspaper, magazine, wire service or broadcast company.

Then, of course, along came the internet and citizen journalism. A great deal of citizen journalism is highly complex and does involve sophisticated reporting techniques. Can a citizen journalist claim a state's shield law if he or she cannot meet that state's definition of "journalist"? Since 2000, an increasing number of cases have been heard involving bloggers and other writers who are not employed by media firms but are seeking the journalist's "privilege" to protect sources. And slowly but undeniably, the courts are shifting the focus of the legal definition: from the person's employment status to the activity itself. Rather than a legal protection for journalists, we're seeing a shift toward legal protection for "acts of journalism."

But if the answer to "Who Is a Journalist?" is simply "Anyone who commits an act of journalism," then we're still in the dark. We now have to define journalism — in a way that, at the very least, will satisfy the courts and the First Amendment.

At this point, it's tempting to throw up our arms and declare everyone to be a journalist, functionally and legally, and move on. Unfortunately, few judges, legislatures or attorneys would support that cause. Could our justice system survive if anyone could invoke the journalist's privilege whenever he or she is called to testify in court? As Wimmer has written, "A privilege held by everyone can be held by no one" (Wimmer, 2014). No, the legal system is still motivated to define journalism in a way that doesn't allow everyone to claim its privileges.

With his definition, legal scholar Ivor Shapiro (2014) wisely focuses on behaviors: "Journalism comprises the activities involved in an independent pursuit of accurate information about current or recent events and its original presentation for public edification" (2014, p. 555). That definition would exclude a great deal of garbage the internet shares every day, but it would also welcome in millions of (unpaid, irregular) citizen journalists.

For a young blogger or part-time website contributor, does any of this legal discussion matter? Well, there are situations where journalists may need extra help. Certainly the protection of confidential sources is vital to investigative reporting, and in covering public disasters, journalists often need to show press credentials to gain first-hand access. Leslie (2009) adds that in many states, citizens requesting to see government records can have their processing fees waived if they can show that they're journalists.

But these legal situations are not everyday situations for most journalists. In journalism, as in most aspects of human life, the law regulates only a tiny fraction of everyday activity. The rest is up to us — our own values, ethics and principles, individually and collectively. For this book, then, the real answer to "Who Is a Journalist?" lies in the adoption of a set of principles that embrace not only Shapiro's "independent pursuit of accurate information" about recent events for public edification but also principles that put citizens front and center.

Today's Journalists: A Continuum of Roles

In order to thrive, democracy needs journalism; more specifically, democracy needs people to do the work of journalism. But if journalism is ever to build up the civic capacity of citizens, as we discussed in Chapter 1, then journalists must do more than disseminate accurate information and hope for the best. Journalists are needed to help citizens recognize the problems that hinder progress, help them discover what they actually have in common and then help them make decisions together that will lead to solutions to shared problems. An increasing number of media observers and media innovators are embracing this idea. In fact, Matthew Ingram believes the "service to citizenship" idea is so important that it should be part of our elusive definition: "Journalism helps communities organize their knowledge so they can better organize themselves," he wrote in 2011. "So anything that reliably serves the end of an informed community is journalism" (Ingram, 2011).

But it's not enough to implore professional journalists to change their attitudes and techniques in better service of citizenship. If the internet age, the emergence of social media and the emergence of citizen journalism have shown us anything, it's that journalism now operates in a complicated **ecosystem** of news and information. Think of all the ways, especially in local communities, that people can find out what's going on. Organizations have e-newsletters; neighborhoods have "hyperlocal" email groups; activists and advocates for certain causes have websites and newsletters; individuals have social networks of personal friends and families; government, the public library, the school district and other public institutions electronically publish their own versions of the news; occasionally, people even use their mouths and ears to communicate news. The mainstream media outlet is now only one node in a communication network that flourishes mostly on digitally powered networks. Journalists once monopolized a community's — even a nation's — current information, but in truth, those days are past.

So now, in this complex ecosystem of news producers and distributors, who is a journalist? If journalism is to be as effective as it can be in supporting democratic practices, we'll need a range of different journalists, performing a range of different journalistic duties — from the traditional, professionally trained journalist all the way over to the renegade, independent citizen journalist. It will take this entire range of journalists to inform and inspire a community of citizens to make democracy work.

Professor Joyce Nip has provided a useful way to look at this continuum of journalists in a citizen-empowering information system (Nip, 2010), which we've adapted for this book's purposes. We can begin one end of the continuum with the traditional, professionally trained journalist.

Professional Journalist

This term describes the traditional work of journalism, with all aspects of gathering and reporting news and information controlled and performed by trained professionals. Despite this group's tendency to work in elite circles and keep a safe distance from the people for whom they produce news, their contributions to any journalistic enterprise are undeniable. As Sonja West has pointed out (2014), professional journalists develop specialized knowledge about the subjects they report on; they focus on what's important to the "public interest" and what's not; they provide context to issues and events; they work hard and fast to provide timely, accurate updates; they adhere to ethical standards and stand accountable for their mistakes or any ethical breaches; and they take the time to investigate complex issues, sometimes exposing wrongdoing at the highest levels of institutions. We would add that professional journalists also can be highly skilled storytellers; they fact-check, that is, verify or debunk rumors and claims that fly around the internet; they are able to navigate complex bureaucracies and other power bases; and they can aggregate and curate the cacophony of information that assaults citizens every day, separating the essential from the banal. In Part II we'll see several examples of how highly trained professional journalists can contribute to relational journalism. Chapter 6's presentation of Solutions Journalism, for example, describes the rigorous investigative techniques required to report on "what seems to work elsewhere" in addressing a complex problem.

We don't mean to imply that untrained bloggers or citizen journalists are incapable of performing any of those professional tasks. It's just that professional journalists are trained, and paid salaries, to do them regularly, so they're the most likely type of journalist (on this continuum) to do so.

Unfortunately, their numbers seem to be decreasing. The Pew Research Center analyzed the workforce data of the U.S. Bureau of Labor Statistics in 2019 and concluded that from 2008 to 2018, newsroom employment in the United States dropped by 25 percent, a significant decline for any occupation in so short a time. In 2008, about 114,000 newsroom employees — reporters, editors, photographers and videographers — worked in the bureau's four sectors that produce news (newspapers, radio, television and "other information services" like web-based news sites). By 2018, that number had declined to about 86,000, a loss of about 28,000 jobs (Grieco, 2019). Some observers have noted, however, that the government's statistics fail to capture the new kinds of jobs that certainly qualify, according to our discussion here, as journalists. LinkedIn, the social network that focuses on employment opportunities, analyzed its own records on company hiring and found that podcasters, digital producers, content providers and social-media managers are nowhere to be found in the government workforce data sets, but demand for their work was increasing (Grieco, 2019). The job outlook for journalism grads is not as bleak as the headlines suggest, because they're building skills that will be needed in all manner of communication work — and in places all along this continuum of "journalist."

Citizen Recognition

Here, the professional journalist recognizes that citizens are producing sometimes-useable content, in three ways: (1) social-media content that they may wish to use as tips or other resources for the stories they're working on, (2) citizens' responses (such as comments at the end of web-based stories or letters to the editor) to content that the professionals originated, or (3) by contacting citizens for quotes — to add humanity, color, flavor or other appealing aspects to a story the professional reporter is working on. Jennifer Brandel at Hearken refers to this journalist as an "AskHole," as the behavior still appropriates the citizens' experiences for the journalist's limited purpose. "We don't thank them. We don't ask what they need. We just ask for what we need from them," she told journalist Kim Bui (2019," Building Relationships" section). It all smacks of extractive journalism, which we discussed in Chapter 2, but at least it involves citizens and moves us down the continuum toward more citizen-respecting forms of **collaboration**.

Citizen-Assisted Reporting

Here, citizens are invited by journalists to help identify new issues to cover, understand new perspectives on existing issues, and otherwise inform journalists at the earliest stages of their reporting rather than the final stages. Hearken is helping news organizations across the country (and increasingly across the globe) develop techniques for getting journalists to respect the innate wisdom of audience and community members, and for getting community members to rebuild their faith in journalists who may have seemed "extractive" in the past. Bui (2019) refers to this change as "power-sharing," in which journalists willingly pass along the formerly exclusive power of "news judgment" to folks who have a stake in the issues at hand — but no formal training in journalism.

Guided Citizen Reporting

Here we see a much fuller immersion of the citizen in journalistic practice. The news outlet publishes content written and produced by citizens with no previous training. At the most basic level, the news organization publicly solicits photos or video from a certain event. In some places, however, the news organization trains a small group of citizens in production techniques, reporting techniques and ethics, so the citizen content will match the look and content standards of the professional content. City Bureau, a nonprofit news outlet on the south side of Chicago, which we'll meet in more detail in Chapter 7, trains "documenters," citizens who then cover city government meetings and other public events that the city's mainstream newspapers or broadcast stations would not cover. Media observers and practitioners share in the conviction that involving citizens in doing journalism increases their investment more generally in the work of citizenship. Nip wrote that "the act of giving opportunities to the audience to participate in news making is itself a democratic gesture, one which affirms and facilitates the exercise of the individual's freedom of speech" (Nip, 2010, p. 139). Bui, who participated in similar projects in Los Angeles, noted that "as the cohort gets better at telling the stories of their lives and communities, whether through storytelling or traditional journalism information gathering, they become more confident that their voices matter, and their work crystallizes how the community views itself" (Bui, 2019). If media work can simultaneously increase people's confidence in the news media, in their own power to effect change, and in their respect for other citizens, we can envision a far brighter future for both journalism and democratic practices.

The Independent Citizen Journalist

This is the type of journalist who completes the continuum on the far side from the traditional, professional journalist. We discussed the assets and advantages (as well as some drawbacks) of citizen journalism above. Their influence in this new ecosystem of news is undeniable. Can some part of citizen journalism be harnessed for positive contributions to the democratic enterprise? We believe so.

The Sweet Spot: "Journalist" as a Collaborative Combination

Our final answer to the question of "Who Is a Journalist?" lies not in the description of one type of person or one set of behaviors but in a network of different types of people doing various aspects of journalism. Whether you're a highly specialized professional reporter or an eager-to-learn novice with a desire to build community, you occupy an important place in the ecosystem of journalism — and the community of journalists.

The overriding theme of our research for this book has been the benefit that accrues to communities whose journalists encompass an inclusive array of collaborators, and whose journalism empowers people to succeed as citizens. By way of summary, let's imagine the synergies by which different skill sets can enhance journalism.

It starts with a new journalistic mindset. When journalists shed the role of "detached outsider" and start to care about a community's people and issues, the quality of their reporting can't help but improve. Part of that improvement, however, is achieved by listening to what issues residents feel are important, listening to their feedback after their stories run, and, when it makes sense, enlisting their help in writing and gathering information for stories. Another part of that improvement is when citizens begin to realize that the journalist actually wants to help people reach decisions and take actions that will improve the community, not just the journalism. This is not biased or partisan reporting, we must be careful to note. This is journalists' advocating for democratic activity that results in community improvement, regardless of which particular people or set of ideas ultimately prevail.

Another part of the new mindset is that journalism shifts from *product* to *process*. Extractive journalists work hard to produce a package or story that they hope will be read or seen and then leave those sources as they move on to the next story and a new set of sources. The relational mindset requires a commitment to a process of problem-solving that doesn't stop with the release of the one story. Again, citizens' contribution is obvious. People who have lived with a situation for years understand the community's power structure and dynamics better than a journalist newcomer — and can navigate, with the journalist's help, toward a solution. The stories along the way will be more interesting because they're more authentic.

Media scholar Jeff Jarvis (2014) envisions a collaborative network whereby trained journalists serve as educators. They don't write "white papers" or lecture citizens on what they should know about an issue. Rather, they guide and inspire citizens to find things out on their own, injecting expertise only when necessary. They become facilitators in other ways, like facilitating community conversations, organizing multiparty searches for information, using their internet-search and "synthesis" skills to share "here's what we know so far" — a form of curation. They publish results on their news outlet's website, or on other platforms that will reach different kinds of audiences in the same communities.

Citizens, from interested residents to occasional comment-writers to dedicated bloggers, can all contribute their authentic experience to any shared reporting on a local situation. They can help prioritize journalistic energy by pointing to the community's most pressing issues. They can serve as eyewitnesses in multiple locations when a single professional journalist can cover only one event at a time. They can contribute analysis and opinion, again based on their local, personal experience. And if journalism does its job, these same citizens can participate in the difficult deliberative work that citizens need to do, to solve shared problems.

Media scholars Jack Rosenberry and Burton St. John (2010) see a cold reality in today's journalism: Neither professional journalists nor citizen journalists, acting in their own universes, actually contribute much, if anything, to improving public life. But if they should join forces, the scholars assert, they could make a positive difference. Professional journalists can't possibly match the authenticity of the citizen journalist. But they do bring a great deal to any collaboration: They know how to verify or debunk claims and rumors. They can craft compelling narratives that can captivate readers or listeners. They know how to design and manage complex reporting projects. They know how to provide context, background and analysis for fast-moving issues. They have investigative-reporting skills when those are warranted. They know the ethics of fairness, truth-seeking, respect for subjects, transparency and accountability, independence from undue influence and minimizing harm to those a story may hurt. They can prompt and manage community discussions with advanced social-media technologies.

Will people working in this new network of collaborators qualify as journalists in the legal sense? If the trend holds in the lower courts, to define journalists as persons who independently pursue accurate information about current or recent events and present it for the public good, then yes.

It's no accident that the collaborative journalism described in this chapter exemplifies many of the qualities of the relational journalism that was described in chapters 1 and 2. Our "new kind of journalism" will be practiced by a "new kind of journalist."

KEYWORDS

Citizen journalist: Someone with no ties to news-media organizations who utilize the convenience and low cost of social computing technologies to publish their own content.

Collaboration: The process of working with others to produce something of greater value than if the partners had worked on their own. The process relies on the identification of each partner's strongest contribution to the project.

Democratic professionalism: According to political theorist Albert Dzur, an attitude of professionals' working closely with the public by co-creating knowledge, sharing decision-making, and serving as an intermediary between citizens and institutions.

Ecosystem: The network of institutions, collaborations and people that communities rely on for news, information and engagement.

Reporter's privilege: A conditional right of journalists to refuse to reveal certain information, such as notes taken in strict confidence or the identities of anonymous sources, to the courts or to law enforcement.

QUESTIONS FOR DISCUSSION

1. What do you see as the benefits of professional journalists' collaborating with nonjournalists, as described in this chapter? What do you see as the drawbacks? Do the benefits outweigh the drawbacks? Explain.

2. In granting certain legal rights to journalists, do you think the court system is wiser to offer protection to individuals who meet certain criteria (i.e., employed, professional journalists), or wiser to offer protection to anyone whose behavior fits a definition of "journalism"? Why?

3. Ivor Shapiro's definition of "acts of journalism" focused on the "independent pursuit of accurate information ... for public edification." His conception seems to exclude those with an explicit point of view, whose primary purpose is to persuade, not to inform. Should advocates be considered journalists as well? What other types of public communication have you observed that Shapiro would not consider "journalism"?

PART 2

The Relational Skill Set

CHAPTER 5

The Five Principles of Relational Journalism

THIS IS WHERE WE TURN OUR EYES FROM THE STARRY HORIZON TO THE unpaved road ahead. In the first four chapters, we introduced a new kind of journalism, based on some ancient ideas, some historical perspective, some underdeveloped theories and a large dose of optimism. We have distilled those thoughts into what we call the five principles of relational journalism.

In the next five chapters, we'll explore the application of these five principles to the real-world, everyday doing of journalism.

In the course of our research for the book, we discovered dozens of innovative news organizations whose work embodies these five principles. We traveled to observe six of them in action, and we conducted in-depth video interviews with an additional 13. In the next five chapters, we present the journalists we've met and share their work in the form of case studies to illustrate the principles.

In Part I we shared our view that journalism is not reaching its important potential of empowering citizens in a democracy. It's not just that the 20th-century business model is broken. The profession's approach to doing journalism, in many ways, does not help citizens assert their problem-solving abilities. In some ways, modern journalism can actually hinder democratic practice. Now is the time for a transformation of American journalism. We see a great opportunity for the development of journalism's facilitative role, which asserts that merely informing an audience is not enough to serve democracy in the way journalism can. In this role, journalism can help citizens to recognize their shared values and shared problems and to deliberate in ways that bring them to shared public judgment.

With this theory as a backdrop, we introduced a new mindset that we term relational journalism. This is where journalists commit to a long-term involvement with groups of citizens and their challenges; they do what they can, starting with providing reliable background facts, to help citizens deliberate; they share the work of journalism with citizens whose own perspectives, experience, and knowledge can enhance the journalism; they work with radical levels of transparency about their processes; and they work to achieve authentic diversity in the way they choose stories to cover, sources to engage and citizens to ask for feedback. "Relational" journalists do these things with the confidence that the First Amendment defends the freedom of all Americans — from the highly trained reporting specialist to the social-media newbie — to share new, truthful information for the purpose of serving the public good.

Is any of this actually happening in the 2020s in American journalism? We're about to find out.

First Principle:
Journalism Is in Itself an Essential Democratic Practice

In order for any democracy to function as it was meant to, public communication must play an essential role. Citizens must understand what their elected leaders are doing, and those in government must understand the concerns and priorities of their constituents. Just as importantly, citizens must know what other citizens are saying and doing, in order to exercise the full powers that a democracy invests in citizens. The authors of the Bill of Rights seemed to acknowledge these basics when they included freedom of speech, press and assembly in the First Amendment.

In previous centuries, the constitutionally guaranteed expressive rights of the news media seemed quite separate from the constitutionally guaranteed expressive rights of citizens. Now, however, because acts of public communication are a blend of the professional and the volunteer, and of the huge corporation and the tiny nonprofit, freedom of the press belongs to every citizen as never before.

But if freedom to express ourselves is all we're talking about — if the dissemination of trivia, sensation and lies, with no accountability, is all this right entails — then this "first freedom" is missing its democratic promise. As adherents of the social responsibility theory of the media have argued since the 1940s, freedom does indeed come with great responsibility. For the authors of this book, this means that 20th-century journalism ethics is only the beginning of news-media responsibility. The heart of journalistic responsibility lies in journalism's facilitative role in a democracy.

Chapter 6 will introduce the myriad ways in which journalists are coming to realize that they can be facilitators for citizen action — not just suppliers of material that may produce informed voters. They are willing to swallow some 20th-century competitive pride, willing to expand their reporting range to include all kinds of different citizens — not just the power holders — and willing to be transparent about what they do not know and what they need help with. We will meet the leaders of Your Voice Ohio, a collaborative of more than 40 news organizations that explores the issues that the citizens of Ohio tell them they are concerned about. It operates on the assumption that reporters and editors recognize the wisdom and experience of ordinary people — and the limitations of their own professional activity. And if, in these contentious times, there should arise a challenge to the motivations or support of this kind of journalism, journalists may not have to stand alone. As Doug Oplinger, the coordinator of Your Voice Ohio, asked, "How do we build a kind of journalism that is so meaningful to citizens that they will want to defend it?"

We will meet other journalists in Chapter 6, including some leaders of the Solutions Journalism Network, which is finding that journalists and citizens alike prefer the kind of investigative reporting that doesn't stop at exposing a wicked problem but continues on to show what kinds of efforts to solve the problem have succeeded. We will meet the leaders of the New Jersey News Commons, which has brought together dozens of news organizations who, in years past, would never have thought of each other as partners in common cause but who now support each other with business-growing ideas as well as shared reporting. We will meet the leaders of Zócalo Public Square, a nonprofit based in Los Angeles that believes in "ideas journalism," whether that takes the form of in-depth articles or highly informative panel discussions and other events for community members.

Second Principle:
Journalists and Citizens Are Collaborators

As we discovered in Chapter 4, a journalist is no longer defined by employment status. Thanks to technological developments of the early 21st century, anyone who wants to share new, truthful information for the purpose of serving the public good is now able to "commit an act of journalism." We described a continuum of journalistic collaborations ranging from the highly trained professional reporter to the lone blogger, but we've discovered that the collaborations that have taken root among successful citizen-centered outlets are those we described as "citizen recognition," "citizen-assisted reporting," and "guided citizen reporting." In Chapter 7, we'll explore in depth the art of listening, in ways that exceed the standard listening for good quotes or for answers to interview questions. We'll explore what it means to listen with a high level of respect, without preconceptions of the best answers to our questions, with an ear for background and context that a database could not supply, and with an ear for citizens' priorities for their communities and for their feedback for journalistic work that is ongoing. With truly deep listening, journalists not only provide nuance to stories but now know how they might collaborate with a nonprofessional in ways that enhance the journalistic process and product.

Professional journalists are usually good writers; good photographers and videographers; diggers of reliable information; good sleuths for verifying or debunking suspicious claims; good curators of what is generally known so far about a given trend, issue or controversy; and good at navigating bureaucracies and halls of power (and the people who work in them). But we'll consider what collaborating citizens can bring as well: lived experience in the issue under study; honest, transparent opinions; expertise on the subtle social networks and relationships that define a neighborhood or community; and the ability to identify community resources that may not be visible from the newsroom or from City Hall.

In Chapter 7 we will meet the leaders of Hearken, a journalism consultancy that believes in inviting citizens into virtually every stage of the reporting process, starting with the generation of story ideas. Their working hypothesis is that by aligning the interests of journalists and citizens, the news will be more useful and relevant — and will ultimately build more trust between journalists and citizens. We'll meet the founders of GroundSource and the Listening Post Collective, both of which use mobile technology to enable residents to identify unreported issues and eventually collaborate with professional journalists to bring the stories to light. We will meet the leaders at KALW radio in the San Francisco Bay Area, which trains residents of low-income neighborhoods to report stories alongside professional reporters. The residents uncover stories the journalists never would have found, and the journalists add professional polish to the work. We'll also meet the leaders of City Bureau, a nonprofit news outlet in Chicago that trains and pays citizens to monitor the goings-on in neighborhoods that mainstream media simply cannot cover, and certainly not as authentically as residents themselves can. We'll see why Darryl Holliday, founder of City Bureau, thinks of journalism as citizenship.

Third Principle:
Journalists Facilitate the Work of Citizens

Of all the innovations we explore in this book, this principle describes the greatest departure from 20th-century norms of professional journalism. Ironically, it rekindles some of the most controversial tenets of the public journalism of the 1990s (Chapter 3). The idea here is that beyond informing voters with comprehensive reports and analyses, journalism serves democracy by helping to build the civic capacity of a community. As described throughout Part I of the book, civic capacity develops when citizens begin to feel they have the understanding and the strategies to resolve conflicts and effect positive change. To do this, they first need to identify shared problems and then the shared values that will enable a group to see its way to a solution to the shared problem. They need to be aware of that elusive goal known as "the common good," or "the public good." They need to know how to listen to people with whom they think they disagree — sometimes people they think they dislike.

That all may seem far afield from the doing of journalism, but in Chapter 8 we will meet journalists who are discovering the spots where journalists can contribute to these capacity-building activities. We will meet the leaders at AL.com, one of Alabama's leading news websites, which provides ways for the diverse (and often divided) population of Alabama to feel better connected to each other. For example, editors invited readers to reflect on the Walt Whitman poem "Song of Myself" and then to write their own, similar reflection on their identity in the context of Southern culture. Michelle Holmes, former vice president for news, said, "It allowed people here to see each other as worthy, as authentic." AL.com also produces a humor-based website entitled "It's a Southern Thing," which again encourages readers to see *shared* values more readily than cultural or social divisions. We'll meet the leaders of Spaceship Media, the pioneers of "dialogue journalism," in which journalists organize and then moderate conversations involving people with differences, often polarized differences, regarding public issues. It works, they believe, because they give the discussions a journalistic structure, with fairness and accuracy as the key dynamics. We'll meet leaders at *The Tennessean*, Nashville's top newspaper, which has partnered with the Nashville Public Library to sponsor forums on complicated issues like affordable housing in Nashville. Over the course of several months, the journalists blended expertise with residents' opinions on problems (and possible solutions) and gave those ideas prominence in the paper. We'll meet the editor at *The Times Record News* in Wichita Falls, Texas, which guided a community-wide effort to solve their county's chronic water shortages.

Fourth Principle:
Relational Journalism Updates Time-Honored Traditions

The foundations of American journalism are solid and worthy. As we searched for innovative ways to better serve democratic practice, we realized we simply cannot jettison the practices and principles that have made journalism the positive force it has been since the founding of the republic. We especially value the traditions of truth-seeking and accuracy; fairness and the battle against bias; independence and the avoidance of conflicts of interest; the role of journalism's "watchdog" on government and society's most powerful institutions; accountability; and a consistent sense of what is newsworthy.

But with each of these time-honored elements of journalism, we suggest hitting the "refresh" button so that the traditions are (a) still relevant and meaningful in a fast-changing media environment and (b) amenable to a journalism that is more citizen-centered. For example, in the hierarchy of values that comprise traditional newsworthiness (currency, impact, proximity, etc.), we urge that the element of "conflict" be downgraded when determining whether a story leads the broadcast or front page. Conflict must be acknowledged in presenting a contentious situation, but often it can be presented in a larger context of potential solutions. As another example, we update accountability: Traditional journalism has not always embraced transparency, as journalists in the 20th century preferred to build up a professional mystique as to how news was gathered. We urge a "refresh" that expands accountability to the point of drawing back the curtain on the processes that produce journalism. Research suggests that trust in media will likely follow.

In Chapter 9 we'll meet some of the most creative innovators in journalism — innovators who never lose sight of the disciplines of traditional journalism. Radio station KPCC in Pasadena, California, for example, has a voter guide like no other. Its advice to voters grows largely from questions the reporters receive from listeners — questions most journalists would never anticipate. But the answers to the questions are meticulously researched, and they are never couched in terms that would favor any one candidate or position on a ballot measure. We'll meet a journalist at Storyful, a company that uses emerging technologies to verify or debunk newsworthy content from a variety of social-media sources, so that its journalism clients can avoid basing their reports on "fake" claims. We'll meet the founder of the Milwaukee Neighborhood News Service, which presents hyperlocal news and features for (and sometimes by) residents of some of the city's poorest and most overlooked communities. Yet its standards of reporting, writing and photography are so high that the service's work is often picked up by larger mainstream outlets.

Fifth Principle: Journalism Must Follow New Paths to Financial Sustainability

Is journalism dying? Chapter 10 represents your authors' attempt to put that question to rest. As we discussed in Chapter 3, American journalism has been resilient in adapting to new economic, technological and political conditions. At the beginning of the third decade of the 21st century, journalism once again is faced with a challenge to adapt — most urgently, to deteriorating business conditions. Local newspapers have closed at a rate that by 2019 had created 171 "news deserts," that is, U.S. counties without a local daily or weekly paper. Given the inability of a printed product to compete with a digital product, and an advertising system that has ignored 21st-century business trends, it's hardly surprising that print news is fading.

But that doesn't signal the end of journalism itself. At this stage it is far too early to know what combination of strategies will sustain journalism, but in Chapter 10 we'll take a look at a few that offer promise.

We don't pretend to offer business analysis or business strategies in this book, which after all is about a new approach to the doing of journalism. But the business and the ethos of journalism are not unrelated. Part of the success of any journalistic business, of course, is the appeal of the product. In this book we suggest that a new approach to journalism, a citizen-centered approach, is likely to attract trust and readership in new ways, to new audiences. If a news outlet proves to be essential reading to a large number of citizens in a community, it only stands to reason that those citizens will be willing to contribute to the sustenance of that news organization, and that businesses will be willing to advertise their goods and services with that news outlet.

And because in any democratic system journalism is, first and foremost, a public service, the most promising innovations seem to be emerging from not-for-profit strategies. When return on shareholders' investments is no longer the driving force behind every managerial decision, editors, publishers and managers can focus more appropriately on true community service.

In Chapter 10 we'll meet the editors of *The Texas Tribune*, one of the most successful of the "new" news outlets of the 21st century. As a nonprofit organization, the *Tribune* has developed a strategy of blending six revenue sources, some of which would have struck 20th-century publishers as preposterous. We'll meet one of the researchers behind the Membership Puzzle Project, a consortium of news startups that celebrate a new understanding of "member-supported." Here the members not only support the outlet financially but also serve as part-time, volunteer consultants on stories. They suggest newly published readings and story ideas, they catch errors in early drafts of stories, and they even share their own original documents, where appropriate. We'll also meet the organizers of 100 *Days in Appalachia*, a news organization that reports thoroughly and authentically on various aspects of that region, but in partnership with the Reed College of Media at West Virginia University, which provides space, equipment, editorial management, student talent and various other resources.

The purpose of Part II of the book is to propel the ideas of relational journalism into the real world, and that includes hands-on experiences for our readers. In each chapter we also suggest exercises to enable readers to try their hand at these new techniques, either on their own, with classmates or co-workers, or with the guidance of an instructor.

CHAPTER 6

Journalism as Essential Democratic Practice

W HAT WOULD TROTWOOD, OHIO, LOOK LIKE IF EVERYONE THERE WAS living a happy, fulfilled life?

For one thing, imagined Bruce, a farmer and former Trotwood City Council member, Trotwood would have plenty of "collision opportunities."

"You know," he explained, "all kinds of opportunities for people to run into each other, say hi and get caught up."

That was Bruce's vision of an ideal Trotwood: Amenities like a rec center or a pool, more parks, squares, shops and other gathering places, and lots of fun annual events. Places for "collisions."

Others shared their ideals for Trotwood, including:

- People of diverse backgrounds getting along well
- Schools with funding equal to that of wealthier districts nearby
- Access to healthy food and affordable health care for all
- An effective local news and information system

Trotwood is a city of 24,000 about five miles west of Dayton, in southwestern Ohio. Bruce and several other Trotwood residents had gathered at Trotwood's community center one autumn evening in 2019 to talk about making their community better. What made the event truly unusual was that it was initiated not by the city government or a traditional civic organization but by local media outlets: The *Dayton Daily News*, WHIO-TV

(Dayton's CBS affiliate), WYSO (Dayton's public radio station), and "Soapbox" (an online magazine in Cincinnati).

Inspiring and overseeing the exercise was Your Voice Ohio, a nonprofit coalition of 59 news media outlets across Ohio. Your Voice Ohio was originally conceived as a vehicle for collaborating on statewide coverage of the 2016 election, but it quickly developed a more ambitious and innovative mission: to create a kind of journalism that recognizes and supports the central role of citizens in a democracy. For that reason, Your Voice Ohio is a powerful illustration of this book's first principle in practice: the notion that journalism is an essential democratic practice.

Ohio is well-trodden terrain for political journalists seeking to gauge the mood of the public at election time. That's because it has long been considered a "swing" state that also could serve as a bellwether for national and other states' political contests. Local journalists, however, had long been frustrated by outsiders' superficial reporting. They worried about a type of civic paralysis caused by increased polarization, uncivil talk and what appeared to be a disengaged public. Journalists over the decades had tinkered with ways to change their reporting practices in an effort to better serve the public. But still the public seemed disengaged and, worse yet, mutual distrust was increasing between the media and citizens.

Doug Oplinger, the managing editor of *The Akron Beacon Journal* before he retired and became project manager of Your Voice Ohio, saw this new coalition as a means not only of sharing coverage of the state's most complex stories but as a way to share a new approach to reporting those stories.

FIGURE 6.1 Doug Oplinger, project manager of Your Voice Ohio, leads a community forum in Trotwood, Ohio.

(Photo by Paul Voakes.)

The evening in Trotwood (Oct. 2, 2019), which Oplinger moderated, was one of about 30 that Your Voice Ohio sponsored in its first two years, involving a total of about 1,200 Ohio residents in conversations like Trotwood's. The primary objective was to discern a news agenda, for the months leading up to the 2020 elections, that is not generated exclusively by candidates, governmental bodies or other centers of power. Priorities on what qualifies as an election story are set, at least in part, by what the journalists at community meetings have heard directly from the citizens who attended.

"This is how we (as journalists) can say, 'We know you,' when we go out to cover the election campaigns," Oplinger said. "'These are what we hear you identifying as the issues in the upcoming elections.'"

It's the first major step in a larger project of strengthening bonds between journalists and citizens. And it goes to the heart of this book's new understanding of the media's role in a democracy.

More Than "Just the Facts"

As we discussed in Chapter 2, the vastly overlooked but vital role for media in a democracy is the facilitative role: What are the major tasks by which media can help build civic capacity, that is, the capacity for citizens to succeed in building community, solving problems together and affecting public policy? Our response is relational journalism, a set of procedures — informed by a "relational" mindset — that not only restores people's trust in media but increases citizens' power in the democratic process.

As an editor for decades at one of the Midwest's top newspapers, Oplinger began to realize that certain practices and routines were driving journalists and citizens apart from each other. For him, this helped explain people's loss of trust — and loss of interest — in the news media.

Traditionally, journalists have felt they needed to get as close as possible to centers of power, on the assumption that the most powerful persons and institutions in a society would have the most important information — the "news" that everyone else would be eager to learn. While Oplinger doesn't deny the need to cover officials and their offices, he noticed that that kind of reporting leads to the chronicling of "insider" minutiae that interest only the community's elite. The elite naturally give feedback — perhaps even exclusive tips — to the journalists, which encourages further reporting that's of interest to relatively few. The budgetary constrictions at news organizations have aggravated the situation. Most news organizations have had to produce ever more content with less staffing, which causes reporters to resort more often to a short list of sources — those same insiders — who can be counted upon for a quick call back and a juicy quote.

Journalists in the past have justified this focus on officialdom by citing the "watchdog" role of the media. This is the function by which journalists hold the powerful accountable for their stewardship of public funds and for acting in the interests of the public. The "watchdog" is rewarded especially when journalists find abuses of power — and scandals blossom in the public eye. When he began the community meetings on behalf of Your Voice Ohio, however, Oplinger saw a different reaction. Citizens in focus groups showed much less interest in the in-depth political coverage than the journalists had assumed. They had had enough of bad news, conflict and scandal.

"They were telling us, essentially, 'Stop telling us how bad our politicians are, and start giving us ways to solve the real problems in our communities.'" Especially the second half of that sentence was not lost on the leadership at Your Voice Ohio. Too many journalists had adopted a sports-reporting mentality; that is, that civic life has winners and losers, and there are scores to be kept — often tallied in polls or elections — along the way. But above all, the implication is that the public sphere, where ideally citizens discuss and solve common problems, had become a spectator sport for all but the very powerful.

Other fallout occurs from journalists' focus on the elite. Oplinger also saw in many journalists an attitude of subtle disrespect for everyday folks. Because experienced reporters know how to develop a "beat," they know the history, the issues and the power dynamics of that sector of public life. But that doesn't translate to omniscience about the community. Your Voice Ohio's first major initiative was a collaboration on coverage of the opioid crisis, which had hit rural Ohio particularly hard. In one rural community meeting, citizens told Your Voice Ohio journalists about an article about citizens' urging a hotline that those with opioid-related emergencies could call. The reporter dutifully went to an official source, who said the county already had such a hotline. Traditionally, that would be a balanced, full report. The problem, the citizens told Your Voice Ohio, was that the hotline closed at 5 p.m. every day and was thus unavailable when people needed it most. Oplinger said that after several Your Voice Ohio community meetings, journalists have expressed surprise at the knowledge and depth of experience citizens have shared. That's a sharp contrast, Oplinger said, to the traditional assumption that "ordinary citizens" have little knowledge to offer reporters covering complex issues.

At most community meetings, he added, citizens prove that they not only know a great deal about issues through their "lived experience" but that they already are involved in civic actions that the journalists were unaware of. "Citizens are already doing something," he said. "Journalists focused almost exclusively on politicians and institutions just don't see it."

Others working in this field have supported Oplinger's impressions of the journalist-citizen disconnect. For example, Your Voice Ohio has partnered with the Center for New Democratic Processes, a nonpartisan, nonprofit organization whose mission is to partner with citizens and communities "to design and implement informed, innovative, and democratic processes to address today's toughest challenges" (Center for New Democratic Processes, 2021). Andrew Rockway, who was the center's Your Voice Ohio liaison for several years, told us the center often partners with the National Institute for Civil Discourse, which in 2015 hosted a conference with citizens, journalists and elected officials. At the end of the conference, journalists seemed to agree that "ordinary" citizens were far more intelligent than they had assumed, and they heard citizens say they felt disrespected and that the journalists they had met seemed arrogant and condescending.

The disconnect between journalists and citizens in Ohio first became obvious in the results of the 2016 presidential election. Oplinger said that nearly all full-time journalists in Ohio have college degrees, but typically only 30 percent of their audiences have college degrees (in Trotwood, it's about 20 percent). He said citizens realize that journalists have enjoyed social privilege, and often they see it in the coverage — and they resent it. Most journalists regarded the Donald Trump candidacy as entertaining rather than a serious expression of frustration with American politics. They assumed, Oplinger said, that citizens would "come to their senses" and reject Trump. In community meetings with Ohio citizens, he said, attendees often express anger and frustration with the way the world — the job market, social trends, politics, etc. — has changed. "And when Hillary Clinton calls these people 'deplorables,'" Oplinger added, it can't be surprising that they would support her opponent.

"Most journalists simply missed that anger in 2016," Oplinger said. Ironically, local journalists bristle at the arrival of "parachute journalists" from national publications or the television networks, when news of national importance breaks in Ohio. The outsiders, the argument goes, know little to nothing of the context or culture of the place they're suddenly reporting from. But Oplinger argues that most local editors and reporters have

FIGURE 6.2 Doug Oplinger, project manager of Your Voice Ohio, listens to a citizen's vision for Trotwood, Ohio.

(Photo by Paul Voakes.)

become "parachute journalists" in their own communities — so great has the chasm grown between even local journalists and the people about whom, and for whom, they're reporting.

How can journalists revise their approach to reporting and writing about local life in ways that bridge the gap? Your Voice Ohio would say it starts with relationship building and community building.

What Does Community-Building Journalism Look Like?

Community meetings like Trotwood's are meticulously planned at Your Voice Ohio. No one wants meetings that citizens and journalists consider a waste of time. Your Voice Ohio titled the Fall 2019 exercise "What's Your Future, SW Ohio?" and organized six meetings in various community centers in and around Dayton — including Trotwood. The local media had run stories to advertise the meetings, and readers were urged to register (online) to attend, so organizers would know how much food to order.

To begin the Trotwood meeting, Oplinger led the Trotwood group through a sequence of four questions:

1. How would Trotwood look if everyone was able to live a happy, fulfilled life?

2. What needs to change in Trotwood so that everyone might begin to live a fulfilled life?

3. What are the strengths and assets of Trotwood that might help bring about the needed changes?

4. Regardless of existing laws or restrictions, what actions will be needed to bring about the most important of these changes?

Oplinger organized the attendees into small groups, and in answer to each question, each group "reported out" a consensus to the whole group. In Trotwood on this particular night, the group seemed focused on the quality of the local public schools. The high school was an athletic powerhouse, everyone agreed, but academic quality could be better. The group came up with 10 suggestions for improvement, from local volunteer programs to a statewide overhaul of the school-funding system.

The evening ended with a "call to action" of sorts. Each attendee was asked to write on an index card the answers to two final questions:

- Who do you know in town who is already working on the solutions we've been talking about?

- What do YOU feel compelled to do tomorrow, as a result of tonight's conversation?

BOX 6.1 "Using Journalism to Save Civic Life"

Chris Horne is an innovator in local journalism, but unlike many other innovators, he's not interested in saving journalism. Instead, he says, "I want to use journalism to save civic life."

He sees the health of journalism intertwined with the health of a community. In his case, that community is Akron.

Horne, who spent two decades working at traditional daily and weekly news outlets, founded *The Devil Strip* in Akron in 2015. It began as a familiarly formatted "alt-weekly" with an arts orientation, but under Horne's guidance it has evolved into a broader-purpose local news site, with an overall mission "to connect Akron citizens to their neighbors and their city." He wants *The Devil Strip* to participate with — at times even lead — citizens as they make Akron a better place to live.

Without using the term, *The Devil Strip* stimulates civic engagement. It starts by creating a "commons," he explained, where stories and local events help residents get facts, and then deeper understandings, and then values that they hold in common. This subtle journey of awareness, Horne believes, is the antecedent to civic action.

The Devil Strip encourages people to care, basically, about where they live. One campaign the *Strip* began was to encourage residents to "shop local," rather than purchase from national chains — but to change habits incrementally. "Shop 10 Percent" was the project — just be intentional about making at least 10 percent of your purchases from local merchants.

"And then just ease into more of that," Horne said, which can become civic pride in the form of activism to help promote public policies at the city-government level. One of the goals of *The Devil Strip*, he said, is to encourage the development of "co-creators," his term for novice political activists whose commitment grows out of a "shared Akron identity" that emanates from the *Strip*.

Horne sees the "civic narrative" as needing to change. When traditional local reporting focuses on crime, bad weather, sports and controversies that divide residents in opposing camps, people gradually adopt a civic narrative that is negative.

"Akron has a lot to offer," Horne insists. "We need to start telling a more comprehensive truth about our community." To help with that, Horne hires Akron residents from neighborhoods throughout the city to write articles or shoot photos or video.

Horne is also careful not to "leave good stories on the page." When a story has garnered attention on the web site, Horne arranges an event at a local community center, bookstore or coffee house, where citizens can meet the author and "main characters" from that story in person, and the issues in the story can be further discussed.

Traditional journalists, or skeptics of all stripes, might immediately wonder "How does any of this Trotwood meeting possibly qualify as journalism?" It does only if one accepts a nontraditional role for journalism: to facilitate citizens' work in democratic processes. To be sure, the Dayton newspaper published several articles on the meetings, but by traditional standards that would be highly irregular: There was no official action taken, officials were not quoted, the subject matter was complicated and the discussion largely unfocused. But the articles, Oplinger would insist, put larger points across. The media were listening because they value the perspectives of the region's residents, and they want to use this as a basis for reestablishing relationships with citizens. Oplinger calls this the "We Live Here Too" phenomenon, and this could be the most important reason for these community meetings. Not only do the journalists admit to surprise at how knowledgeable citizens are, but citizens as well have commented that, having seen reporters in action and talked to them about their challenges, they have new respect for what journalists do. And they

BOX 6.2 Beyond the Bad News: Journalism Researching Solutions

In 2013 *The Seattle Times*, concerned about the quality of public education, decided it needed to take a new approach to reporting on the persistent challenges that bedevil the systems from prekindergarten through college. It found just the right partner in the Solutions Journalism Network, a New York-based nonprofit that is developing and spreading the practice of solutions-oriented journalism. *The Times*, known for investigative reporting and reader innovation, became an early adopter of Solutions Journalism. In 2013, when the Education Lab was born, its aim was to broaden Seattle's conversation about public education and engage community members in generating solutions. In addition to keeping a steady reporting focus on the issue, the newspaper hosted community meetings with parents, students, teachers and education advocates.

But the journalism didn't stop there. Solutions Journalism was building a network of reporters and communities with similar challenges, in order to share what seemed to be solutions. The Seattle journalists had learned of parents in low-income neighborhoods of Chicago who had dealt with similar issues: poor academic performance and uneven discipline policies, to name a few. Solutions brought a handful of Chicago parents west to meet with Seattle parents.

They shared their experiences, which included their success in lobbying for change in the Chicago school system. The meetings led to *Times* stories reporting the Chicago solutions, some of which were adopted by Seattle parents. The effort led to successful reforms in Seattle public schools' detention and expulsion policies and in recruitment of a more diverse swath of students into the program for gifted and talented children.

Solutions Journalism Network has blossomed into an organization that has served hundreds of news organizations with resources and advice on this increasingly attractive approach to covering public affairs issues. It's an approach that directly supports democratic processes in that it supplies citizens with new resources for solving problems together. It strikes back at what Keith Hammonds, president of the Solutions Journalism Network, calls "learned helplessness" — the lack of civic efficacy that today's citizens too often assume after reading the news (news that thoroughly documents how bad things are). With a more traditional approach to reporting, Hammonds said, people see their world as not only broken but unfixable. On the other hand, if journalism is truly an essential democratic practice, it can help citizens feel they can do something about seemingly intractable problems.

understand that most local journalists live in the communities they cover. They shop at the same stories, send their children to the same schools, and share in the same civic pride. Trust, as we know, is a key antecedent to civic action among disparate groups; journalism has a ready opportunity to partake in that trust.

The vast majority of what happened at each meeting in southwestern Ohio went unreported, but the newspaper, magazine and two broadcast stations were investing in a process that they think will result in more authentic, more comprehensive and more accurate stories in the long run — and increased audiences for those stories. They have also indicated interest in solutions, not just conflict and hopelessness, and they have planted the idea that citizens themselves are vital contributors to solutions.

The journalism of Your Voice Ohio now takes several forms. In addition to community conversations in several regions in Ohio, the group organizes collaborations among major media in the same region to cover a single topic, very thoroughly. Since

So how does it work? A true Solutions Journalism project has four elements:

- A well-documented description of a shared public problem in a local community.
- In-depth evidence of a response elsewhere to that problem, with special attention to what the results have been and how those results were achieved.
- Details on the limitations of that response.
- Insights into how the response might be applied in other communities, starting with the journalists' own.

Solutions trainers are quick to point out what Solutions Journalism is not. It's not a story that celebrates the heroic efforts of one individual or group. It's not a report on someone's suggestion for a quick, simple or complete solution. It's not a favorable feature on a well-intentioned organization in the community. It's not a report on a proposal that has never been tested. It's not a cute or feel-good story, like a feature on the kids who will donate their lemonade-stand proceeds to a local charity.

And above all, it's not cheerleading or "advocacy journalism," where journalists abandon any thorough search for evidence and editorially urge one position at the expense of others. Sara Catania, Solutions' director of journalism school partnerships, said Solutions endorses essentially old-school investigative journalism in that it is independent, with rigorous standards of evidence. Solutions journalists present their research findings to a community, Hammonds said, but what happens next is up to the citizens of that community.

The network amasses results and findings that address various problems, from access to health care and public-school reform to racial tensions and gun violence — and makes these available to any journalists who join. The network actively urges journalists to submit their own work, to add to the database. (See Story Tracker, at https://storytracker.solutionsjournalism.org/.)

Solutions Journalism has been active long enough for media researchers to assess its impact. Media scholars at the University of Texas at Austin's Center for Media Engagement conducted detailed experiments on readers of stories with the four elements of Solutions Journalism (Murray & Stroud, 2019). They concluded that readers of the solutions stories felt the quality of the journalism was better than with the nonsolutions stories, they were more likely to become involved with the issue, they expressed heightened interest in the issue and they felt greater overall "positivity."

This comports with a study Doug Oplinger conducted for Your Voice Ohio. He found that stories in *The Akron Beacon Journal* that included possible solutions to problems led to more "time on site" — reader attention to the story — than those that only described a problem.

its initial in-depth, collaborative coverage of the opioid crisis in Ohio, it has organized collaborations to cover the fast-changing economy in Ohio, entitled "Building a More Vibrant Ohio." It has organized a retreat for news managers on "news equity" to discuss their own roles in "marginalizing populations, creating tension and preventing constructive problem-solving." It has created a handbook (in partnership with the governor's office) for journalists on how to cover addiction.

But in this renewed focus on citizens and communities, is collaboration among media necessary? We believe so. If journalism is truly a public good, in service to the greater goal of successful democratic practices, it must also shed some of the attitude that served it so well in the fiercely profit-driven environment of the 20th century: the attitude of competition.

Swallowing Some Competitive Pride

Until the digital and economic upheavals of the 21st century, journalists rarely saw a need for collaboration. Several news organizations could easily afford to send their own teams to cover the same events, each confident in its ability to outshine its competitors and thus gain market advantage over them.

But with the decline of traditional revenue sources, news managers in the 2000s have come to realize that once full-service news products cannot cover the territories, the topics or the populations they once did. And with a new focus on the audience's genuine information needs, as Your Voice Ohio has championed, we begin to see the emergence of collaborations.

Your Voice Ohio was created to provide enhanced statewide coverage of the 2016 elections, but Oplinger said that model proved difficult to coordinate for ongoing issues. Your Voice Ohio still advocates collaboration, but on a regional scale — over a handful of counties, say, instead of the entire state. As one example, *The Akron Beacon Journal* joined forces with WKSU, the public radio station in nearby Kent, and *The Devil Strip*, an alternative weekly in Akron, to explore housing in the city and beyond, in northeastern Ohio. They had discovered hints of widespread problems related to rental housing and absentee landlords.

Andrew Meyer, WKSU's news director, said the community deserves the best possible coverage of important issues but that no single news outlet can match what the three of them can do together. And it's more efficient.

"None of us has the powerhouse staff to do it all," Meyer said. "We now can freely admit that. So now our work becomes better for it. We don't have to all send our own top reporters to the same news event."

The key is agreeing who does what best, according to Chris Horne, the publisher of *The Devil Strip*, (whose title, by the way, refers to Ohioans' term for the strip of grass between the sidewalk and the street). The *Beacon Journal*, he said, can provide the daily announcements of government meetings, and it has a crackerjack squad of investigative reporters skilled in data analysis.

"But our role at *The Devil Strip*," he explained, "is more the product of realizing that our readers don't always know the basics of how a situation got to be a major problem, let alone the details of policy proposals. So we provide the primer, or the 'first few chapters' of the ongoing story. And we'll highlight our content on our site for a much longer period of time than the others can, so we can provide almost a library-like resource on the issue." For its part, WKSU adds a new human dimension to its researched stories, with natural sound and the actual voices of decision-makers and those affected by housing issues.

BOX 6.3 **Collaboration, and Beyond**

With 565 cities and towns to cover, the need for local journalism in New Jersey is huge. In a time of dwindling budgets and staffs, New Jersey journalism was falling well short of that challenge. In 2012, out of a shared desire to avoid "news deserts" in Jersey, a collaboration like no other was created.

Stefanie Murray is the director of the New Jersey News Commons, one of the major projects of the Center for Cooperative Media at Montclair State University. The News Commons has about 260 media members, ranging from the established (e.g., New Jersey Public Radio or *The Newark News*) to the less established (e.g., *Weird New Jersey*, *New Jersey Hispano* or Hot from the Kettle, a news site for foodies). The News Commons shares reporting on investigative projects, but it does much more as it fulfills its mission to "grow and strengthen local journalism for the benefits of the citizens of New Jersey."

Murray says the News Commons addresses members' business concerns as well as its journalistic challenges. It has held popular "Revenue Summits," which provide guidance on managing a small business, especially on growing revenue. It provides trainings and workshops for members' staffs, and it sends members a daily newsletter on the news business in New Jersey. It even helped forge a New Jersey law (the first of its kind in the nation) that allocates funds to groups meeting the information needs of underserved New Jersey residents in innovative ways.

And it converts longstanding media rivalries into collaborations. News Commons members have joined forces to produce, among other projects, "In the Shadow of Liberty," on immigration issues in New Jersey, and "Dirty Little Secrets," on toxic contaminants in plain sight. Murray said there are still challenges in getting longstanding rivals to compete: print, broadcast and online outlets are sometimes still wary of each other, as are weeklies vis-à-vis dailies and local vis-à-vis regional publications. And she insists that all members adhere to a basic code of journalistic ethics, which can be another kind of challenge. But Joe Amditis, the News Commons' associate director, said "the truth is, there are a lot of journalists and publishers out there who are more than willing to set their competitive tendencies aside and work together to create something useful, meaningful, and good" (Amditis, 2016).

The News Commons values collaborative investigative projects because of their impact, Murray said. Strong reporting leads to strong audience reaction, which in turn leads to strong civic action. But the News Commons supports local outlets' journalism in ways that engage their communities more directly and more in line with relational journalism. It trains members to organize "Voting Blocks," where journalists join a small group of neighbors over a summer and fall, as they assess the candidates and issues in a political campaign. But some local outlets are staffed so thinly that they cannot afford to converse in community meetings when there are "bread and butter" events like local government meetings to be covered. The News Commons offers grants to those outlets to hire freelance reporters to cover the meetings, so the staff can engage more deeply with the community.

Doug Livingston is a reporter with the *Beacon Journal* who is excited not just by the basic dynamics of collaborating but by the citizen-centered approach the collaborators agreed to take.

"We're going to spend time with the people who must live with the result of whatever policies are adopted," he said. "The traditional institutions of power will frame the housing issue in a certain way, but that's not the only way. Legislation looks a certain way at City Hall, but how does it look as it lands on somebody's front doorstep?"

As we discussed in Chapter 1, the arrival of interactive media technologies has changed the flow of news and information from a one-way stream (professional journalists' content to the mass audience) to a new information "ecosystem" in which the professional journalists play but a part. Now, even within the larger community ecosystem, we see a subsystem of only the professional journalists — with each collaborator contributing what it does best, with the goal of a better-informed community than their competitive pride would have produced. Meyer, at WKSU, is sensitive to the criticism that collaboration seems to be a luxury that can be addressed only after each news outlet's own basic coverage needs are met. He agrees to a point but adds that when the approach is citizen-centered — attending to the information needs of the audience members — then the benefits of collaboration are too great to ignore.

"It's symbiotic," he said. "We need larger audiences to stay afloat, and if we deliver information that the audience is seriously looking for, and in a comprehensive way, then we all win."

The Importance of Inclusion

Returning for a moment to our understanding of the First Amendment in the 21st century, we recall that one of the longstanding, underlying rationales for that first guarantee in the Bill of Rights is to enable a "marketplace of ideas." In Chapter 1 we learned that as early as during the Age of Enlightenment, political philosophers asserted that only with freedom of expression can the full breadth of ideas in a society come forth. By enabling citizens to listen to or read about a vast inventory of arguments and claims, citizens are able to look past mainstream truisms to see more creative ideas. They can then promote the most sensible, while the least worthy will fall away — just as in a "marketplace" for goods and service. The evolution of the news industry in a capitalist economy saw a tightening of control over content so that, by the late 20th century, perspectives that didn't reflect mainstream thinking were largely excluded. The internet's interactive features, however, brought new hope for a true marketplace of ideas that had been, up until the 2000s, mostly a theoretical ideal.

The result has been disappointing once again, however, with the massive presence of fabrication, defamation, exaggeration and titillation subverting the internet's potential for the honest exchange of new discoveries and diverse ideas and experiences. By an entirely different means, digital media have excluded many of the same kinds of voices that traditional mass media excluded. And yet, in Chapter 2, listed among the duties of journalism that are fundamental for a successful democracy, we saw the duty to "help citizens understand others whose experiences are different from their own." It's a tall order, but citizen-centered journalism must find ways to expand its reach — and give voice — to all citizens, not just certain pockets of audiences.

Your Voice Ohio has experienced the challenges of inclusion in what Oplinger described as a disconnect between journalists and the citizens they are meant to represent. The primary example was a gap between journalists and Ohio citizens who voted for Donald Trump in 2016. That, unfortunately, is only one of many gaps that keep journalists from connecting with citizens. It wasn't just a group of low-income rural residents whose displeasure with media coverage caught the attention of journalists at the community meetings. There are several groups of citizens with characteristics that have historically left them in the shadows of media communications — and therefore without much power in the world of media communications. These include race, gender, religion, sexual orientation, physical ability, geographic origin, socioeconomic status and age. Robert Maynard, founder of the Maynard Institute in Oakland, a pioneer in expanding diversity in journalism, called these sets of characteristics "faultlines." The faultlines provide the basic frames of references by which most people, including journalists, view a situation. The Maynard Institute has taught that journalists should not deny or ignore these faultlines but rather attempt to recognize their presence in every story they begin to report (Lehrman, 2019). After all, awareness of difference is a crucial beginning step toward celebrating difference, which is the hallmark of a tolerant and pluralistic society.

Media scholars have generally seen three areas in which journalism can improve its inclusiveness. The profession itself can diversify its staffing demographics; journalists can approach their work with new framing and reporting strategies that will result in the inclusion of more perspectives; and the content of the journalism itself can become more accurate, more sensitive and more respectful toward groups that historically have been excluded.

As much as some journalists would like to think that they can cover any group that is unlike themselves with fairness and sensitivity, most journalists today would agree that colleagues with lived experiences matching those of underrepresented groups produce high-quality journalism because of that shared life experience. The good news on the staffing front is that the profession, historically dominated by white males, is becoming more diverse. A study in 2018 by the Pew Research Center (Grieco, 2018) found that relatively few — 38 percent — of journalists between 18 and 29 are white males.

What does more inclusive coverage look like? Professional organizations like the Society of Professional Journalists (SPJ, 2020), the Online News Association (ONA, 2016), and the American Press Institute (Jackson, 2019), to name a few leaders, have spent the last few decades creating and revising thoughtful guides to help editors and reporters in this regard. A few tips:

- For starters, journalists are urged to expand the sourcing of every story to include not only persons with power or expertise (traditional sources) but also those whose lives are being directly impacted by the story. When reporters interview new, more diverse sources, they should share those names and contact information with staff colleagues, so that the expanded sourcing

BOX 6.4 Connecting People Through Ideas

"Zócalo" is the Spanish word for public square, and it seems the perfect title for the journalistic experience Gregory Rodriguez has been developing since 2003. The public square, Rodriguez believes, is the necessary setting for nurturing a democratic culture. But he doesn't take that nurturing for granted. Far from it.

"At a time when our country's public square and our global digital conversation have become ever more polarized and segregated," Rodriguez wrote in Zócalo Public Square's mission statement, "Zócalo seeks to create a welcoming intellectual space and engage a new and diverse generation in the public square" (Zócalo Public Square, 2019, Mission Statement).

As a website, Zócalo Public Square offers a number of features we'd identify with arts journalism or "culture journalism": feature articles, essays, photo essays, illustrations, poetry and recommended readings. But Zócalo is unusual in its underlying purpose: to connect people to ideas while it connects them to each other. It strives to do that even when no article is published.

Zócalo, based in Los Angeles, takes great pride in the quality of its published journalism, but it also strives to connect people to ideas by organizing public events. The editors choose a topic and find a panel of speakers with expertise from diverse perspectives. The moderator is usually a professional journalist. One evening in October 2019, for example,

the question was "What Can Everyday Angelenos Do About Homelessness?" Admission is always free, and participants often attend a reception with the panelists before the program begins. By the end of the evening, Zócalo's hope is that all in attendance will have enjoyed a community conversation about the topic. Does it make for an article on Zócalo's website? "Sometimes," Joe Mathews, Zócalo's California editor, replies. "If the event is well done, it becomes a story."

Zócalo Public Square connects people, Rodriguez explains, with "ideas journalism." Instead of focusing on the identity or credentials of the journalists or their interview subjects, he said, Zócalo wants to focus first on their ideas — especially ideas that bring clarity to complex issues. This, he believes, is journalism's great gift to the nurturing of democratic culture.

But is a community event, in and of itself, journalism? Rodriguez answers with an emphatic "yes."

"Even if nothing is published, if it's community-building, if it's educational, if it's social in terms of people meeting new people, then it's what we want to do."

Zócalo Public Square has built an impressive blend of high-quality content with appealing public events. Its articles are syndicated to 290 other media outlets, and since 2003 Zócalo has hosted more than 600 themed events, in 33 cities.

---

doesn't die after one story. Few journalists would disagree with the notion that the more sources a story has, the more accurate that story is likely to be.

- Who is pictured in photos or videos? Whose voices are heard on radio reports? Journalists are urged, again, to move away from the easy-to-find head shot of the elected official and search instead for faces and voices of those directly affected, or with "lived" experiences providing a different sort of expertise.

- Traditionally, persons of color are overrepresented in entertainment and sports journalism, and women are overrepresented in arts and lifestyle journalism. And both groups have been woefully underrepresented in public affairs reporting.

The most difficult, but most effective, way to include more of a community is in the approach to reporting. The American Press Institute (2019) suggests a set of strategies that echo what we are calling relational journalism in this book. This includes strategies that focus on the experiences, perspectives and information needs of groups traditionally overlooked (even when they are the subjects of the story). The API suggests that reporters embrace empathy: attempt to understand why interviewees feel the way they do. Traditionally, the assumptions of the reporters and their assigning editors have dictated the framing of a story. Instead, API urges, use empathy to adjust the focus of the story. There is a difference, by the way, between empathy and sympathy, which many journalists reject as the unethical adoption of a bias toward a source. Empathy is an attempt at objective understanding, in much the same way a psychotherapist attempts to understand the feelings of a patient — but without taking sides.

In the course of reporting a story, the API offers several other empathy-guided tips:

- In approaching sources unfamiliar with media interviews, begin with an off-the-record conversation, not only to establish rapport but to get a feel for what a formal interview might yield in terms of information or opinions for the story. Then, at the appropriate moment, shift gears to a more formal Q-and-A mode, on the record.

- Ask the subject, especially if the subject is on one of Maynard's "faultlines," if he or she is happy with the media's coverage of his/her community. If the answer is no, probe for reasons and background stories. This can save a great deal of unintended misunderstanding later on.

- Think through the probable impact of your story upon the least-powerful communities involved in the story. If harm is likely from the story, can adjustments in the reporting be made without affecting the veracity of the story?

- Spend time in an underrepresented community without a particular story in mind. This is known as visiting "third places," places like barber shops, coffee shops, beauty salons, church halls, homeless shelters, senior centers and the like. Here relationships are forged between journalists and community members, and, usually, story ideas are found as well.

- Especially with subjects in underrepresented groups, conduct interviews face-to-face, not via text messaging, email or telephone. Those shorthand methods may be useful after the first several face-to-face encounters, but using them as a default reporting method will strike subjects as extractive, not relationship-building.

- Conclude an interview with the questions "What am I missing, as we start to wrap up here?" and "For my story to be really thorough, who else should I be talking to?" The answers to those questions may result in the key strengths of the ultimate story.

FIGURE 6.3   Sara Catania directs journalism school partnerships for the Solutions Journalism Network.

(Photo courtesy of Sara Catania.)

And finally, the attention to inclusion is good for the future business sustainability of journalism. One of the most important reasons for ignoring "fault line" groups in 19th and 20th century journalism was that those groups typically did not provide advertising revenue to the station or publication. Publishers and broadcasters were building businesses, first and foremost, and the content of the news needed to be relevant to the business community and to audience members wealthy enough to purchase the goods and services they saw advertised. There was no reason to include others, according to that model. But with the advertising model fast disappearing, other models (which we'll explore in Chapter 10) are emerging that require membership or participation from a full array of audience members. In an age of declining audience size, where journalism needs to attract new audience members, inclusion along the faultlines makes good business sense.

These, then, are the new and promising means by which journalism can fulfill its role as a facilitator for citizens in their vital roles in a democracy: focusing on what citizens want to learn from their media; making meaningful, long-term connections with the communities they serve; working hard to include groups that journalism has traditionally overlooked; stopping not at discouraging descriptions of wicked problems but instead researching possible solutions to those problems; and collaborating with traditional rivals to improve on their offerings to their audiences.

In Chapter 2 we discussed the social responsibility theory of the First Amendment, an outgrowth of the Hutchins Commission report of 1947. The theory acknowledges that the First Amendment, in guaranteeing freedom to the press, does not literally require any particular behaviors of the news media. But it also implies that in exchange for such great leeway in their work, the news media ought to perform certain functions in support of democratic practice. And over the last 70 years, journalists by and large have appeared to be perfectly fine with the notion that their work should somehow serve the public good. In the disruptions of the 21st century, though, those duties have become obscured. The examples in this chapter, we hope, have provided some clarity as to how today's journalists can help their audiences become more effective citizens. It's a challenge, to be sure, to get journalists and citizens somehow to see each other as partners in democratic practice. Doug Oplinger at Your Voice Ohio put it this way: "How do we build a kind of journalism that is so meaningful to citizens that they will want to defend it?"

BOX 6.5 A More Optimistic Journalism Major

Are journalism students open to an approach that's radically different from the coursework of the early 2000s? Sara Catania, who has traveled the country helping professors incorporate Solutions Journalism into their teaching, responds with an enthusiastic "yes."

Today's students, Catania has observed, are ready for something different.

"Students today come into a Journalism program with a different mindset," Catania, the director of journalism school partnerships for Solutions Journalism Network, explained. "Their context is that of news aversion, news avoidance, and a general but real sense of despair." They have grown up reading and listening to a kind of journalism that too often is fixated on what's wrong, repeatedly reporting on massively complicated, intractable problems without reporting on what's being done about them. They don't want to invest in careers that simply add to that despair.

But an increasing number of faculty, whose observations Catania has shared on her Solutions Journalism blog, have found that the solutions approach reinvigorates the students. Gail Wiggins, an assistant professor at North Carolina A&T University, told *The Atlantic* she sees Generation Z students making a special connection with solutions.

"This generation really wants to make change," Wiggins said. "They're often feeling like journalism in its traditional form doesn't always do that" (Quoted in Catania, 2018a).

Kathryn Thier, who pioneered Solutions pedagogy at the University of Oregon School of Journalism and Communication before pursuing doctoral studies at the University of Maryland, told Catania that she had her students complete a survey about solutions, at the end of the term. "I had several students say to me, 'Well, I wasn't even sure if I was going to stay in journalism. I began to wonder: Did I choose the wrong major? And then I heard about solutions journalism'" (Catania, 2018a).

Theresa de los Santos, an assistant professor of communication at Pepperdine University, said her students leave with such enthusiasm that they mention solutions in their job interviews. "Most of the news directors and editors they're sitting in front of are really excited," she said, even if those journalists haven't engaged themselves in solutions journalism (Catania, 2018a).

Kim Walsh-Childers, who has taught journalism at the University of Florida for 30 years, agreed. "My students like this approach. They're excited about the idea that they can learn to tell stories that don't make everybody want to give up — just throw up their hands and quit. They themselves have that experience of 'Why do I even want to go to a news web page when it's all just going to be bad?'" (Catania, 2018b).

With a solutions approach, Walsh-Childers said, "It's much more encouraging for students to be thinking, 'OK — maybe there are ways out of these problems.'"

The number one aspect that students cite in their praise for solutions journalism? The professors told Catania that it's the rigor of the solutions method. It doesn't help them become solutions journalists, they said; it helps them become good journalists, period.

EXERCISES

1. During class, identify a significant, ongoing issue on campus or in the local community off-campus. Then, individually:

   - In one sentence each, describe the perspective or "frame" that local or campus news media reports have used to cover the issue.

   - Now think of a different perspective or frame about this issue — another way of looking at things — that has not appeared in the media coverage.

- Describe benefits that readers/listeners might gain if your new perspective were included in the coverage.

- Compare your new perspective to other new perspectives in the class. Taken all together, what benefits would derive from inclusion of most or all of these new perspectives?

2. During class, develop a list of communities on campus or in the off-campus community that most everyone in the class is "not" personally familiar with. Such communities might include military veterans, disabled persons, ethnic or religious groups, persons in gender transition, senior citizens, extreme right-wing activists or extreme left-wing activists. Have your instructor assign a different one of these communities to each student. Then, outside class:

- Locate a member of your assigned community and arrange an interview.

- In the interview, ask him/her to discuss a story in the media recently whose coverage s/he found unsatisfactory. Probe as to why it was unsatisfactory.

3. Some media stories have the effect of supporting "democratic practices," while other stories do the opposite — they have the effect of undermining democratic practices.

- On the web, find a recent news or feature article whose likely effect will be to inspire or motivate readers/listeners to act as citizens in a democracy. Explain why this effect is likely.

- Now find a recent news or feature article whose likely effect will be to discourage or undermine important democratic practices. Explain why this effect is likely.

4. With the class, develop a list of all the sources for news and information about the campus. These should be independent sources — radio stations, newsletters, blogs, newspapers, online news sites, television programming, etc. — and not public-relations offices for the university or parts of the university.

Now imagine a collaboration among those independent news outlets.

- What major topic or issue would be suitable for a collaboration?

- As with the collaborations of Your Voice Ohio or New Jersey News Commons, assign a different aspect of coverage of your issue to each of the collaborating news outlets.

- What challenges — logistical or ethical — would you foresee in this collaboration? How would you overcome them?

- Do you think this collaboration could produce more valuable information for the campus community than an effort by a single news outlet? Why or why not?

5. Choose any article on a student-led Solutions Journalism project, described by Sara Catania from The Whole Story, a Solutions Journalism Network resource on the website Medium: https://thewholestory.solutionsjournalism.org/tagged/jschools

   - In one paragraph, describe why the project Catania described qualifies as Solutions Journalism.

   - In the second paragraph, describe a way you might adopt the methods described in the article, to explore a similar problem and solution on your campus.

CHAPTER 7

Journalists and Citizens as Collaborators

O N A TYPICALLY GRAY AND ICY FEBRUARY DAY IN CHICAGO, TWO DOWN-town news operations eschewed the rough and tumble we-know-best banter that typifies newsrooms and instead focused on love and caring for their communities.

Valentine's Day was nearing, and WBEZ's Curious City team was doing what they always do: asking residents to weigh in with their questions. Saya Hillman, a Chicago native, wanted to know what people who moved to the city from elsewhere loved about it. The love letters poured in from transplants who waxed poetically about fireflies aglow, fast walkers, big band music at neighborhood bars, forest preserves and streets lined with magnificent towers, turrets and bay windows. "To Chicago, with love," a podcast and feature story on multiple platforms, was welcoming and warm.

Like their counterparts down the road at Hearken, journalists on the radio station's pioneering Curious City team believe that ideas for news should come directly from the community and that journalists' job is to midwife them.

Beth Braun wanted to know what was going on with lead pollution at the massive ArcelorMittal steel mill on Lake Michigan in Burns Harbor, near where she has always lived in Northwest Indiana. She asked Curious City to find out. "I lived here, grew up here and I'm probably going to die here," she told Curious City. "I love it here, and that's why I wanted to reach out to Curious City."

After listeners voted in favor of her question, a reporter began digging. A 2018 *Chicago Tribune* investigation had found that the plant emitted more lead than any other industrial plant in the country. Braun wanted to know more and asked how she could find out if her neighborhood was contaminated. Curious City connected her with a researcher to test the soil and reported on her journey of discovery and action. "I'm hoping that one small person like me trying to reach out to other people can make more awareness and maybe make some sort of change, at least in this small town," she told a reporter (Stark, 2019).

Each day, Curious City gets a handful of questions that are phoned in or posted on the website. The questions are about the Chicagoland economy, education, environment, governance, history, culture and more, and the staff invites listeners to vote on which ones reporters should investigate. The issues are easy to track on the website, which hosts the public voting rounds, retains the answers to old questions on an easily searchable platform and details new questions being investigated.

Alexandra Salomon, a seasoned reporter and producer with impressive credentials and overseas experience, leads the Curious City team. She's convinced that journalism is more relevant and connected when people from the community suggest news ideas, framed from their personal experiences. "It allows us to apply the rigorous standards of journalism directly to where the public wants to apply them," she said (A. Salomon, personal interview, Feb. 12, 2019).

Curious City has learned that community members are great tipsters when it comes to recognizing a shared problem. The best questions come from "somebody who is concerned about something in their neighborhood and has tried to get answers," Salomon said. By working with them, "we've connected with the citizens and we've deepened their own connection to their community."

These connections don't begin and end with the question. Curious City reporters like to involve the individual who brought the public problem to light throughout the reporting process as new information develops and people respond to it. The reporting process is open and transparent, beginning with the public rounds of voting on questions and ending with the website's archive of past questions and answers.

FIGURE 7.1   Intern Mackenzie Crosson, left, producer Katherine Nagasawa and editor Alexandra Salomon discuss a story for WBEZ's Curious City.

(Photo by Paul Voakes.)

This type of accountability to the audience is important to Jesse Dukes, an audio producer who helps write, record, edit and mix the pieces. "The depth of our relationship to our audience ensures that we have constant points of confirmation that we are doing what the public wants," Dukes said. "In the old model there is not a lot of confirmation that decisions based on 'news judgment'" meet the needs of the public (Dukes, personal interview, Feb. 12, 2019).

Curious City was founded in 2012 on a simple insight after WBEZ journalist Jennifer Brandel wondered aloud about the professional practice of news judgment. Why are journalism professionals in newsrooms asking all the questions that become news? Why not ask the people?

Curious City was her answer to those questions, and the Curious City approach and brand have spread to public radio stations across the country. Brandel moved on from WBEZ to found Hearken, to increase her commitment to community-powered journalism and to help catalyze a growing movement of journalists who want to collaborate more fully with the public to create relevant and trusted news.

Brandel and her successors at Curious City want journalists to be in an ongoing relationship with members of the community and to show that they care about their well-being. They are practicing relational journalism, a new approach that respects and values citizens as co-producers of news and knowledge. Relational journalism, introduced in Chapter 1 and explored more fully in Chapter 4, recognizes that journalists should facilitate the work of citizens in a democracy and invite citizens to share in that work. The relationship is two-way, meant to build trust over time.

We'll return to Brandel's story and the transformative work of Hearken. But first, let's explore what it means for journalists and citizens to collaborate.

In Chapter 4 we discussed "who is a journalist" in these times of fluid boundaries and a rapidly changing news ecosystem. In today's technology-enabled environment, more people are equipped to perform duties that once were the sole province of professionals. Effectively supporting citizens and their democratic work now is the job of many people, each fulfilling different journalistic duties.

We outlined a continuum of ways in which this is done ranging from the standard professional model to the independent producer. The models outlined are: professional journalist; citizen recognition; citizen-assisted reporting; guided citizen reporting; and the independent citizen journalist. In this chapter, we suggest that communities are best served when journalists collaborate broadly, not just as a way to produce better web, print and broadcast reports but to also help citizens succeed in the democratic work they must do. The principle explored here applies ideas from the citizen recognition, citizen-assisted reporting and guided citizen reporting models.

Some of today's innovators are less academic in their descriptions of the stepped-up role citizens should play in the creation of journalism. They are inventing ways to give

BOX 7.1 Chicago's "J School of the Streets"

Journalism is citizenship, best produced by the people. That's the guiding light that inspires every groundbreaking innovation at City Bureau in Chicago, where co-founder Darryl Holliday and team "disaggregate the skills of journalism and distribute them to the citizens to build civic capacity" (Holliday, personal interview, Feb. 13, 2019).

The nonprofit news outlet, founded in 2015, does more than listen to community members to find story ideas or extract opinions and perspectives. It puts citizens in the driver's seat.

"Journalists need to learn how to share their power," Holliday said, adding that City Bureau is "looking for ways to rewrite their contract with the public."

Clearly news stories are more complete, accurate and relevant when members of the public help identify and report them. But City Bureau's ambitions

are about more than simply improving the quality of the news. It aims to spread the skills of journalism throughout the community as a way of also increasing residents' involvement in public life.

City Bureau explores how to do this through three innovative programs: civic reporting fellowships, "documenters," and the public newsroom. Headquartered in Chicago's Woodlawn neighborhood, the work is strongly community based, inspiring *Politico Magazine* to dub it "the J-school of the streets" (Blau, 2019).

City Bureau hires and trains neighborhood folks to attend and monitor local government meetings. Known as documenters, these residents also contribute to larger news projects and help build "a common pool of knowledge," which City Bureau says is designed to "democratize news and information at the local level." Their "documenter" work, which includes a directory of meetings and training opportunities, is housed on an easy-to-use database at documenters. org. A "city scraper" technology toolkit also is available to anyone who wants to create a database of public meetings to inform community members and encourage them to attend.

Early in its evolution, Holliday called this work monitorial journalism, noting that "the traditional version of monitorial citizens are people who are outside the dominant paradigm and get involved when they need to." Often, he said, the documenters' work is an on-ramp to greater engagement in the civic life of a community.

Public newsrooms — free weekly workshops for journalists and members of the public — also are meant to reframe the contract between journalists and the public, partly by breaking down the barriers of mutual distrust.

FIGURE 7.2 Darryl Holliday is the co-founder and News Lab director for City Bureau in Chicago.

(Photo by Paul Voakes.)

citizens more power to fix what they see as journalism's imbalance in power. Among the most vocal is City Bureau of Chicago, which is redesigning who makes journalism and how, as it seeks to demonstrate that "journalism belongs to everyone."

Darryl Holliday, co-founder of City Bureau in Chicago, asserts that "journalism is citizenship." Holliday, who is trying to refunction journalism, speaks for many other innovators who think that by doing journalism, citizens become better citizens, and by seeing themselves as citizens, journalists become better journalists.

Bonni McKeown, a blues educator and documenter, wanted to get to know the Austin neighborhood better so she dropped in to City Bureau's 95th public newsroom event, held a couple of months before the 2019 mayoral election (McKeown, personal interview, Feb. 13, 2019).

At the Austin Family Community Center, she joined other residents for an early-evening "Public Newsroom" led by City Bureau reporting fellows who had partnered with *The Austin Weekly News* to produce "The Austin People Powered Voter Guide."

Austin, the city's largest West Side neighborhood, once a thriving, suburban-like majority-white enclave, fell victim to the white flight and disinvestment that began in the '60s and persisted. Today it is predominantly African-American, low-income and saddled with a reputation for crime and a homicide rate that is among the city's highest.

Austin's challenges and opportunities were very much on the minds of those who gathered for the election conversation that focused on issues rather than on the horse race between contenders. As a result, the group was able to more constructively explore "a range of solutions from candidates," said one grateful attendee.

Attendees weren't there just to listen and learn though. They also were asked to engage. The group was divided into smaller groups and, using a guide designed by City Bureau, they discussed income and jobs, recommended solutions and figured out how to pitch their alderperson. City Bureau said it would mail the pitches to the appropriate alderperson.

The public newsroom, open to all, brings to life City Bureau's declaration that "We don't empower community, we create space for interconnected learning and the expression of communal power" (City Bureau, 2020a).

FIGURE 7.3 Annie Nguyen and Michael Romain, civic reporting fellows at City Bureau, present survey findings with community members.

(Photo by Paula Ellis.)

Providing more equitable coverage of Chicago neighborhoods that often are referred to as distressed, underserved or marginalized is at the heart of City Bureau's origin.

"Austin is not seen as a tight community," a City Bureau reporter said. "We need to explain and reveal the strength of this community," she explained as residents worked in their small groups.

The work of City Bureau is guided by its commitment to work "with" the people, not just "for" the people. As the preamble to its list of community engagement guidelines states, "We define community engagement as any interaction with the people we not only serve but work with" (City Bureau, 2020b,). All the guidelines can be found in Appendix 3.

By bringing journalists and community "together in a collaborative spirit," City Bureau's goal is "to produce equitable media coverage, encourage civic participation and hold powerful forces to account" (City Bureau, 2020a).

What It Means for Journalists and Nonjournalists to Collaborate

Successful collaborations rely on a clear understanding of who is best suited to do what. It is a relationship of interdependence that holds for as long as all participants deliver their best, thereby creating bonds of trust and mutual reliance. A collaboration succeeds only when collaborators understand and carry out an efficient division of labor.

Thinking of community members as collaborators rather than as the audience or as sources requires a shift in a journalist's mindset. Once a journalist reorients his or her approach to a relational one, new avenues for newsgathering and storytelling open up, and it's possible to see how journalism is a process meant to help communities learn and succeed rather than a one-and-done product.

So who does what when citizens and journalists collaborate? Innovators across the country are continuously trying to figure that out. Clearly, though, trained journalists come to the collaboration with a certain skill set, just as citizens come with a different skill set.

Citizens bring unique and often overlooked abilities to community problem-solving and thus are a generally untapped source for journalists, who have become overly reliant on institutions and official sources of information. Citizens bring their personal experiences to discussions about shared problems. And as they tell their story, they reveal what they hold valuable. Citizens bring historical perspective and, unattached to officialdom, they bring honesty. At times they share needed expertise on specific topics and their networks of relationships. Citizens are able to identify resources in the community that could be applied to a problem. Importantly, citizens can advocate for a cause, a policy or a solution.

Trained journalists with a mission to educate the public bring a unique set of skills to the potential collaboration. They are immensely curious and trained to seek out facts by interviewing expert sources, searching documents, using data and persistently following where the facts lead. Journalists have an orderly and questioning mind. They are trained observers who report news as it is unfolding, connect and synthesize complex streams of information, and provide context to aid understanding. Journalists, employing a host of technical skills for print, online, television, radio and magazine news reports, are skilled storytellers. They are guided by legal and ethical responsibilities.

Journalists who want to codesign, cocreate and coproduce news with citizens as partners take on additional roles. They find ways for citizens to help define the "news agenda" and gather relevant information. These journalists inspire and lead citizens to do great work, often for little or no pay. They scout for emerging stories and issues that citizens can pursue, and train them in writing, reporting and creating for multiple media platforms. To support the community's broader democratic work, journalists guide the community in curiosity, verify facts, move everyone away from "fake news" accusations and curate what is known so far.

With this understanding of who brings what special talents and skills to the collaboration, it's possible to examine some practices that have gained heightened importance as journalists recognize the importance of partnering with citizens to coproduce the news.

BOX 7.2 As Diverse as the Communities They Serve

Amid the San Francisco Bay Area's crowded media scene, KALW stands out for working hand-in-hand with the residents of diverse communities to produce news and ensure that the radio station and webcast truly belong to the public.

KALW isn't the area's largest public radio station, but it is its oldest and most community minded. Building authentic relationships and coproducing news and entertainment with community members is an essential part of the job at KALW, which continuously experiments with ways to be more representative, relevant and engaging.

News director Ben Trefny is committed to diversifying everything about the news report and how it is produced. He's worried that people don't trust media institutions, but more troubling, he says, is that people don't trust each other. One way to remedy that, he believes, is to produce media with the people (Trefny, personal interview, July 30, 2018).

A seemingly simple decision to ask listeners what they thought about a controversial issue produced an aha moment in 2016 that Trefny enthusiastically recounts when he describes the station's journey toward greater inclusion.

Developers had just announced plans to demolish existing buildings on Treasure Island and build up to 8,000 housing units that would be rented at market and below-market rates. The land, however, was contaminated with toxins and radioactive materials. Journalists, worried that economically disadvantaged people would be taken advantage of, were beginning to frame the issue in stereotypical binary terms. KALW turned to its listeners and asked: Would you live on Treasure Island? The public's nuanced responses helped reshape the reporting and led to a discussion about the tradeoffs involved. Members of the public had suggested they needed housing and would live there if assured the land was safe.

Trefny emphasizes that the relationships with the public aren't meant to be a one-and-done. "It's when we can continue engaging that we see success."

Differing perspectives and experiences matter when tackling a shared public problem. That's one of the many reasons news leaders worry that the backgrounds of those who report the news aren't as diverse as the communities they serve. For help with this, Trefny turned to the Maynard Institute's "Voices" program to work with his station as they had done with *The Oakland Tribune* under the leadership of then-editor Martin Reynolds. The institute trains residents from diverse neighborhoods to tell the stories of their communities. Reynolds, now with the Maynard Institute, calls it "news from the inside out," a term coined by Sandy Close, former executive director of New America Media and the Pacific News Service (Reynolds, personal communication, Nov. 18, 2015).

Trefny explained that the neighborhood reporters contribute community knowledge and context that are invaluable for naming and framing news reports, while "we bring a lot of the professional skills to them." Professional journalists "can't tell the story as completely" without help from people in communities who are willing to share their truth, he said.

In addition to the improved reporting, Trefny said "the value has been a real change in how we view the community."

Listening More, and Differently

Listening has always been part of the journalist's toolkit, but in these changing times, it plays a starring role in the mindset shift toward working with citizens to provide more relevant and accurate news.

Professional journalism groups, academics and practitioners have expounded on the necessity of listening at the beginning of the reporting process, throughout it and after the piece has appeared. There are numerous listening methodologies packaged in toolkits, hosted on technology platforms and filling the pages of journalism trade publications. In addition, journalists are learning about how to listen

BOX 7.3 Community Listening via Text and Talk

Andrew Haeg, an accomplished journalist and media innovator, wasn't satisfied with the traditional methods he had mastered for reporting about communities. So, like most inventors driven to explore unfamiliar terrain, he set out to learn from the experience of others. He dove into the fields of organizational behavior and user-centered design. "That flipped my view of journalism to listening first," Haeg said.

With that one insight, Haeg, already a co-founder of the Public Insight Network, launched GroundSource, a technology platform to make it easier to source news stories from the ground up. GroundSource enables news organizations to engage directly with people through SMS texting.

A serial entrepreneur with a missionary zeal, Haeg understood that the technology was a tool for fundamentally disrupting the top-down practice of journalism. To do that, Haeg and like-minded journalists, over a period of years, advocated for listening first. They launched news outlets as practical experiments that generated new ways journalists could better connect with citizens and align their work with community needs and interests.

In New Orleans, for example, GroundSource was used to develop and maintain a network of phone subscribers who opted in to receive text-message news items and answer questions about pressing social problems.

Employing GroundSource technology developed in 2012 and building on the success of Listening Post New Orleans, Haeg launched Listening Post Macon, in central Georgia, in 2016 while he was an entrepreneur in residence at Mercer University's Center for Collaborative Journalism.

Haeg, who helped pioneer the Public Insight Network, a network of citizens who share their experiences and knowledge with journalists, and Jesse Hardman, a journalist and media developer who founded Listening Post New Orleans, are arguably the greybeards of the reborn movement to encourage and help journalists listen more carefully to members of the community.

---

from other professionals. From the therapeutic fields focused on healing a disorder come techniques applied to the coverage of trauma and motivational dialogue meant to strengthen an individual's motivation to change. From the field of positive psychology comes appreciative inquiry and other techniques that focus on building strengths and resilience rather than identifying and fixing deficits.

The listening we are discussing here is a continuous process, an ongoing feedback loop with the community that helps journalists shape their coverage. It is a mode of listening for understanding with empathy, which builds relationships over time and is therefore a cornerstone of what we have referred to as relational journalism.

It stands in contrast to what has been called extractive or transactional listening. These journalists are no longer content with transactions that value people's input narrowly and last for only as long as needed for a story. In other words, they are looking to build a relationship built on mutual interest and trust rather than only to extract a quote that will illustrate their article.

"We're helping people understand the things they see every day," explained Hearken engagement specialist Janine Anderson. "That's a valuable relationship" (Anderson, personal interview, February 6, 2018).

Today, the Listening Post Collective, which evolved naturally from its New Orleans roots, captures what's learned from other community media projects across the country, provides training and peer-to-peer support and evangelizes for listening first, a value now embraced by numerous journalism professional groups and practitioners with their own set of tools and tips.

The revolution Haeg and Hardman helped launch is about more than listening to improve journalism though. It's about building community by inspiring and enabling residents to engage in public life.

Haeg thinks of journalism as one of the foundational rungs on a ladder of engagement that strengthens an individual's ties to the community and deepens their involvement. He calls it the engagement cycle, which begins "with a simple invitation to action." It all begins with a question, crafted to elicit conversation about tangible issues drawn from people's personal experiences. (See Box 7.4 "To Listen, Ask Better Questions," p. 118)

"We have to have a lower barrier to entry so someone with low motivation and low ability, or low confidence in their own ability, will feel ok with stepping up and saying something," Haeg said. (Haeg, 2017).

The mission of the Listening Post Collective Hardman created begins and ends with people in the community. It promotes a seven-step process for the media to effectively engage with the community. "Our work is predicated on doing an information ecosystem assessment of a community" that identifies "what people want to understand and how they feel represented in existing media," Hardman explained (Hardman, personal interview, March 5, 2020).

"The health of any community is tied to information access: people's ability to understand what's going on in their community and their place in it," he said.

Through its partnership with Internews, Listening Post Collective members also learn from news organizations around the globe about how media can be an essential agent for development.

Josh Stearns, a philanthropy program officer and communications instructor, has outlined five models that move journalists from transactional to transformational listening (Stearns, 2014). The first is traditional listening to sources and interviewees, plus listening to find new sources and perspectives. The second is listening for story ideas, but also listening for community priorities. The third is listening for feedback and creating multiple avenues for real-time and ongoing feedback that extend beyond a website's comments section. Next is listening for understanding and context. Stearns encourages listening to "the concerns, passions, challenges and hopes of local communities," which, he adds, will make other forms of listening easier. Last, but certainly not least, is listening for relationships. "Listening for the sake of listening, for the sake of showing up and being present for others, is critical to building trusting relationships," Stearns said.

Raising Questions

Journalists take great pride in being known as tough questioners who are able to ask just the right question to elicit a previously undiscovered fact. Often these exchanges are filled with conflict as is sometimes necessary to get to the truth. At other times, journalists may only be seeking a juicy quote to illustrate or humanize their story. This is what critics call extractive interviewing.

Journalists listening for the kind of context and understanding that builds relationships ask different kinds of questions. The questions are generative, free of judgment and not driving to any preordained conclusion. They can be appreciative, shifting the focus from deficits to strengths and defining problems as opportunities for innovation and change. And they can be deliberative, focusing on "What should we do?" when judgment is needed to resolve the tensions between competing options.

Traditional journalism training and practice emphasized careful backgrounding on the subject and preparation for the interview. There are direct questions, open-and-closed-ended questions and tough, sometimes personal, questions. All of that remains good journalistic practice, but today's innovators pushing to realign their reporting with the interests of people in the communities they serve are experimenting with the approaches drawn from the other fields listed above.

In these newsrooms, you're likely to hear more "what if" questions than direct, closed-ended questions that suggest a simple answer.

There's even an institute dedicated to helping people learn to ask good questions so that they can participate in decision making. The Right Question Institute works across a number of domains but its "micro-democracy" focus is of particular interest here because it aims to help people turn everyday encounters with public institutions into opportunities for participation and democratic action.

Putting People First at Hearken

At the Chicago nerve-center of Hearken, the ongoing buzz is about asking and listening. The company's engagement specialists from around the country have Zoomed in to a video-conference meeting to review their clients' efforts to shift their news routines. More than 250 organizations have employed Hearken's "people-powered journalism" approach in an effort to better align their work with the interests of the public, for both service and business reasons.

Hearken founder Jennifer Brandel worries a lot about the relationship between media and the public. The lack of trust is corrosive and stems in part from the fact that newsrooms have increasingly adopted the lens of "consumer" over "citizen," she said. The dynamics of social media have exacerbated this trend by equating

FIGURE 7.4 Jennifer Brandel is CEO and co-founder of Hearken.

(Photo by Paul Voakes.)

consumption metrics with success, she explained. Hearken believes that serious stories can be shareable and works with its clients to show how. Listening, carefully and respectfully, is at the core of what Hearken advocates. Its transformational goal is to create reciprocal relationships between community members and the media makers who serve them.

FIGURE 7.5 Bridget Thoreson, left, and Summer Fields, engagement strategists at Hearken, lead a video staff meeting with Hearken strategists around the country.

(Photo by Paul Voakes.)

"If newsrooms want to be good 'for' democracy, they need to be better 'at' democracy," Brandel has famously said. Opening up the reporting process, structuring routine ways for ongoing listening and being transparent redistribute power in the relationship by giving it back to the people.

Brandel has helped catalyze this growing movement to reinvent journalism by putting the people first. Hearken spreads its gospel far and wide, but it does more than proselytize. The firm offers consulting services and a technology platform to help news organizations transform their reporting processes and place a higher value on the wisdom of everyday people. Its website is a treasure trove of ideas, tools and case studies. (For Brandel's reflections on putting citizens first, see Box 11.2 "What She Didn't Learn in School.")

Hearken and like-minded journalists are either upending the practice of journalism or returning it to its preprofessional roots. Most likely, it's a little bit of both.

Bridget Thoreson, Hearken engagement strategist and industry insights leader, said the shifts in approach and philosophy bring her closer to what motivated her to get into journalism (Thoreson, personal interview, Feb. 12, 2019). She believes in service to readers and said that these reimagined practices "have deepened" not diminished journalism's traditional values. "If the customer is no longer the advertiser but the person using the news, you get much more aligned with their values." When the professional values of journalists are more closely aligned with public values, democracy is better served.

BOX 7.4 To Listen, Ask Better Questions

Some reporters just seem to have a knack for knowing where to go, who to talk with and how to listen to learn from community residents. They may make it look easy and natural but there's art, science and a lot of practice behind what they do.

Listening Post has some great advice on how to start an ongoing conversation with people about the things that matter most to them. Its advice appears in its "Guide to Crafting Great Questions," which can be found at https://tinyurl.com/GuidetoCraftingGreatQuestions.

Here are the highlights:

- **Look for experiences over opinions.**

  Avoid questions that begin with "What do you think" or "What's your opinion on," and go with questions like "What happened to you when ... ?" or "How were you impacted ... ?" For example:

  Don't ask: What do you think about gun laws?

  Do ask: How are guns a part of your life? What negative or positive impact have guns had on your life?

- **Make abstract issues tangible.**

  Ask questions people can readily answer based on their experiences. Turn complex topics into accessible questions that speak to issues people are dealing with. For example:

  Don't ask: How are you impacted by gentrification?

  Do ask: What percent of your income goes to rent or mortgage?

- **Ask people to tell their story, not fill out a survey.**

  Ask questions the community has been begging to answer and give people space to answer by telling their story. For example:

  Don't ask: Are you satisfied with the public school system?

  Do ask: Tell us about the last time you were proud of our public schools.

- **Stick to the 5Ws and H (Who, What, When, Where, Why and How).**

  Start your questions with Who, What, Where, When, Why, and How as often as you can. For example:

  Don't ask: Are you in favor of new federal immigration policies?

  Do ask: How are you impacted by new federal immigration policies?

  Do ask: What's the impact of new federal immigration policies on your community?

  If you ask a yes/no question, follow it up.

- **Have some fun.**

  You want your project to feel like an extension of the community — vibrant and engaged.

  To learn more about how Listening Post designs and implements a reporting project with the community, check out its playbook at www.listeningpostcollective.org/playbook.

EXERCISES

1. Find an article about a community problem. Who is missing from the article? What would you ask them? How would you ask questions not to "extract" a quote but to contribute to your learning and reporting focus?

2. Find an article written by a nonjournalist — a member of either the campus community or outside community. Edit the story for clarity, correctness and accuracy. Write a hypothetical memo to the writer, as if you were editing the article for a new community publication you were starting up.

3. As a class project, start an "information partnership" with a campus organization that has voiced concerns about a current campus issue. The goal is for the class to coproduce meaningful journalism with community members, whom you'll assist in "committing acts of journalism."

   With guidance from your instructor, create a class website for this project and complete the following tasks, individually or in small groups:

   - After attending a public meeting about the issue, summarize the issue, as expressed by those who spoke at the meeting. Then add your own analysis, based on your own research. Be sure to include background, context and as many different points of view as you can identify. If no one else has organized a public meeting about the issue, organize and publicize a meeting yourselves.

   - From what you heard from the "nonjournalist" community members, develop a list of "what we still don't know" — the information needs of the community.

4. Move the "information partnership" in Exercise 3 from the preliminaries to the reporting stage.

   - Write a reporting plan for a reporting project that will involve both community members and class members as reporters and writers. Divide the tasks among both groups, making sure no one person is asked to take on a massive, weeks-long project.

   - Now divide graphic, photographic and video tasks among both groups (class members and community members).

   - Once you have revised the graphics, images, videos and articles, meet with the community contributors to discuss "What we're still missing," to make the reporting project more insightful and informative. Revise again as needed.

   - Post the package on the class website, inviting the larger community that has been interested in the issue to post their comments on your website.

5. In a short essay, compare your work in Exercise 3 (and/or 4) to that of Hearken, or any of the other news organizations whose work was described in this chapter. How would you have done this project differently?

CHAPTER 8

Journalists Facilitating the Work of Citizens

R ECKON, ALABAMA MEDIA'S SHOWCASE BRAND FOR TACKLING ITS COMMU-
nities' public problems, is a far cry from the public affairs reporting of yore.
It is brilliantly named, conversational and relatable.

Ya reckon? The question rolls so naturally off the tongue. It offers a welcoming invitation for community members to exchange their personal views
and experiences about issues of the day.

Born in the playful, fast-moving spirit of social media, Reckon was a
startup built in 2017 by a handful of print and video journalists inside a legacy
media operation that was aggressively experimenting with new ways to
attract people to news that's too often characterized as dull-but-important.

Its launch was a key moment in the news organization's ongoing journey
to discover how journalism might better serve the needs of citizens.

As it moved from "journalism as outrage" to "journalism as a catalyst for
solutions," AL.com editors began to see journalism as a process, not merely a
product. As a result of its work, on multiple technology platforms and under
an array of creative brands, the news organization hoped to foster connection between people, encourage understanding of differences, uncover the
values people held dear, promote a sense of belonging and provide multiple
opportunities for this to occur.

"Helping people feel part of something and find a way into it" is the
challenge and opportunity, said Michelle Holmes, vice president of content

for Alabama Media Group, who guided the course of continuous innovation before retiring in 2019.

John Archibald, a Pulitzer Prize-winning columnist at AL.com who was on the Reckon startup team, confessed he was nervous at first. After all, he had been working for newspapers for 30 years and hadn't envisioned doing podcasts, video commentary, cartoon histories, news comedy sketches and memes like those that launched Reckon. "We mixed old schoolers with young people and there was magic there," he recalls, noting that underpinning it all was solid reporting with traditional journalism ethics delivered to "readers and viewers, scanners and listeners in ways they would pick up." It was fun too.

So, what about that name? What does it mean? Thirty minutes into a team brainstorming session, it popped into Archibald's head. When he shared it with the group, they instantly knew it worked.

"Reckon, to come to terms with. Reckon, to face consequences. The day of reckoning. Reckon, in the South, to consider or think. I reckon so. Reckon has weight and regional flavor at the same time," Archibald said as he reflected on the inspiration.

In a distinctly authentic voice that is of the community, Reckon connects and supports citizens as they prod and poke each other to share facts and opinions that over time gel into the public's judgment about how they can make progress on the complex challenges they face together.

It is a platform for deliberation, which, as we explored in Chapter 4, is at the heart of democracy.

A Reckon editor said the team intentionally chose provocative topics and the toughest issues "to bring them to some moral reckoning." Among the topics were: longstanding problems with the prison system, the decision not to expand Medicaid, Confederate monuments, racial divides, inequity, the wage gap and women's rights.

If democracy is problem-solving, then deliberation is the process by which citizens engage with each other to choose what to do. Only by weighing different options for action and working through inescapable trade-offs can citizens choose a direction that maximizes what they most value and minimizes

FIGURE 8.1 Reporter Anna Claire Vollers makes a point at a staff meeting of Reckon.

(Photo by Paul Voakes.)

the negative consequences. In many ways, this process of deliberation or coming to public judgment is the public reckoning.

As Reckon was evolving, AL.com also looked for ways to join the conversations it found women across the state were having about matters of public concern framed and expressed from their own experiences.

After a few fits and starts with other ideas, Reckon Women was born in the crucible of the inflamed public debate that erupted after Alabama in 2019 signed into law what was then the country's most restrictive abortion ban. Absent, however, were the voices of women. "We decided to dedicate ourselves to journalism that elevated the voices of women," said Kelly Scott, vice president of content. "We decided to focus on reporting that heard the concerns of women and exposed the broader gender disparities in our state; a state where male lawmakers have failed to consider maternal health, workplace discrimination and other policies affecting women."

In the opening chapter of this textbook, we defined democracy as the process by which citizens, acting in association and as part of fluid interdependent community networks, work together to solve shared problems and pursue opportunities. Citizens may work with and through institutions, but, in a democracy, the sovereign authority rests with them, not the state.

In Chapter 2, we asserted that to support citizens in their essential democratic work, journalism must shift to a more facilitative role — one that we call relational journalism. Relational journalism refers to a style of journalism — both a skill set and a mindset — that facilitates the building of relationships with citizens, and among citizens. Deliberation studies have shown that relationship-building is a reliable requisite to collective problem solving — as is shared access to reliable information.

For almost a decade, spurred on by an urgent need to build tighter ties with its community as it transitioned from print to digital platforms, Alabama Media has been innovating in ways that illustrate this shift to facilitation and relational journalism.

Fostering a Deliberative Perspective

In many ways, journalists need to unlearn long-taught habits of the mind and shift their own perspectives away from an institutional mindset that enshrined their expertise, authority and distance. Only by changing their own stance to one of collaboration with the public can journalists authentically engage with the community in mutually beneficial exchanges over the long haul. This often-wrenching change in attitude and role is the essential foundation on which to build a deliberative perspective.

Focusing on the future, while learning from the past, also is key to a deliberative perspective. Citizens deliberate when they need to choose a path forward in the face of disagreement and uncertainty. The deliberative talk catalyzes action. Through

BOX 8.1   **The "Triangle of Trust"**

If the issue is seething hot, Spaceship Media digs in. Just when others might walk away from the conflict inherent in wickedly complex and emotional public issues, Spaceship invites citizens from all walks of life to talk it out.

Guns and gun violence. Enforcement of immigration laws. Disparities in health policy. The future of agriculture. These are a few of the deeply polarizing topics that Spaceship has explored with residents of communities across the country in partnership with other news organizations.

Founded by two experienced media professionals in 2016, Spaceship is pioneering what it calls dialog journalism to bridge across differences and reduce polarization.

The founders were disheartened by the vitriol that had overtaken the public sphere during the fractious 2016 presidential election campaign. Journalists were accustomed to dealing with conflict and reporting on it. But co-founders Eve Pearlman and Jeremy Hay had a hunch that there were more constructive ways for journalists to deal with conflict and better serve democracy.

Spaceship designs sustained online dialog that are lightly moderated so that the conversations flow freely and in whatever direction the group decides. Journalists provide information and facts as needed and report stories as they emerge. But the stories aren't the focus of the work; the people are. "Journalists serve as guides into the dialog," explained Pearlman, chief executive officer (Pearlman, personal interview, June 25, 2018).

To do this, Spaceship has evolved a seven-step dialog process. They are: The Build, The Gather, The Welcome, The Experience, The Carry, The Nourish and The Share.

The first step is to build a collaborative relationship with partner news organizations and decide what conversation will be most valuable to the community. What are people in conflict about or what aren't they talking about? The second is to gather community members by asking them to volunteer to join the conversations, provide some background on themselves and suggest what they want to know about other communities. The group is then culled to ensure that both "sides" and all views are represented and that no one feels outnumbered.

Next Spaceship works with news organizations to welcome participants. It identifies communication platforms (i.e., Facebook, in-person gatherings) that work for the specific groups and create content to launch the conversations. After the group is selected, conveners design the experience by creating spaces where people can talk and learn from each other. The fifth step is the carry, Spaceship's term for moderation. Here they pay careful attention to mod-

their actions, citizens shape their shared future. More simply, together they answer the question: What kind of place do we want this to be?

News organizations that have made these transitions first recognized that their understanding of public needs and wants is out of sync with the way members of the public see things. This fundamental misalignment can lead to maladies ranging from irrelevance to mutual distrust.

To sync up with the public better, journalism innovators have proclaimed the value of listening more, to more people and more carefully. But if journalists want to support public problem solving and help citizens deliberate, they must ask: Who are we listening to? What are we listening for? Those questions remain open-ended and not definitively answered, but the Kettering Foundation, working with journalists and practitioners of deliberation, is developing some useful insights.

eration and focus on the personal and informational needs of the participants. The term carry is meant to convey that moderators help people with differing views have a respectful dialog . As the conversations ensue, the job of Spaceship and other journalists is to nourish them by providing information, posing questions and encouraging others to do the same. FactStacks are unique and critical to the process because they provide a shared set of facts on which to base a conversation, Pearlman explained. These FactStacks are produced to answer specific questions that arise during the dialogs. The final step is to share. Spaceship works with newsrooms to produce content developed from the dialogs. Stories may be based on something in the FactStacks or about the conversation and what was learned. A summary of the seven-step process can be found at https://spaceshipmedia.org/about/#-method.

Using this process, Spaceship tries to create what it calls a "triangle of trust" between divided communities and the media organizations that serve them. The triangulation involves media on one side, a group of protagonists (i.e., pro-gun, pro-choice) on another and antagonists (i.e., anti-gun, anti-choice) on the other. "As people on opposite sides of difficult issues begin to talk and understand one another, and as journalists support those conversations with reporting and moderation, a trusting community is formed," Pearlman explained.

FIGURE 8.2 Eve Pearlman of Spaceship Media speaks to journalists at Mercer University's Center for Collaborative Journalism in Macon, Georgia.

(Photo by Ivie Marie Clarke.)

The mistrust between citizens and journalists goes both ways, Hay said. "News organizations often mistrust their audiences ... and citizens don't trust news media."

Pearlman recalls that she was in journalism school when she first thought the discipline was misaligned with the needs of the public. Since then, she's learned that "putting the community in the center, putting listening in the center, and thinking about service and connection is very meaningful."

Chief among the things Spaceship Media has learned over its years of experimentation is that "connection has to come before the facts," Pearlman said.

In Chapter 2, we described how deliberation differs from discussing or debating an issue. The process incorporates six democratic practices identified by the Kettering Foundation and outlined in that chapter. Those practices offer journalists clues about what to listen for when people are talking about public problems that are important to them.

The foundation's Journalism and Democracy work group has been researching how journalists can promote and listen for democratic discourse. Alabama Media is part of this learning collaborative. From those sessions, David Holwerk, a longtime journalist and Kettering senior scholar, extracted the following suggestions about what journalists might listen for as citizens discuss prison overcrowding, the label most commonly used by experts and professionals to discuss that complex problem. Everyday people might describe it differently.

- Listen for people renaming a problem in terms of things that are important to them, rather than in the language of experts and public policy. For example: "The problem isn't prison overcrowding. The problem is that we have too many people in prison. My nephew is serving 10 years for selling two joints. He should never have been in prison in the first place."

- Listen for people talking about things that they can do to help solve the problem. For example: "Too many of these guys come out of prison with no skills and no support, so they go right back in. That's something we could all help on."

- Listen for people talking about resources they can bring to bear on a problem. For example: "The women's group at my church could organize a mentoring program for women getting out of prison."

In fact, when Alabama Media partnered with the David Mathews Center for Civic Life in 2014 to host community forums about overcrowded prisons as part of its coverage, journalists heard many comments similar to these.

Modeling Deliberation and Creating Spaces for It

More and more news organizations are hosting community forums to uncover shared concerns and help citizens figure out how to solve them. Some of the sessions are strictly informational and allow for limited discussion or debate. But others are truly deliberative.

Deliberative forums are designed to help citizens solve a public problem using a framework with three or four options for action. The options, or key questions, push people to consider a range of possible solutions rather than a polarizing one or two. They are designed to encourage a conversation about the tradeoffs inherent in each possible solution and in the process help people discover the values they hold most dear. This type of structured deliberation for tackling hard problems can work in virtual and physical spaces.

When Alabama Media wanted to engage with the public to find solutions to the urgent prison overcrowding problems it was investigating, it turned to the Mathews Center. Working more closely with the public already was becoming part of the newsroom culture. Journalists quickly discovered that what government officials would not tell them, the public could. Reporters asked members of the public to help them find out what was going on inside the prison walls. Personal stories, useful information, and thoughtful questions flooded in.

At the deliberative forums they hosted around the state, journalists found that even deeper wisdom resided in the public. To bring it to the surface, they relied on a deliberative framework the Mathews Center designed for forums they facilitated.

Helping Nashville Solve a Housing Crisis

As a result of pro-growth policies, Nashville has become known as an "it" city. But prosperity isn't widely shared.

In a 12-part series entitled "The Cost of Growth and Change," the *Nashville Tennessean* explored the downsides for residents who couldn't find affordable housing or support their families with typically low-wage tourism jobs. As related problems with the transportation and school systems surfaced, the news outlet began to ask if Nashville was in a "new urban crisis."

To tackle these complex, interdependent and persistent public problems, the staff wanted to foster a two-way conversation with members of the public and involve citizens in both reporting on the challenges and solving them.

David Plazas, opinion engagement editor, said the journalists' mission was three-part: to hold a mirror to Nashville; to give voice to the voiceless; and to provide solutions in addition to identifying problems.

"People kept trying to figure out who to blame. We explained here's how we got here and here are some ways out," Plazas said.

Plazas believes the news organization has a role to play in creating deliberative spaces in the community and online. In addition to creating spaces, Plazas said journalists need to seek out and join those that already exist.

Working closely with the Nashville Public Library and interested citizens, the *Tennessean* sponsored a forum on affordable housing and launched a book club to ask if Nashville, growing in prosperity and inequality, was the type of "New Urban Crisis" author Richard Florida had written about. The book club did more than spark talk. Members came up with ideas that the newspaper shared with the mayor's office and the public. Throughout the year-long project, citizens joined the discussion, and the newspaper published 40 op-eds on different aspects of the affordable housing crisis. The newspaper gathered a diverse group of citizen activists to join the mayor for a discussion that appeared in a documentary it produced as the series concluded.

These efforts motivated more than 50 organizations to create a new coalition called "Welcome Home!" to advocate for concrete solutions on affordable housing.

Plazas believes that traditional ideas about editorials and editorial boards are passé. "We have to be out and in the community. Because we are opinion editors, we can be activators," he said. "It's not about saying here's what we think. Instead it's here's what we know and help to guide you."

The public seemed to reward this more relational form of journalism. Readership — both in print and online — grew.

"We have a responsibility to help spread the word about how democracy works and how to participate," Plazas said. "It's a different type of journalism, but I think it's journalism still."

The deliberative framework offered three approaches for discussions on state prisons: increase capacity and improve basic conditions; address root causes through education, support and rehabilitation; and implement alternative approaches to incarceration (AL.com, 2014). These three approaches were published in print and online. Citizens were asked to rank the options they preferred, and hundreds did. Eight action-oriented themes emerged, and citizens also volunteered ways they could help (AL.com, 2015).

The groundbreaking work that combined tough-minded reporting with relational journalism approaches garnered national awards. And the public's focus on it "helped to set the table for 2015 legislative actions that were designed to reduce overcrowding in prisons," said K.A. Turner, a senior editor who helped lead the effort (Turner, personal communication, March 30, 2020).

Alabama Media and the Mathews Center were teaming up again in 2020 to look at disparities in K–12 educational achievement. They worked with citizens to identify and name the problems in terms that every community member can relate to. They created opportunities for citizens to deliberate about potential solutions that can engage the entire community.

Cristin F. Brawner, executive director of the Mathews Center, appreciates the partnership in which each organization learns from the other. Deliberation brings a solutions orientation to journalism, she said, because it "focuses on opportunities for addressing deep-rooted challenges while providing hope that options do exist for moving forward" (Brawner, personal communication, March 30, 2020).

Uncovering Hidden Community Discourse

Formal deliberative structures and events can help communities tackle tough problems and show people how to walk the talk. Informal reckoning is going on all around us.

If journalists listen carefully and attune their ears to deliberative talk, they'll find people deliberating at their kids' soccer games, at the bus stop, in coffee shops and other informal gathering spots. In other words, citizens already are engaged with public problems in their communities. Journalists need to listen in on those conversations and train their ears to hear citizens exchange views, learn from each other and suggest actions that most everyone finds acceptable, if not perfect.

In his book *For Communities to Work*, David Mathews explores how a public forms within a geographic community. He offers three gateway questions (Mathews, 2002, p. 19) that citizens, drawing on their own experiences, ask as they become aware of a problem.

- Is this a problem that affects me?
- Can I do anything?
- Who will join me?

Reporters are accustomed to "gathering string," that is, collecting information and knowledge to be used in future reports. But what if they gathered string about the public from members of the public by asking some different questions? The answers to the following questions, which build on Mathews' gateway questions for citizens, could illuminate how the community works.

- Who else have you talked with about your concerns about the neighborhood and its future?
- What did they say?
- When did you talk to them?

jesikah maria ross, senior community engagement strategist at Capitol Public Radio in Sacramento, has written a helpful guide to practicing what she calls participatory journalism, which is closely aligned with this book's mindset. Ross' guiding principles emphasize inclusion, cocreation, face-to-face events, public service and developing civic infrastructure.

To ross, participatory journalism means that you select and develop stories in conversation with the communities most affected; design a reporting process that generates understanding, connection and trust; and strengthen existing networks and forge new alliances that build community resilience beyond reporting.

With Internews and the Listening Post Collective in 2020, ross released a playbook that outlines her five-step process for journalists and community members working together (Ross, 2020). The playbook is built around CapRadio's documentary series about a south Sacramento neighborhood viewed from the outside as troubled and crime-ridden but, the series found, on the inside is a diverse and resilient community with unique assets. The playbook blends the tools of community organizing and journalism. While all the steps found at https://internews.org/sites/default/files/2020-07/JMR_playbook_07-10-20_V3.pdf are worth visiting, we call attention here to the third step — bringing people together. After holding listening sessions throughout the community, ross says, it's important to "use your momentum to bring people together" and share what the journalists are learning. In one neighborhood, the journalists partnered with an elementary school to host a community fair that included a series of brainstorming activities and opportunities for journalists and community members to get to know each other in a festive and fun setting. To share back with the community, the station set up a mobile story booth and offered community media workshops.

- Where did these conversations occur?
- Why did you bring it up with that particular person or group? And why in that location?

Holwerk suggests that adding these questions to the standard practice of who, what, when and where would certainly make the immediate story richer, "but its main value would be cumulative."

Journalists who ask these questions could develop a deeper understanding of the community and the networks of relationships that comprise its essential, invisible architecture. "If they made a routine of asking these questions at the end of *every* interview, over time they would begin to hear the hidden discourse of residents as they make choices about shared public problems — which is to say, how they do the work of citizens in a democracy" (Holwerk, personal correspondence, April 20, 2020).

Narratives That Build Community

Communities that have actively engaged residents do better. It's that simple.

And journalists, by the stories they tell, help shape the community's perception of itself and its residents. These perceptions matter because they influence how people feel about their individual and collective ability to solve problems.

BOX 8.4 **Through a Drought, Together**

In 2014, Wichita Falls, Texas, was three years into such a bad drought that city officials feared they would run out of water in two years. The reservoir that supplied water to the town's 104,000 residents was down to 28 percent of capacity.

Deanna Watson, editor of *The Times Record News*, recognized immediately that this urgent problem required a public response. She instinctively knew that her news organization would need to respond and lead differently. The newspaper threw all its resources at the problem and engaged the entire community to find and implement solutions.

The Times Record News published more than 230 stories in print and online as part of its yearlong coverage entitled "Lifeline," a reminder that the threat could destroy the town.

The newspaper reported on official actions, investigated potential wrongdoing and explained the complex challenges in understandable terms. But it didn't stop with these traditional journalistic approaches. "When you live in a community, you're part of it. We all felt the desperation," Watson said as she explained why the newspaper had to do more to show everybody in town how they are involved.

To help residents see what they could do, the newspaper asked readers for their ideas about how to conserve water. They published an idea a day on the front page. A favorite suggestion was to conserve water by showering with a friend!

The newspaper promoted saving water, and it created community consensus around building a treatment plan that could take sewer water and make it drinkable.

Eventually it rained, but Wichita Falls will never be the same again, say city officials who note that water consumption was down significantly. Looking back, Watson sees that as evidence of "people taking a hold of their own situation."

Russell Schreiber, public works director, credits a resilient citizenry for surviving the drought and helping to solve the water crisis. And he praised the newspaper for its essential role.

"The biggest reason [is that the newspaper] did a great job expressing what a dire situation we were in," he said in 2017. "The public responded in a tremendous fashion," he said, adding "It's because of them that we got through the drought."

With the immediate crisis behind them, Watson and her team "transitioned to a more hopeful narrative" with a project they called "Imagine Wichita Falls."

In addition to conveying information, news stories transmit culture and values. They reflect the world back to its residents, subtly suggesting who is in and who is out; who matters and who doesn't. This is why inclusion matters so much. To engage in the community, residents must feel that they belong to it, can care for it and share in its future success.

In the opening chapter, we talked about the importance of social capital and the relational networks that undergird it. Communities look different to journalists when understood as networks of relationships rather than as institutions bound by a confusing mix of geographic boundaries. Earlier we suggested a way to report on these noninstitutional community structures known as relational networks.

News is in the identity business. People want to be heard, acknowledged, understood and have their actions witnessed. News stories do all of these things. They help us decide if we belong or not. They help us choose our communities.

The rise of narrowcasting and social media outlets amplifies this point. People are willing to pay for news, a Michigan State University study found, but not to be informed or entertained. People paid for news to reinforce their social identity in groups to which they belong (Chen & Thorson, 2019).

Can community news outlets counter this trend by finding ways to foster a sense of belonging to a geographic community?

Holmes has thought a lot about the importance of connecting people and the news organization's unique opportunity to weave together the community's abundant networks. "Whitman, Alabama," a stunningly beautiful and moving video series in which Alabamians read verses of Walt Whitman's "Song of Myself," reminds us that our differences are our strength and that together we make a whole.

In these times of alienation, loneliness and polarization, journalists, through the stories they tell, can encourage the sense of belonging that people long for. "To me it is the same problem — alienation and lack of connection," Holmes said. "That is the essential problem of both journalism and democracy, it is feeling part of the whole."

BOX 8.5 City Bureau's Community Engagement Guidelines

City Bureau in Chicago sparked lively conversations among journalists interested in facilitating the democratic work of citizens when it published its community engagement guidelines. The guidelines that follow are consistent with the principles outlined in this book and among the most sophisticated we have seen.

At City Bureau we define community engagement as any interaction with the people we not only serve but work with. To ensure our engagement approach both reckons with traditional journalism's violent past and creates a future where journalism belongs to everyone, we've developed the following guidelines:

1   We believe community engagement is a pillar of journalism — it's not a tool, single job, one-off project or a means to saving traditional news institutions.

2   We believe authentic community engagement takes time, intentionality and space to evolve. We resist rushing this process and will not operate on timelines that don't accommodate our community.

3   We cultivate relationships, not transactions. The status quo is extractive reporting and has led to distrust between the public and journalists, dehumanizing the interaction between community and media. We believe journalism should cultivate a network of relationships that generates accountability and shares resources.

4   We take an asset-oriented approach to our work. We honor and acknowledge that there are existing communities with resources that we can learn from and skills that journalists should share in return. This practice helps to build civic wealth and makes local information systems more resilient.

5   We produce work that is nondominant (democratic in its nature) and nonbinary (resisting a single truth or narrative). To combat journalism's history of paternalism and white supremacy, often dressed as objectivity, we must unlearn the notion of a singular truth.

6   We don't empower communities, we create space for interconnected learning and the expression of communal power.

They can be found at www.citybureau.org/community-engagement-guidelines.

BOX 8.6 Don't Go It Alone

Journalists aren't likely to become experts in facilitating community conversations, dialogues or deliberations. There are plenty of places to look for help both on and off campus.

Here are just a few of them and you'll find more as you look closer to home.

- Sustained Dialogue Institute https://sustained-dialogue.org/
- National Coalition for Dialogue & Deliberation (NCDD) https://ncdd.org/
- Essential Partners https://whatisessential.org/
- National Issues Forums https://www.nifi.org/
- Everyday Democracy https://www.everyday-democracy.org/
- Living Room Conversations https://livingroom-conversations.org/
- Campus Compact https://compact.org/

As you look around for partners to lead community conversations, consider checking with the state humanities council or centers for public life like the David Mathews Center for Civic Life featured in the AL.com case study (https://mathewscenter.org/programs/).

Some universities have centers, institutes or programs dedicated to deliberation and community conversations. Examples are: Center for Public Deliberation at Colorado State University (https://cpd.colostate.edu/); the Westmont (College) Center for Dialogue & Deliberation (https://www.westmont.edu/westmont-initiative-public-dialogue-and-deliberation/resources-wipdd); the University of Chicago's Parrhesia Program for Public Discourse (https://college.uchicago.edu/academics/parrhesia-program-pub-lic-discourse); the University of Iowa's Program for Public Life (https://ippl.sites.uiowa.edu/); Kansas State University's Institute for Civic Discourse and Democracy (https://www.k-state.edu/icdd); and Franklin Pierce University's New England Center for Civic Life (https://www.franklinpierce.edu/institutes/neccl/).

Faculty members who work in this area can be found in a wide variety of departments including communications, political science, psychology, history, social work and agriculture extension.

A Community of Actively Engaged Women

Few legacy news organizations have expanded the definition of journalism and its practices as aggressively as Alabama Media, the publisher of not only AL.com but also the state's three largest papers, and part of the privately owned Advance Publications group. It has eagerly embraced and worked with other experimenters, many of whom populate this textbook.

Using all that it had learned about how to create community spaces for the type of public dialogue and deliberation needed to solve tough, complex problems, AL.com was fully prepared to quickly launch Reckon Women when the moment arrived in May of 2019.

It began as "the women's project," a collection of essays from women across the state who responded overwhelmingly in 36 hours to Alabama Media's invitation to describe what it is like to be a woman in Alabama. "The powerful, raw collection represented women who were conservative, liberal, black, white, young old, straight and lesbian," explained Scott, who published the essays on the front page and main sections of Alabama Media's newspapers and shared it across its digital platforms, choosing to turn off comments "so the women could be heard, not attacked."

AL.com next created Reckon Women as a Facebook group, which 1,000 women joined immediately to identify and discuss the issues Alabama needed to address to help women thrive. Spaceship Media was asked to guide the conversations, as it had done with previous exchanges about hotly contested issues about health care and guns. Moderators encouraged people to share their personal experiences "to re-humanize the 'other,' a skill that's been left behind as we migrate into our social communities," explained Rebecca Walker Benjamin, senior managing producer who leads the effort.

FIGURE 8.3 Kelly Scott, editor and vice president of content at AL.com, leads the morning news meeting.

(Photo by Paul Voakes.)

Next came a Reckon Women e-newsletter, an investigative reporting project on motherhood informed by the growing Reckon Women community and the launch of "A Seat at the Table," a series of two-hour events held across the state. At each event, journalists share an overview of recent news that affects women, and a panel explores the issues. A community listening session in which attendees are asked if the issues that matter most to them have been identified follows the informational sessions, and the event concludes with a tutorial on the legislative process that emphasizes why it's important to have your voice heard.

"The most interesting moment at each event was to see when the lightbulb turned on for participants about what this movement can become and how they might see themselves involved with it," Scott said.

Alabama Media clearly sees that supporting citizenship and connecting deeply with community members are central to its mission, even if traditionalists raise alarms.

Benjamin, who has been innovating at Alabama Media for years, thinks journalists must know how to adapt to ever-changing circumstances. "Journalism has changed for as long as it has existed," she said. "Maybe supporting dialogue in this time is journalism."

EXERCISES

1. Listen to a personal story told by a classmate. Ask questions; take notes.

   - When the classmate has finished, organize what you've heard into a compelling, narrative version — and read it back, the following week, to the person you've listened to. Then listen to his/her appraisal of how you did.

   - Repeat the previous exercise, but with a member of the community beyond campus — someone you know very little or not at all.

2. Have the class facilitate a meeting about a particularly difficult issue of concern to college students. The instructor will assign role-playing "points of view," including radically oppositional roles, for most members of the class. Assign two students to take turns facilitating a 40-minute discussion. Take turns rotating in and out of the facilitator role.

   After the discussion, have each student write a report in which they describe the topic and summarize the dialogue .

   - Describe whether people were listening carefully to understand the other person's view and asking questions of those on the other side.

   - Describe any turning points in the conversation. Did anyone make a pivot in their view as a result?

3. Each student identifies a "listening post" on campus to learn of new issues — issues that have not been prominently covered in the news.

   - How is each issue being framed by community members? How else could it be framed?

   - Each student then draws up a list of potential stories, based on what s/he has heard at his/her listening post.

4. Organize a group of students from outside your class to meet and talk about one of the issues the class members' listening has identified — an issue the class believes has potential for a community-engendered solution.

   - Agree upon which three class members will make a presentation about citizenship, deliberation and role of journalism in helping communities reach solutions. Apply the concepts and processes described in this chapter to the issue at hand.

   - At the meeting, moderate and facilitate. By the end of the meeting, you will have led the group to these steps:

     - Agreement on what would be the outcome, in terms of public policy, that would ideally result from the group's public deliberation

- Agreement on the process that will best guide the group to that result

- Agreement on a list of "information needs" that a team of journalists might address

- Agreement in identifying the various points of view that have shaped debate or disagreement on the issue

- Suggestions as to whether there is yet any "common ground for the common good" apparent from the discussion

CREDIT

Fig. 8.2: Copyright © 2019 by Ivy Marie Clarke. Reprinted with permission.

CHAPTER 9

Updating Time-Honored Traditions

At most news organizations, a voter guide for upcoming elections is not unusual. But at radio station KPCC in Pasadena, California, the voter guide walks and talks — and answers listeners' questions. Lots of them.

Mary Plummer is the founder of the Human Voter Guide at KPCC, which provides a variety of election-related tips for Southern California citizens. But because of the personal touch she has brought to the project, she also earned the nickname "Human Voter Guide."

Instead of relying on seasoned political reporters to provide summaries of the ballot-measure arguments and candidates' positions and qualifications, the station invites citizens' questions about an upcoming election. Voters are curious about pros and cons and candidates, of course, but the station fields even more questions about the mechanics of voting. When the voter guide was launched during the 2016 political campaigns, it received 47 questions from voters. During the Fall 2018 election campaigns, that number rose to 430 questions. Plummer has fielded questions about how to change party preference before a primary; how much postage is needed for a mail-in ballot; whether people can vote if they're homeless; even whether your ballot is valid if your toddler has scribbled all over it (answer: yes, as long as it can still be read).

The guide serves as an example of KPCC's innovative approach to journalism — and of the next of our principles of relational journalism. Even in times that demand radical new approaches to reporting and presenting

FIGURE 9.1 Mary Plummer is the founding editor of KPCC's Human Voter Guide.

(Photo by Paul Voakes.)

the news, some traditions of American journalism deserve to be kept. In this chapter, we'll briefly explore the most important of the "tried-and-true" principles and practices that have made journalism such a vital component of American democracy. But as KPCC and other exemplars will demonstrate, these traditional notions have been refreshed in ways that support citizens and democratic practice in the 21st century.

As one example, journalism (even when it focuses on new ways to engage citizens) must still commit to the relentless pursuit of the truth. KPCC, a nonprofit, NPR-affiliated station, makes extraordinary efforts to build relationships with listeners and to connect listeners with other residents in their own communities. Its staff works hard to discern the informational needs of those communities, and then to address those in compelling new ways. Yet Ashley Alvarado, the station's director of community engagement, insists upon the discipline of information-gathering that has characterized journalism for more than 100 years. The answer to each one of the questions submitted to the Human Voter Guide, for example, is meticulously researched. The station wants listeners' input on what questions to ask the candidates during interviews, but the suggestions are carefully vetted by experienced journalists. Citizens' informational needs can be met without sacrificing sound news judgment, Alvarado says. "We're not breaking away from important standards of journalism," she says, "we're just making standard journalism more inclusive."

The station engages in many of the practices of relational journalism we explored in the previous three chapters. It hosts "Feeding the Conversation," community meetings in which editors, producers and reporters lead discussions of topical issues with residents. It's a little different, Alvarado explains, as it purposely strengthens the station's relationship with Southern California communities, but it's also an old-fashioned effort to gather ideas for stories that will resonate with listeners and to build a roster of sources who have authentic experiences for those new stories.

Plummer, who previously worked for ABC News in London and Los Angeles, also insists that accurate information is paramount.

"Accurate information, yes," she adds. "But information for whom? That's what's different here. We let our listeners and readers help shape the coverage, because that's our goal: Meeting people where they're at."

We could probably identify dozens of tried-and-true traditions of journalism, but in this chapter we'll focus on the six journalistic traditions of the 20th century that we deem most important and most worthy to be continued:

- Seek the truth, with objectivity and verification
- Be fair, especially by overcoming bias
- Be accountable
- Be independent
- Monitor society's most powerful institutions, especially for abuse of power
- Be consistent in determining newsworthiness

With each of these traditional principles, roles or practices, we'll explore not only their enduring value but also how they are being "refreshed" — modified for a contemporary mode of journalism that also values the work of citizens.

They need refreshing. With the increasing role of social media in recent years, for example, misinformation spreads at dizzying speeds, and it travels faster than factually correct information does. This is why the pursuit of truth now must include strategies of verification and fact-checking, and why citizens must be recruited for some important corrective procedures. We have all learned about the values that underlie editors' decisions on whether a story is newsworthy, but the hierarchy of those values has distorted journalism in unhelpful ways in recent decades. We need to re-examine those values in light of journalism's current need to build community by helping citizens solve shared problems. And a few of the principles listed above, such as accountability, have enjoyed little more than lip service. It's time to explore how useful they could become in restoring citizens' trust in media, simply by developing new ways to practice those old ideas.

Truth and Truthfulness

In their book *The Elements of Journalism*, Bill Kovach and Tom Rosenstiel describe the element of truth as journalism's "first and most confusing principle" (Kovach & Rosenstiel, 2014, p. 47). Philosophers have debated the meaning, and even the existence, of truth — for centuries. We're not about to enter that debate in these few pages; however, there's no denying that the relentless pursuit of truth is one of journalism's distinguishing characteristics. So we'll take Kovach's and Rosenstiel's advice and focus on a practical approach to truth, beginning with the concept of truthfulness. This is a state of mind by which the seeker of truth acknowledges that a universal, ultimate truth may be impossible in a world of highly subjective human beings, so it's the honest pursuit — not the result — that matters. The truthful journalist is one who attempts to build representations of the world one fact at a time. Gradually the accumulation of agreed-upon, verifiable (accurate) facts leads to the creation of context, and with context the journalist can begin to find and share the meaning of events and trends. Each day's account, Kovach and Rosenstiel assert, is "valid for now, subject to further investigation" (p. 58). Note how different already this humble attitude is from the arrogance of omniscience that Walter Lippmann, 100 years ago, would have journalists adopt.

And where does "objectivity" fit in? We think of objectivity as a process of honest inquiry, not unlike the scientific method employed by researchers. Consider each accurate, verified fact the piece of a vast jigsaw puzzle that, if completed, would represent truth. Every news article or package that discloses new, factually verified information contributes yet another piece to that jigsaw puzzle. Like scientists, journalists must honestly consider whether new evidence supports a hypothesis — and if not, correct the hypothesis. Like scientists, journalists must disclose their methods of information-gathering and must do so in a way that invites others to embark on the same inquiry. Consider how different this is from 20th-century objectivity, where journalists took the cognitive shortcut of finding two sides to a controversy and then devoting equal space or airtime to both sides. This enabled false equivalence whereby, for example, equal space would sometimes be given to activists denying climate change or denying that the Holocaust ever occurred. Yet journalists would take no responsibility for spreading such ideas because, they thought, they were being objective.

The internet age has made the pursuit of truth, already elusive, incredibly more difficult. As Kovach and Rosenstiel observed, this is one of the great ironies of the 21st century: Knowledge becomes more difficult to find because the seeker must sift through so much more raw information and misinformation than ever before, simply in order to find meaning. For journalists in particular, we see added challenges. In a high-speed digital environment, there is increased pressure to post a story first, even knowing it's incomplete and it quite possibly contains factual errors. And because of the massive layoffs in journalism, editorial oversight — questioning of reporters' assumptions and assertions, or fact-checking in the newsroom — is diminished, or gone.

So this pursuit of truth is difficult, but not impossible. Media ethicist Stephen A.J. Ward has proposed a "pragmatic objectivity," whereby journalists should honestly strive for accuracy in every detail, honestly strive to be comprehensive and thorough with each story and test alternative explanations as a scientist would (Ward, 2009).

And it all starts with day-to-day accuracy — getting the facts straight. Only then can the journalist, and ultimately the citizen, make sense of what's happening at a deeper level. Former editor and professor Gene Foreman (2016, pp. 195–196) offers a checklist for reporters and editors:

- Ask your sources and yourself, often: "How do you know that? Where did you get that?"

- When reporting with documents, especially government documents, read all the way to the end before making conclusions about their conclusions.

- Ensure that every controversial statement is attributed, and attributed accurately.

- Update and correct information throughout the life of the story, especially after it was first posted.

- When appropriate, provide your audience with links to your source material.

- Ensure that the headline, teaser, or promo to the story accurately reflects the intended meaning of the story.

And as a "refresh" for the internet age, Foreman also recommends that journalists consider any social-media posting of a factual claim to be "not" a fact, but rather a news tip to be checked out. We would add that social media provides a marvelous fact-gathering resource known as crowdsourcing, whereby a virtual community helps with a research task or verification. Again, because the journalist must ultimately vouch for the accuracy of his or her piece, the crowd's work as well should be painstakingly verified.

Speaking of verification, this element of truth-seeking has risen to a level of extreme importance in recent years — simply because social media have enabled avalanches of misinformation (inaccuracies in general) and disinformation (deliberate inaccuracies). The good news is that resources have developed to help reporters and citizens detect misinformation on the internet and, where necessary, correct rumors and falsehoods.

Craig Silverman, media editor at BuzzFeed News and a leading expert in online fact-checking, and Rina Tsubaki, a former manager at the European Journalism Centre in The Netherlands, have identified seven categories of "online fakes" that both journalists and citizens should recognize (Silverman & Tsubaki, 2019):

- *Actual photos, but from unrelated events.* Gullible viewers are led to believe they illustrate a current story. Remedy? Run a reverse image search (available from a number of providers) to see if there's an earlier version — and where and when it was created.

- *Video or photo that's staged* — then presented as an actual news event. Remedy? Again, verify the origin of the image file.

- *Manipulated images.* Technology has made it increasingly easy to alter elements with a photo, or to slow down video speed, for example, to make the subject seem impaired. Remedy? Check out the origin of the image file.

- *Fake social media accounts.* People of ill will can easily create an account using the name of a celebrity or politician and then post false information. Remedy? Facebook and Twitter display a "blue tick" on every profile page that they've verified as authentic. No blue tick visible? Ask the sender to send you verifying information.

- *Manual retweets.* If the retweet was not automatically sent but instead done manually, it's possible the receiver copied and pasted a tweet into their own message field, enabling them to alter the content of the original. Remedy? If you see an "RT" at the top of the message you received, it has been manually retweeted. Try to find the original tweet.

- *Fake social-media posts.* A number of readily available apps can create posts that look as if they've been sent from legitimate accounts. Remedy? Go to that account independently to see if the same suspicious post can be found there. In general, just be suspicious of social-media content, especially if it seems provocative or controversial.

- *Fake websites.* It has become fairly easy to copy the look and structure of a legitimate website and set it up with a different web address. Remedy: Search on different search engines to find the site's URL. If different URLs turn up, the situation is suspicious. Use the free program WhoIs to look up the domain owner and when the domain was first registered.

The Poynter Institute, a leading resource for journalistic training, has provided a wealth of materials to help journalists cope with manipulations and fakes. One of them is the booklet created by Aos Fatos, the respected fact-checking platform in Brazil (International Fact-Checking Network, 2019). It offers several tips for fact-checking an article or other content that seems suspicious:

- For any news report that seems suspicious, check the source. Look for the same set of facts on the websites of trusted news organizations. Just be aware of the possibility of fake websites made to look like those of actual news organizations, as Silverman and Tsubaki (above) advised.

- Read the suspicious report carefully. Are they using specific sources, or vague references that can't easily be checked up on? If the report offers source links, click to see if their sources seem legitimate. How recent is the post? You could be reading a legitimate but out-of-date report. Does its language use adjectives frequently, or inflammatory language? These are red flags that professional journalists did not write the piece.

- Check out the author of the piece. What else have they written? Can you find a bio on this person, and at what site? Can you contact this person directly? If you feel you need to contact them, do so. The service accountanalysis.app helps evaluate Twitter accounts quickly and reliably.

- Google it! In addition to using relevant search terms to verify information, images can be checked on Google. Drag any suspicious image or video to the Google search box to see if Google knows its origin and other facts.

- Look carefully at any statistics being used. If a data set can be reached, check to see whether the main findings in the data match the findings described in the text. Are key numbers being misinterpreted, or omitted?

- Check your own bias. We tend to believe social-media content that reaffirms our own biases, ideological or otherwise. Trolls and manipulators are clever at posing as someone who seems to share the same opinions as their targets.

- Still confused? Get help from the professional fact-checkers at FactCheck (factcheck.org) or PolitiFact (politifact.com).

If the journalist does find a falsehood or manipulation of some kind, does that mean he or she must expose the fake and correct the misinformation? Journalist Susan Benkelman (2019) offers sound advice in a guide written for the American Press Institute. There is a danger, she warns, in amplifying the falsehood and thereby making a damaging situation worse. In general, she advises: If the falsehood has been broadly disseminated already, if the general public would benefit greatly from knowing the claim is in error, if the source of the falsehood is in itself newsworthy and if the falsehood already seems to be having a negative impact, then it's time to expose and correct the fake. Even then, she writes, some readers may remember only the falsehood and not the journalist's careful unmasking of it. She recommends a "truth sandwich," by which the journalist surrounds the false statement — before and after — with the statements of correction and keeps the repeating of the falsehood to a bare minimum — even if this means "burying the lead" by not beginning the article with the false statement.

When Kelly Jones first went to work for Storyful in 2016, she couldn't help but notice a sign on the office wall: "Truth in Context." She finds she's just as committed to that tenet than ever.

Storyful is a for-profit company that adapts fast-changing technologies in the service of one of journalism's oldest traditions: the pursuit — and defense — of the truth. It uses proprietary technology to quickly verify, or debunk, possibly newsworthy content from a variety of social-media sources, in order to protect the credibility of its media clients. Storyful also trains journalist clients (as Jones sometimes does) in how to conduct their own verification of incoming content.

The company was founded in 2010 by two Irish journalists who wanted to help news clients curate information about breaking stories that was arriving on social media. With the explosion of misinformation, a huge part of their business has become ver-

ification. Its success was so immediate that in 2013 Storyful was acquired by News Corp for $25 million (Owen, 2019), and by 2020 the company employed 55 journalists.

The work is unlike any other journalism she has done, Jones said, in part because her team's greatest successes will never be publicly appreciated. That's because success involves the stifling of an erroneous story that would have gone viral in seriously harmful ways if Storyful had not discovered the fakery and alerted its news-organization clients. It's tough as well, she said, keeping up with the technologies of disinformation, which in recent years have become prolific.

But the battle on behalf of "truth in context" is still worth the struggle, she told us. The work of verification, she hopes, will re-establish a culture that values evidence and reliable fact, and a culture that values transparency in the gathering and sharing of information.

Fairness (and Overcoming Bias)

A lack of bias has long been a hallmark of excellent journalism — and a primary component of what is considered journalistic fairness. Multiple reporting and media ethics texts have ample advice to young reporters trying to establish habits of fairness:

- Show empathy and compassion for your subjects, especially for children, victims of crimes and anyone obviously inexperienced in dealing with the news media.

- If the content of a story seems to criticize someone, seek out the target and get their response.

- Make sure any quotes or soundbites used in the story are given appropriate context (Foreman, 2016).

- Make sure the "frame," or "angle," with which you began reporting the story is continually subjected to open-minded revision, and make sure the frame was not based on pre-existing stereotypes or assumptions about a type of people.

- In general, apply the Golden Rule: Be sure you would feel comfortable being treated the same way you are treating your subjects for the story.

But most texts have not addressed the complex, persistent barrier to fairness: the challenge of overcoming biases that we've all grown up with. So here's the "refresh" for this principle: Over the last few decades, a good deal of research in human cognition has created new knowledge about how humans form biases and how they shed their biases. Media educator Sue Ellen Christian has applied many of these findings to the work of journalists and has developed a process she calls "debiasing" (Christian, 2012). It's a way to provide news and information "as free from preconception and assumption as possible" (p. 182). Research shows that biases are overcome most easily when the person is honestly motivated to be free of bias. This plays well into the journalist's situation. Christian also sees several "external" prompts for debiasing even if the journalist is not "internally" passionate about freedom from bias. For starters, occupational norms demand that journalists be neutral in their assessments of others. Most newsroom cultures champion the challenging of stereotypes. Vocal pressure from just one voice, one colleague who is passionate about freedom from bias, can rein in others' attitudes. And thoughts of your organization's reputation, not to mention your own reputation, can also be a motivator.

How does debiasing begin? Christian recommends five "cognitive strategies":

- Consider the opposite. Every story starts with a frame, or narrative. What if the opposite were to be closer to the truth? Identify the conventional wisdom on your topic and deliberately consider the opposite. If more journalists did this while covering the bombing case during the 1996 Olympics in Atlanta, Richard Jewell probably would not have been falsely accused in the news media.

- Consider alternative assumptions. Like the first guideline, ask what the alternative explanations could be, no matter how ludicrous. Christian recommends a two-minute brainstorm, in which a reporter jots down every conceivable possibility or explanation for the situation being covered.

- Slow down. Biases are shortcuts in the thought process, and cognitive shortcuts are extremely tempting to those on tight deadlines.

- Get better at data analysis. Statistical analysis is a valuable form of critical thinking, and understanding the numbers is a great fact-based way to challenge early assumptions.

- Walk in the shoes of your subject. Take the perspective of your subject and ask what your priorities would be if it were you being reported about. Be careful, Christian warns, not to create new bias by swinging all the way to an entirely sympathetic perspective.

Independence: Freedom from Conflicts of Interest

The strategies above can be enormously helpful, but we're all human. To assume that debiasing strategies have removed all bias from any given journalist would be folly. One of the sources of bias, and indeed one of the greatest threats to a journalist's pursuit of truth, is a loyalty to someone other than citizens (or other than truth in the abstract). Since the beginnings of journalism itself, conflicting loyalties have threatened the craft's integrity. Consider the variety of forces that can undermine independence: Journalists can be unduly influenced by their own political or ideological predilections; by deep, heartfelt support for a social or political organization; by informal "consulting" a reporter may do for a politician "off the record"; by private financial relationships that may influence or be affected by the story (and yes, that includes receiving valuable gifts or free tickets from the companies being covered); or by such aspects of personal background as race, social class, religion or any of the other "faultlines" Robert Maynard outlined (see Chapter 6). The remedies of the past five decades are still sound: (1) Be transparent and disclose any such biases or conflicting loyalties, at least to your editors and if necessary to your news audiences, and (2) ask for reassignment so that the outside loyalties will not directly influence your journalistic work. An ethical journalist can't really expect to cover people they are close to or beholden to.

Those rules, however, don't address the more complex challenge to independence: Journalists can't slough off their own personal backgrounds, the stories of who they are. In many cases, personal background enriches their journalistic work in profound ways. So it's not as simple as saying, "I won't cover immigration or border issues because of my own Latino heritage; that way I'll stay independent." The extent to which a true conflict of interest exists could be debated endlessly. Kovach and Rosenstiel (2014) urge a more pragmatic approach: Stick to what's important about good journalism (starting with the principles and practices outlined in this chapter), and it will be obvious that the journalist's loyalty remains with citizens and their need for impartial, accurate information. They recommend an attitude of "I'm an excellent journalist who also happens to be (Latino, gay, disabled, or any other 'faultline')."

"When that happens," Kovach and Rosenstiel write, "racial, ethnic, religious, class and ideological background 'inform' that journalist's work but do not 'dictate' it" (2014, p. 163) (emphasis added).

The "refresh" we need to address for this principle is this book's admitted fervor for helping citizens. As we saw in Chapter 2, public journalism (this book's conceptual grandparents) took a great deal of criticism for its supposed loss of objectivity. Conservative editors feared the movement would soon have reporters becoming activists — supporting one community outcome over others — and would lose credibility. We believe that fear misunderstood — and still misunderstands — the goals of citizen-centered journalism. If the journalist is attempting to convene as well as inform, so that citizens together can make sense of new information and deliberate over possible solutions, that is still independent journalism. The journalist should be, as Kovach and Rosenstiel argue, "a connector, a translator, a contextualizer and interpreter — but not a combatant or activist" (p. 68). The ultimate goals of American journalism are to produce an informed electorate, and, in the process, to help create and sustain community. Relational journalism does that more deliberately than in the past.

Monitor the Powerful; Expose Their Abuses

The role "watchdog" finds its justification, as we saw in Chapter 4, in First Amendment theory. Citizens in a modern, complex democracy cannot all monitor the conduct of government themselves, but that conduct must nonetheless be monitored — to ensure that those in power are upholding their constitutional and legal duties. The news media — the so-called Fourth Estate of government — perform that task on behalf of the citizens. The exposés of the early 1900s led to laws enacting social and economic reform, and investigative reporting has been a staple of American journalism ever since. This form of journalism lost some of its luster in the late 20th century, when so much of its focus turned to exposing personal wrongdoing — politicians' and celebrities' extramarital affairs, for example — and away from systemic injustices whose remedies would impact large numbers of citizens.

Our "refresh" for this tradition has to do with the role of citizens in public communication, which has grown significantly in the 21st century. In earlier times, trained journalists would typically get a tip from a source among the political elite, scour relevant documents, and eventually interview those they were investigating. They still do that, of course, but social media have enabled citizens to lend a hand. Reporters with substantial followings on social media can let the community know parts of their investigative projects and ask for tips — rumors they can check out. Citizens collectively can look in more places, and have more knowledge and experience, than any one or two reporters on any given topic. At KPCC, the "Feeding the Conversation" meetings in community centers have led to several investigative projects, Alvarado said, as journalists listen for both story ideas and possible sources.

FIGURE 9.2 Ashley Alvarado is director of community engagement at KPCC in Pasadena, California.

(Photo by Paul Voakes.)

BOX 9.2   Hyperlocal, Hyper-Rigorous

Sharon McGowan is one tough editor.

Before becoming the founding editor-in-chief of Milwaukee Neighborhood News Service (NNS) in 2011, she had been an investigative reporter and managing editor at *The Chicago Reporter* and later was assignment editor for WBBM-TV and managing editor at WBBM-AM, both in Chicago. She taught journalism at Northwestern's Medill School of Journalism for 20 years. She was a 2019 inductee into the Milwaukee Press Club's Hall of Fame. She retired in 2019, and her successor, Ron Smith, has equally impressive credentials. He came to the job from *USA Today*, where he was a managing editor.

Given that leadership, it's hardly surprising that the NNS adheres to the traditional journalistic standards we're outlining in this chapter. But the NNS's range of journalism is anything but traditional. The service was born out of a dissatisfaction among central Milwaukee residents that their lives were being represented negatively, if at all, in Milwaukee's mainstream media. The Zilber Family Foundation and the Diederich College of Communication at nearby Marquette University partnered to launch the NNS, with the goal of covering three low-income neighborhoods. The NNS now covers 18 neighborhoods in central Milwaukee. The university provides newsroom space, equipment and financial services, while the foundation offers grants to cover much of the NNS's operating budget.

Its focus is hyperlocal: It attends to the news needs of the area's residents. Regular features include "On the Block," mini-profiles of persons who live in these neighborhoods, with a minute-long audio by each featured person; "Neighborhood Lens," slide shows of various aspects of life in the neighborhoods; "How To," practical articles on everything from finding a summer job to keeping the utilities on for low-income residents; "Community Voices," opinion pieces by neighborhood residents; and "Post from the Community," notices about upcoming events or local news, submitted by residents.

The service is staffed by part- and full-time journalists, many residents themselves of these neighborhoods, and a host of student interns from Marquette. McGowan said she insisted on "professional standards — everything from values and ethics to proper diction and AP style." Because of that diligence, she said, NNS stories are often used by mainstream news outlets, and the NNS has received awards from the Radio Television Digital News Association (RTDNA) and the Milwaukee Press Club.

In addition to the unusual features with the homegrown flavor, the NNS covers the central city in traditional ways as well. It covers beats like education, health, housing, economic development and public safety. And in keeping with the traditional "watchdog" role of news media, the NNS does investigative reporting as well. With help from the Solutions Journalism Network (see Chapter 6), in 2019 it posted a three-part series called "Tale of Two Cities," an in-depth look at Milwaukee's juvenile justice system, informed by the successful reforms in New York City's juvenile system.

Be Accountable

This is one of the younger "traditions" of American journalism — an inevitable outgrowth of the rise, in the 20th century, of investigative reporting and the exposure of wrongdoing. Journalistic accountability is the only reasonable response to charges of journalistic hypocrisy: How can journalists demand accountability of politicians, bureaucrats and business executives when they will not hold themselves accountable for their own work?

By accountability, we mean the willingness to answer for one's work — to honestly explain how the work was done, and to own up publicly to any mistakes made. In most journalistic experience, that translates to publishing corrections, which in itself has created great challenges for traditional journalists. For most of the 20th century, editors believed that publishing corrections was an admission of fallibility — a severe detriment to the posture of omniscient expertise. In many news organizations, errors were publicly corrected only when someone outside the organization pressed for a correction, or when the error was so egregious that it could not be ignored, or when someone threatened to sue the organization if the error were not corrected.

Throughout the book we have recommended the alternative attitude of relational journalism, which requires transparency, among many other attributes, as a means of building trust with a community of citizens. As the Society of Professional Journalists' guidebook "Journalism Ethics" suggests, the SPJ's Code of Ethics makes it clear that "journalism does not exist in a self-interest vacuum but in an environment of reciprocity" (Brown & SPJ, 2011, p. 251). Thus we now have specific guidelines for corrections that display more openness and more humility on the part of journalists. Bugeja (2012), for example, urges that journalists identify where and when the error occurred, provide the correct information, display the correction prominently, explain how the error was made, and apologize to the persons affected by the error and (if appropriate) to the public — and to do all of that as soon as possible after the error is discovered.

To refresh for relational journalism, we are seeing news organizations building accountability into their routines — not just when the occasional error must be corrected. Mary Plummer, of KPCC's Human Voter Guide, said she often calls subjects she has named in a story (or in other stories she's written in the past) simply to ask them what they thought of her work. This gives her a chance to explain the decisions that guide political reporting, she said. Alvarado cites this as an example of the listening to citizens that forms the core of KPCC's journalism.

In recent years, correction of online errors has presented a new kind of challenge. It is tempting for editors simply to remove the incorrect content from a website or social-media account. But do citizens deserve a better, more transparent, accounting of what happened? Gene Foreman, along with many other editors, would answer yes. He urges online editors to post a new announcement about the mistake that states when the erroneous content was first posted and, of course,

FIGURE 9.3   Ashley Alvarado, director of community engagement, left, and managing producer Jon Cohn, right, offer suggestions to John P. Smith, a retired Air Force officer and a storyteller for Unheard LA, at a rehearsal in Spring 2019.

(Photo by Paul Voakes.)

to include the correct information (Foreman, 2016). Many news outlets retain the erroneous copy in the archives but attach a note to it informing readers that the story has been updated and corrected.

Apply the Values of Newsworthiness Consistently

What determines whether a story leads a newscast, gets squeezed into the final block or is not reported at all? Newsworthiness is another concept that separates journalism from other forms of communication, but its application has been elusive over the years, to say the least. Media scholars in the 1950s first labeled the process "gatekeeping," and gatekeepers were fond of saying that a story achieved prominence according to how important and/or interesting it was to the editor on duty at the time. Those highly subjective criteria gave way, as more researchers unpacked the decision-making, to an array of factors, many of which are by now familiar to journalism students. Without a doubt, a set of values, applied consistently, helps journalism maintain a consistent approach to daily work. What's interesting to us is the hierarchy by which the factors influence decisions on the newsworthiness of a story. The pecking order, among 20th-century editors, went something like this: timeliness, prominence of persons involved, potential impact of the story, elements of conflict, proximity to the audience, oddity, human interest and emotional appeal, and usefulness.

To refresh for relational journalism, we would need to re-order some of these values. For example, few would argue with timeliness, but with today's pace of journalism, timeliness can lend itself to speed for the sake of getting it posted first, without regard for accuracy, ethics or reflection. Fast news that's mistake-filled news does a disservice to a community. We would also demote the factor of conflict. Valuing conflict can dangerously distort people's view of the world, especially in implying that a public issue is not important unless a fight is involved. This in turn discourages citizen involvement, as it's more entertaining to sit on the sidelines than to get involved in something like that. It also implies that most important public issues involve intractable disputes, which lead to polarization instead of reconciliation. We submit that when people find common ground and propose a solution to a shared problem, that's news as well. This factor's title is better expressed as "Conflict and Resolution." We would demote prominence, simply because it leads reporters not only to experts as their only sources but also toward celebrity news, which rarely helps citizens with the issues they seek help with. We would also demote oddity and human interest as distractions that are usually unhelpful to community-building. We would upgrade the importance of impact, as this is the wheelhouse of a vibrant democracy. If the story inhabits the public sphere, that is, a concern of many citizens whose problems can be resolved by public policy, this deserves the attention of both journalists and citizens. Proximity deserves to retain its value, even in an era where virtual, online communities are often considered as important as geographically proximate communities. We believe that both journalism and citizenship can enjoy a significant revival when people are to address each other face-to-face as well as online.

EXERCISES

1. Find a news claim on Twitter, Instagram, Facebook or another social media platform and, using the (Storyful, Google or substitute other) protocol, verify whether the claim is reliable (fact-based). Show the steps you used.

2. Find a news claim on Twitter, Instagram, Facebook or another social media platform and give it a rating between 1 (utterly biased) and 10 (as fair, balanced and factual as is humanly possible). Explain the process you used to reach that rating.

3. Find a news site on the web that you've never heard of before and is not affiliated with any legacy news organization. Use your research skills to find out who owns, or who is sponsoring, the site. What does this imply about the potential fairness and bias in the site's content?

4. Identify an issue on campus that involves the needs or claims of a group with a different cultural background (or other "faultline") from the majority of students on campus.

   - List the assumptions and stereotypes many students would make about this group in relation to the issue.

   - Using Sue Ellen Christian's "debiasing" method, describe how you would apply her five "cognitive strategies" to plan a feature story on this issue.

CHAPTER 10

New Paths to Sustainability

I MAGINE THOUSANDS OF PEOPLE CONVERGING ON SOUTH CONGRESS STREET in Austin, Texas, during three days in late September, when the heat and humidity are both topping 90. From across the Lone Star State and beyond, people have gathered — not for folk music, not for barbeque, not even for South by Southwest or a craft beer festival — but for an act of journalism.

The Texas Tribune Festival is the biggest of more than 50 annual live events sponsored by the innovative nonprofit media organization *The Texas Tribune*. Founded in 2009 by three Texans who wanted to change the way citizens engaged with important issues, this unique media company sees the annual festival as just one way to connect people to the issues around government, public policy, politics and statewide concerns.

From Congress to health care, from energy to the environment, *The Texas Tribune* provides nonpartisan, digital-first reporting of news, interactive data, and unique live public events like the festival, where people can learn, discuss and seek to resolve challenges that face the communities of Texas.

It's also leading the way in finding imaginative new means to fund the work of journalism for the future.

And that is the focus of this chapter. The economic challenges the industry was facing by 2020 were among its most fearsome, but we find little evidence of the death of journalism itself. Certain distribution systems and business models may be in fast decline, but citizens' demand for news and information is not about to follow suit. The purpose of this chapter is to explore several

How did the economics of the print news industry news decline so sharply in just two decades? At the dawn of the 21st century, much of the way journalism had worked for 150 years began to unravel. The change was prompted, as so often in journalism history, by new technology. The internet, especially with its user-friendly platform the World Wide Web, enabled information and communication that was nearly instantaneous and nearly limitless in volume. And less than 10 years later, social media enabled every media consumer to become a media producer as well.

Consider the impact this had on the 20th-century way of doing business in journalism. With newspapers, the journalism sector hardest hit in the 21st century, barriers to entry (i.e., the cost to a new competitor to enter a market) were huge; who had access to printing presses? This is why most local and regional media enjoyed near-monopolies for most of the 20th century. Also, retail businesses relied almost solely on news media to reach their target markets, and they were willing to pay so much to advertise that readers paid (with their subscriptions or single-copy prices) only a tiny fraction of the true cost of producing a newspaper. The industry was already in precarious shape by the early 2000s, due in part to the recession brought on by the so-called "dot.com bust" of the late 1990s. In cutting expenses, a media company still had to make those debt payments. Health insurance costs

for employees were skyrocketing. Retired employees had substantial pensions, from the business heyday of the 1970s, 1980s and 1990s, which still had to be paid to them. Union contracts fixed personnel costs. Paper and ink still had to be procured no matter how high those prices were rising. The product could be delivered only with a fleet of trucks, which needed expensive fuel.

By comparison, online news was the revelation that became a revolution. The "barriers to entry" of the 20th century came tumbling down. Anyone with a decent personal computer, decent video and audio recording equipment and access to the internet could compete with a news outlet that took millions of dollars to build. One journalist could now, each day, do the jobs of several traditional journalists. And online news was available on demand, any day, day or night. It is produced fast, and it's updated constantly. No more waiting for the morning edition of the paper, or the late-night news on television or radio. The 20th-century model relied on the scarcity of the product: to find out what was happening in the sports world, for example, we would read reports from the paper's sports section, or a handful of magazines, or watch a sports-focused cable channel. Now with the web, we have choices by the thousands.

The revolution didn't stop with web-based dissemination of news. By 2005 millions of internet

of the most promising avenues news entrepreneurs are pursuing in their efforts to build a sustainable financial base for journalism that serves citizens in their democratic work. As with every chapter in the book, this one celebrates innovation.

Ecosystems

A useful way to consider the financial future of citizen-centered journalism is to start with the concept of "news ecosystems." In ecology, an ecosystem is a network of interconnected elements formed by the interaction of a community of organisms with their environment. Imagine such a network of elements supplying current information to citizens. The Democracy Fund, a nonprofit organization dedicated to strengthening the integrity of the U.S. political system, defines a news ecosystem as "the network of institutions, collaborations and people that local communities users were engaging with social media, which was soon becoming integral to digital journalism. Broadband enabled the easy distribution of video (and two-way interactivity in general). Smartphones were becoming ubiquitous, soon commanding more attention in many Americans' lives than any other part of their physical world. Social networks, at first contained as communication opportunities for friends, were then expanded to include anyone on earth who shared a similar interest. Metrics were developed to measure the reach of any particular post (Daly, 2018). And replacing a fairly fixed number of readers or viewers was the phenomenon of "going viral," that is, growing a massive audience rapidly. For a news or opinion piece to do that, the author need only be sure that the piece can be easily shared through social networks, can be summarized at least in part by the audience members who are sharing it, and that it can be explained in one sentence. Better yet: If the content is up-to-date, irreverent in tone and includes visual elements, it will attract great attention in what has become known as "the attention economy."

Web journalism upended a basic, though seldom expressed, fact about traditional news media: Ever since the penny press of the 1830s, the news has been bundled into an omnibus product. Each day, for example, the traditional newspaper has provided a bit of sports, a bit of politics, a bit of news from abroad, a bit of weather, a bit of opinion, a bit of en-

tertainment, and plenty more — in bits. With web-based journalism, the bundle has been unbundled. Niche news sites provide information on every topic the newspaper did, but in greater detail. Historian Christopher Daly has asked, "What is the remaining value of reading merely pretty good coverage (and paying for it) when readers can unbundle the newspaper, go online, and plunge into first-rate coverage, written by real aficionados and provided at a price of zero?" (Daly, 2018, p. 461).

Thus it's hardly surprising that newspapers have lost so much of their formerly exalted presence in the new century. In 1990, the combined circulation of U.S. newspapers was 60 million. By 2019 that had dipped to 28 million — a loss of more than half of the nation's newspaper readers in just 29 years (Grieco, 2019). As recently as 2006, U.S. newspapers employed about 74,000 journalists. By 2018, that workforce had shrunk to 38,000 — again, a loss of about half.

Traditional media managers had plenty of opportunities in the 1990s to embrace internet-based technologies for news. But they were generally unprepared for these technologies. Most declined, on the logic that only a tiny fraction of their customers owned personal computers, and an even tinier fraction could connect to the internet from their homes. Many editors, publishers and managers assumed the internet was a high-tech curiosity that would always remain the domain of the technologists only.

rely on for news, information and engagement" (Morgan, 2019, p. 5). In the early decades of American journalism, the ecosystem was fairly simple: printed matter such as newspapers and organizations' newsletters, and the pronouncements of local political leaders, clergy, postmasters and the like. The advent of broadcast media enriched the ecosystem in any community, but the dominant elements were still, by and large, private companies that controlled much of the flow of public communication. Along came the internet, and social media, and every community ecosystem has quickly transformed into a multidirectional, multimodal network of sources of content. The traditional news media have become, at best, one element among many institutions, collaborations and people comprising the ecosystem. Whereas media companies at one time flourished financially because they dominated the news ecosystem, their financial stability is anything but assured in the 21st century.

Community by community, Americans' news ecosystems are being altered by internal and external forces, making it one of the most turbulent times in media history. Each ecosystem consists of anchor elements, like news organizations, universities, public libraries and government agencies; infrastructure, that is, media ownership structures, access to broadband and the like; and networks, that is, groups of people who interact by using the system (Morgan, 2019). Despite these commonalities, the boundaries of news ecosystems are unique to each community in the country and are understood best by the local people using them. Ecosystems, in this networked, collective way, provide for the basic information needs of a community.

Jeff Jarvis, a journalism futurist and professor at CUNY's Newmark Graduate School of Journalism, sees a complex, interdependent network of news organizations complementing each other's roles — companies that will succeed once they learn to collaborate on distribution and advertising, as well as content. They can include "new news organizations, reformed legacy institutions, not-for-profit investigative organizations, public media, specialists of various sorts, networks, and enterprises I've not yet seen or imagined" (Jarvis, 2014, p. 139). Jarvis envisions ecosystems based in "beat businesses," small news operations that each focus on deep coverage for single communities of interest (Jarvis, 2014). That could include hyperlocal news, or news of specialty topics. He measures beat businesses as "bigger than a breadbox, or blog, but smaller than a general-interest news organization" (p. 139).

The transformation of these news ecosystems is a work in progress with an ever-changing mix of news and information providers rising and falling so rapidly that they can be difficult to track. Their business models vary, as do their ownership structures and sources of operating revenue.

This chapter provides a snapshot of the most popular approaches in the early 2020s to finding financial stability. The rise of nonprofit news organizations is the most important trend. The innovative news organizations described in this book, many of them nonprofits, tend to be recent entrants into their particular ecosystems. Whether working at an established news outlet that is redefining its role in the community, a news startup, or even a small group of dreamers with a great idea for a new "beat business," journalists need to know how to define the ecosystem in which they hope to succeed. The Democracy Fund (Morgan, 2019) offers an organized approach:

- *The Legacy Media.* This is the name given to news organizations that existed before the emergence of the internet, such as local commercial radio stations, low-power community radio stations (often community-, church- or campus-oriented), television stations, daily newspapers and weekly newspapers. There's a helpful database at https://www.usnewsdeserts.com/, and the FCC has a database for all licenses of AM and FM stations at https://www.fcc.gov/media/radio/radio-lists.

- *Ethnic Media*. Many cities enjoy a rich array of outlets — online, on air or in print — for members of certain ethnic minorities, immigrant populations or religious groups.

- *Emergent Digital Media*. From alternative arts magazines to investigative reporting enterprises, creative new digital publications are emerging in most American cities. These often exemplify Jarvis's beat businesses in their degrees of specialization. They may be a bit difficult to identify, but many are affiliated with one of two nationwide organizations: LION Publishers, providing training and technical and legal support to digital news outlets, both for-profit and nonprofit, at lionpublishers.com; or the Institute for Nonprofit News, a network of more than 200 nonprofit newsrooms whose website, inn. org, has a directory searchable by location or subject area. (See Appendix 1 for more complete listings.)

- *Nonmedia Sources of Information*. This is the most difficult group to identify, but often the most influential. It can include community or political leaders' personal media, or the email listservs or digital newsletters of influential advocacy groups; neighborhoods; churches, mosques or synagogues; local government agencies including libraries; and cultural centers and the like.

As America's news ecosystems transition from dominance by a few to interdependence among many, it is important early on to describe the content and style of each element in the ecosystem, so that entrepreneurs can identify gaps or needs — and potential complementarities.

This book can't begin to provide adequate guidance on how to launch a news business, but there are excellent resources (e.g. Briggs, 2012) for those with an entrepreneurial spirit. It is obvious, however, that any community-building, democracy-centered news business — whether a creative startup or a longstanding outlet — must attract sufficient funds to sustain its operation. There are costs to presenting consistently excellent journalism of this kind, not the least of which is salaries and benefits for the journalists who do this difficult work in this labor-intensive business. The rest of the chapter explores what innovators have discovered in answer to the revenue challenges.

Into the Future: Three Types of News Organizations

Massive and relatively sudden changes in communication technology and media economics have devastated the newspaper industry that flourished in the 20th century (see Box 10.1 "How We Got Here"). The advertising that newspapers had easily attracted for 150 years was suddenly moving to social-media platforms, many of which repurpose (but do not produce) original journalism. In the first quarter of 2016, out of every new dollar businesses were spending on digital advertising, Facebook or Google/YouTube was taking 85 cents (Daly, 2018). The industry lost more than half its newspaper readers just from 1990 to 2019 (Pew Research Center, 2019). And in 2020, things got worse, when the COVID-19 pandemic sent shock waves through nearly every sector of the global economy. The pace of the industry's downturn further quickened.

But the decline of the advertising-fueled omnibus newspaper has been inevitable, and thus the rise of alternative avenues to sustainability has been likewise inevitable. In terms of organizing businesses for success in the coming years, we see three basic types.

For-Profit News Companies

Legacy news organizations have struggled mightily over the last 20 years, and the coronavirus pandemic has further threatened already-crippled enterprises. Still, for-profit news organizations, both legacy and startups, will continue to play a significant role in most news ecosystems. Their business models, however, aren't likely to look like those of newspapers in the go-go years when advertising accounted for about 80 percent of revenue. Without advertising to fuel all its operating needs, traditional for-profit news organizations are trying to offset the advertising losses with more revenue from readers and viewers as their business shifts to digital platforms. They also are turning to many of the other revenue sources once considered exclusive to nonprofits: grants and gifts. Ownership structures also have been changing as the need for capital has outpaced what the news organizations could generate internally. The debate about corporate (Wall Street) ownership has been supplanted by worry that the hedge funds and venture capitalists that now own many newspapers outright or finance them don't respect journalism as a form of public service. Private families, for good and ill, have traditionally owned newspapers, although many sold to corporations during the late 1900s. Some private local owners were more community minded than others. Recently, a few regional and national newspapers have been rescued by billionaires, which, while fascinating to monitor, is hardly a formula for sustaining journalism.

However, for the kinds of citizen-serving innovations we're describing in this book, other types of news organizations seem more compatible.

Nonprofit News Organizations

In the growing universe of innovative alternatives to the advertising-dependent 20th-century model, the nonprofit corporation has emerged as one of the most promising. A nonprofit corporation, according to federal law, is an organization whose work in some way benefits the public or a specific group of members. If the Internal Revenue Service affirms that its operation meets those criteria, the organization is exempt from federal taxes (U.S. Legal.com, 2020). Religious organizations, charities, private schools, political organizations and clubs are among the most familiar examples.

Could a news organization qualify as such an organization? For starters, a mission that "benefits the public" is at the heart of citizen-centered journalism. And the idea has a long history. The Associated Press, one of the most venerated institutions in American journalism, has been a nonprofit news cooperative since 1846. Today there are more than 230 nonprofit newsrooms in the United States, three-quarters of which have launched since 2008. And most are oriented to the local: About 63 percent of them have local, state or regional coverage as their focus (PEN America, 2019). Most of the nonlocal nonprofits emphasize investigative reporting or public-affairs analysis. Is their work respected? In 2018, more than half of the recipients of awards from the prestigious Online News Association (ONA) were nonprofit news organizations.

As recently as 20 years ago, a legacy newspaper would have rejected any notion of converting to a nonprofit organization — so strong was the tradition of newspapers as pillars of their local business communities or, for national news corporations, as darlings of Wall Street. Then in 2019, *The Salt Lake Tribune* did the unthinkable: It applied for nonprofit status, and the IRS, bucking a longstanding tradition of denials, approved. In its application, the newspaper had to outline its plans for high levels of public service, which included political neutrality, especially in not endorsing political candidates; distributing its news free to Utah libraries; declaring freedom of the press to be a "human and civil right secured by law;" monthly town-hall meetings in which reporters would discuss their work; and paid internships for journalism students (Hansen & Holcomb, 2020). For any newspaper committed to citizen engagement, that list seems hardly onerous.

News Cooperatives

Far less common in the news business — despite the early example of the Associated Press — is the cooperative. This is an enterprise whose owners are also the people (members) who use its services. Of the 47,000 cooperatives in operation in the United States in 2020, more than 10,000 were credit unions. But food services, health care providers, utilities and child-care providers have often formed cooperatives as well. The members share equally in the control of the cooperative. They elect a board of directors from among themselves, and the board hires a management team to run the business. The startup capital comes, usually, from the members' investment. After the costs of operation have been covered and designated sums are reinvested into co-op improvements, the remaining profit is returned to the individual members (Inc.com, 2020).

A news co-op would, theoretically, gather members at two levels: community members who wished to invest in a news outlet that met their information needs, and possibly a network of local news co-ops who wished to share technology, legal assistance, membership-building expertise, and other resources.

A recent pioneer in news co-ops is Tom Stites, who founded the Banyan Project, a federation of local news co-ops. The pilot co-op was Haverhill Matters, in Haverhill, Massachusetts, which struggled to find financial footing and the necessary digital delivery tools for a few years, until it closed its doors in early 2020. Startup capital is key, Stites told Nieman Lab shortly after Haverhill Matters' demise, and the project didn't have enough to sustain the difficult early days when expenses were high and income sporadic (Kennedy, 2020).

But Stites continues to believe that co-ops offer an appropriate option for those interested in serving local communities. The users and readers of the local news site, in a co-op, are also the part-owners of the site. The readers thus can own a piece of equity in the co-op and a vote in electing the board, but they also get a front-row opportunity to engage with journalists and other citizens in the community conversation. In Haverhill, members would receive an email each week asking for suggestions on what issues needed coverage and for feedback on the journalists' previous work (Kennedy, 2020).

As news companies struggled and the news deserts increased across the country in 2020, Stites continued to reach out to communities, journalists and funders who might want to try the co-op experiment elsewhere in the United States.

Revenue Streams for News

Whether a news organization is about to launch or is 200 years old, whether it's for-profit, nonprofit or a cooperative, whether it's online only or incorporating video and/or print in its output, it must make money. It must find the people or organizations that are willing financially to support its contribution to its news and information ecosystem. Innovators are experimenting with new ideas every year, and by the early 2020s, five strategies for generating revenues seemed to have emerged as particularly viable: philanthropy, memberships, collaborations and sponsorships, specialized content and services, and events.

Jim Collins, a prominent management consultant, is well known for his books on business management. As a follow-up to his best-selling *Good to Great*, Collins wrote a slim monograph called *Good to Great and the Social Sectors* (2011), which recommends a number of strategies not for profit-seeking businesses but for organizations committed to public service — a category we believe includes news organizations. His framework for thinking about revenue generation can serve as a useful guide for news entrepreneurs. Collins identifies two distinct dimensions of revenue: gifts and grants and earned business revenue (see chart below). Some organizations, like the American Cancer Society (in Quadrant II), are high on gifts/grants but low on business revenue; they have excellent fund-raising operations but provide no goods or services that customers will pay for. Other organizations, like a community hospital (Quadrant IV), are high on business revenue but low on gifts/grants; patients and their insurance companies pay handsomely for the services the hospital provides. Other organizations are low in both dimensions (Quadrant I); they offer nothing for sale, and they do no fund-raising for gifts or grants. They often operate with some form of government funding. And then some organizations, like the Girl Scouts or private colleges (Quadrant III), are high on both gifts/grants and on business revenues. Those Girl Scout cookie sales are complemented by other massive fund-raising efforts; a college provides education to students who pay tuition, and it also systematically raises funds from alumni and others. Here's how Collins envisioned the four types:

Where does a news organization fit? Collins doesn't address journalism specifically, but our view is that an innovative, citizen-centered news organization should be able to thrive in Quadrant III with a combination of revenues from both business operations and donations or grants. Let's start with the gifts/grants side.

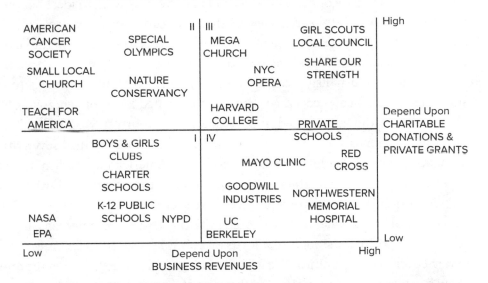

ECONOMIC ENGINE IN THE SOCIAL SECTORS: 4 QUADRANTS

FIGURE 10.1 Collins' Four Quadrants of Revenue Possibilities

(Collins, 2011, p. 21)

Philanthropy for News

The first on our list of revenue sources is certainly on the "gifts and grants" dimension: funding from individuals, families, private companies and philanthropic foundations. Ever since the emergence of alternatives to the standard media business model, foundations in particular have been the key to bolstering their work — and in many cases providing startup capital. By 2020 more than 6,500 foundations in the United States had funded media initiatives or operations. The amount of money philanthropy has poured into journalism has skyrocketed since 2009, when 300 funders made $69 million in grants to about 300 U.S. organizations. By 2017, more than 1,200 funders had granted more than $255 million to 925 organizations, the media-focused philanthropy group Media Impact Funders reported (Armour-Jones, 2019).

For the entrepreneurial publisher, one of the greatest challenges in dependence on philanthropic support is that foundations typically give "seed money" to enable the launch of a publication or specific reporting project, but rarely with any intention to continue funding beyond the first few years. In fact, a growing trend in the 2020s is "impact investment" funding, where foundations' grants are funding not only journalistic operations but also strategizing for the news organization to build long-term revenue streams that can sustain the operation without philanthropy (PEN America, 2019).

In the first two decades of this century, foundations tended to support national, rather than local, news organizations. Despite that nearly two-thirds of the country's nonprofit news organizations are focused on local news, just 4.5 percent of all foundations giving to journalism between 2010 and 2015 went to local nonprofit newsrooms. New outlets in urban neighborhoods or rural regions are especially disadvantaged when the philanthropic dollars find their way to a handful of the largest, most highly regarded nonprofit news outlets (PEN America, 2019).

The leading journalism-oriented foundations have been responding to the shrinkage of local news coverage with unprecedented levels of generosity. The Knight Foundation announced in 2019 that it would invest $300 million over five years to reinvigorate local news in various ways. Knight joined seven other foundations and philanthropists to help create the American Journalism Project, which provides grants and training aimed at financial sustainability, with a focus on news organizations that emphasize their civic responsibilities. Report for America is another philanthropy-backed initiative that places talented early-career journalists in newsrooms that focus on public service and a commitment to under-covered communities. The group said it would place 250 young reporters in such newsrooms in 2020 alone, with hopes of placing 1,000 reporters by 2024 (Stehle, 2020).

Memberships

Now we slide over to Collins' second dimension of revenue, earned business revenue. Many media economists see memberships as the revenue stream that promises the most stable long-term revenue for news organizations. Most news consumers are familiar with subscriptions, by which a customer pays for the regular delivery of a news product. But memberships involve more than a business transaction. Members are asked to support the mission of the news organization as well, by making a renewable financial contribution independent of consuming any news product. Thus, a membership becomes something of a social contract — a relationship between the journalists and members. In many news organizations with memberships, members offer support with their skills, their own social networks and their volunteer time as well as their money. In return, members at times get access to special content, direct engagement with journalists or even input on which topics or stories to pursue.

And it works. In the 2010s, when most for-profit news organizations were reporting dramatic job losses, most membership-funded public broadcasting stations — both radio and television — were steadily growing their staffs and their scope of news coverage. In fact, between 2011 and 2018, the 264 independent local National Public Radio stations increased their staffs by an average of 50 percent (Edmonds, 2019).

The membership approach seems highly compatible with citizen-centered journalism, as it focuses on developing so much community trust that the membership will give its time, talent and money. As Jarvis writes (2014), membership gives audience members "an opportunity to join a cause, and help that cause succeed" (p. 43). In our view, such a cause would be great journalism in the service of citizens in a democracy.

Sponsorships and Advertising

The business dynamic that enabled journalism to flourish for 150 years — and now enables Facebook, Google and other social media giants to flourish — is not about to disappear. For local, civically minded news outlets, it takes on different forms. While the drastic reduction in print advertising — both classified and retail ads — brought huge financial distress to newspapers, many news outlets assumed that retail and classified ads would shift to their websites. That didn't happen to anywhere near a level that would supplant the lost revenue from print ads. More recently, however, these organizations have been working out ways to apply digital technologies, such as narrowly targeting certain ads to just the right potential customers.

Sponsored content, once anathema to many editors, has emerged as a viable revenue source in recent years. In earlier times, a "sponsoring" advertiser would pay

BOX 10.2 **Putting Members to Work**

Most membership plans for news media involve a monthly or annual pledge from the member. Often a mug or tote bag will be involved as well.

Now imagine a plan whereby the citizen must apply for membership. Applicants are accepted on the basis of their expertise in one or more current-affairs topics. Those accepted can expect to be suggesting story ideas, sharing their own expertise with beat reporters, debating with other members the merits of controversial positions within a certain beat and perhaps even editing reporters' rough drafts of stories that directly involve the members' expertise.

Ambitious? Certainly. Far-fetched? Not at all. This is how *De Correspondent*, a Dutch news outlet, has built its journalism — and its revenue. In fact, its budget is based entirely on memberships. *De Correspondent* has 60,000 members, who pay an average of $65 per year to belong.

Beginning in 2018, New York University journalism Professor Jay Rosen and his colleagues attempted to duplicate *De Correspondent*'s success, for a transnational, English-reading audience. After receiving a few grants from foundations to create an early structure, *The Correspondent* raised $2.6 million from a crowdfunding campaign alone, before hiring its first reporter. The news site officially launched in September 2019.

Emily Goligoski is the research director of the Membership Puzzle Project, which seeks to find and share best practices among news outlets — like *The Correspondent* — that are experimenting with membership models. The idea of truly active memberships for news, she explained, is that members enable the news organization to be more comprehensive in its scope of stories, more accurate, and more engaged with the communities it serves (Goligoski, personal interview, Feb. 1, 2019). Members who are actively involved with the journalism, she said, are more like-

ly to dig deep to support the news outlet financially. More importantly, trust grows. "Trust in journalism is key," she said, "and trust depends on transparency in the journalistic practice, and transparency is easier with membership models that bring citizens behind the magic curtain of journalism." In the process of dispensing a bit of their expertise, she said, members learn aspects of the craft of journalism, the fundamental principles of good journalism, and they learn the impact that good journalism can have on communities.

By early 2019, Goligoski was monitoring 163 different news outlets around the world that were using some form of membership to bring in revenue. Her observations so far? It's not enough to declare interest in collaborating with members, she said. The outlets that have seen the greatest success are those with these four attributes:

- Journalists see their audience members honestly as having a great deal to contribute to their news work.

- The journalism is oriented to solutions, not just the exposition of a problem.

- The news organization is selective about its scope of work — its role in its news ecosystem — rather than trying to provide all things to all audiences.

- The journalists are committed to transparency, even to the point of sharing their data and their processes with members and with their public audiences.

In 2020, the Membership Puzzle Project consolidated what it had learned from its meticulous partnering with this global network of membership news outlets into "The Membership Guide," available at https://membershipguide.org/handbook.

---

to provide a feature story on a topic of reader interest that happens to mention that advertiser's product or service prominently and favorably. The implied deception — that an objective-looking, professional-looking article or video package is a cleverly disguised advertisement — disturbed the ethical sensibilities of most editors. But in an era of shrinking ad revenue, sponsored content is getting a second look. A 2016 survey of local independent news publishers found that over half are now selling sponsored content (PEN America, 2019). Today, the ethical reconciliation centers on transparency: Readers, listeners and viewers must be made to understand clearly and immediately that a particular piece of content is funded by an advertiser, not the journalistic staff. Many online publications, for example, provide specialized content, like Vox Media's "Explainers," whose commercial sponsor is prominently displayed on the screen but whose content is entirely staff-produced.

Another new approach to advertising revenue is the business collaboration. In Chapter 7, we saw how Your Voice Ohio was realizing the journalistic benefits of collaboration among news outlets who in the past regarded each other as rivals. The same benefits can accrue in news outlets' business collaborations. Jarvis (2014) describes a growing number of advertising-sales networks composed of members — of various sizes and playing to different markets — in which one sales rep sells ads on behalf of not just her own outlet but every other member of the network. The entire network of outlets shares in that ad revenue. Sometimes, news organizations team up in applying for a grant or gift from a foundation, working on the same journalistic project and sharing the grant revenue. The quality of the work, and the scope of its impact, is usually far greater than if the outlets had applied for grants separately.

The basic, classic logic of advertising in journalism remains intact: If a news organization produces journalism that is interesting and important to a substantial audience, businesses will pay for access to those audience members, in order to put their products and services in front of those potential customers. If citizen-centered journalism, even if it's now narrow rather than "omnibus" in scope, is relevant enough to members of a community, advertisers will want to reach out to that community.

Specialized Content

Innovative news organizations are discovering that they can create more than one informational product. The concept is actually traditional, as newspapers for 100 years have produced occasional supplements such as local histories or book-length summaries of a local sports team's championship year — and sold them. The difference now is that news organizations are providing the supplements more regularly, and on a variety of platforms, and readers are willing to pay a premium to receive them. Examples include "insider" reports such as highly detailed, expert coverage of a professional sports team; detailed notices and reviews of a city's music scene; detailed coverage of an unusual local institution like a large, nationally renowned corporation, university or federal agency; or in the case of *The Texas Tribune*, a daily newsletter with "insider" coverage of state politics, marketed to those who work in state politics.

In early 2016, the Reed College of Media at West Virginia University had been planning to create a faculty-supervised, student-produced digital publishing enterprise that would focus on life in Appalachia.

Then Donald Trump was elected president. The national media descended on the region, dubbing it "Trump Nation" and promoting assumptions and stereotypes about Appalachia that the students, faculty and staff could not abide. "We're actually a microcosm of the United States," WVU Provost Maryanne Reed, the college's dean at the time, said, "and we decided that West Virginia should own the narrative."

The school's digital enterprise swung into high gear, and thus was "100 Days in Appalachia" born: a chronicle of the impact of the first three months of the Trump Era upon their region. The project's ultimate goal, Associate Professor Dana Coester explained, was to "tell a counter-narrative about the region and to bridge ideological divides" among citizens of the region (Coester, personal interview, August 13, 2018).

"100 Days," still operating well beyond Trump's first months, has become an exemplar of the trend among citizen-centered media to collaborate with academic institutions. The project secured immediate financial support in late 2016 from foundations — both local and national — and found immediate professional partners in West Virginia Public Broadcasting and Daily Yonder (a nonprofit, Kentucky-based, nonpartisan digital outlet that covers issues of rural America). It now has a professional staff of reporters and editors (many of whom are media college faculty), and the college has developed a set of courses whereby students contribute to "100 Days" as well. The students curate the professionally produced content for distribution on social media, and they experiment with new ways to build online audiences. Occasionally, students' original stories appear on the "100 Days" website as well. Ashton Marra, an assistant professor of journalism and one of the "100 Days'" editors, said journalism programs are appropriate collaborators because schools welcome experimentation without fear of failure. "You

Events

This is another new twist on a strategy that local television stations and newspapers have known for generations. Traditionally, the news outlet would organize (and usually pay for) the local Fourth of July or Christmas parade, or a summer series of free outdoor concerts, or a 10K race for all categories of runners. The events produce good will in the community, but no revenue. *The Texas Tribune* has pioneered a new style of event that generates revenue: a "festival" that provides not entertainment but stimulating insights on public affairs — and charges admission. The *Tribune* brings to Austin influential political leaders, journalists and public intellectuals from Texas (and beyond) once a year, and attendees gather not only to hear the speakers and panels but to network with the state's movers and shakers. Editor Emily Ramshaw said the festival required a shift in the staff's professional culture, and reporters were not used to taking the stage (as moderators and speakers) themselves but that most warmed to the role after a year or two. The *Tribune*'s "event culture" has expanded rapidly: In 2018 it hosted more than 50 events in addition to the annual festival, which brought in more than 14,000 attendees and accounted for more than $1 million of the *Tribune*'s $9 million budget.

test things out," she told us. "You incubate, and if you have professional partners who are also willing to share some risk, the experiment has sturdier legs." The college also adds value to "100 Days" in the form of campus office space, equipment and the considerable talent of the former journalists now serving as teaching professors.

Provost Reed was careful to point out that "100 Days" is not the "teaching hospital" kind of collaboration that was popular in the early 2000s, where students would produce stories under the supervision of journalists at nearby legacy papers or stations. "That model assumes," Reed said, "that the 'hospital' is on firm financial footing. We want to help the news industry survive and then thrive, but we don't want to train young people for jobs that may not exist in the future."

The plan for revenue for "100 Days" resembles many others at startup nonprofits. Tyler Channell, a lecturer at the college who has taken on a role as engagement and revenue developer for "100 Days," said the project is looking beyond the expiration dates of those startup grants and courting memberships among the site's readership base, trying various levels of a paywall. Channell said the ultimate

FIGURE 10.2 Ashton Marra and David Smith coteach a class in "100 Days in Appalachia" at West Virginia University.

(Photo by Paul Voakes.)

goal in the college's development is to be able to export a revenue model for digital publication to the state's imperiled newspaper industry.

Balance Is the Key

Business guru Jim Collins (2011) advises organizations in the "social sector" to work for a balanced array of revenue streams, with strong components from both the "gifts and grants" and the "earned business" dimensions. It would be difficult to find a better illustration of that balance than *The Texas Tribune*. The outlet has no fewer than six major contributors to its annual revenue of more than $9 million: from foundations, 25 percent; from individual and family gifts, 24 percent; from corporate underwriting and sponsorships, 19 percent; from events like the annual festival, 18 percent; from memberships, 10 percent; and from special services — from daily newsletters for political insiders and exclusive local reports for use by news media elsewhere in the country to renting office space in their downtown Austin location and writing a supplement on Texas government for a high-school textbook — 5 percent (*The Texas Tribune*, 2019, p. 18). Compare the *Tribune*'s income streams (Fig. 11.3) to newspapers' norm in the late 1990s (Fig. 10.3), where a combination of retail and classified advertising accounted for 79 cents of every dollar received.

The innovative nature of the *Tribune*'s financial structure echoes the citizen-centered innovations in its newsroom. Emily Ramshaw, the editor-in-chief from 2016 to

Newspapers, 1998

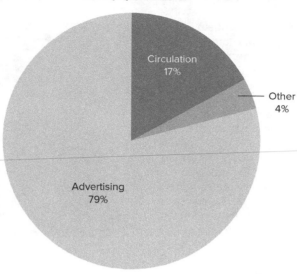

Circulation
17%

Other
4%

Advertising
79%

FIGURE 10.3   Newspaper revenues in the late 1990s

(Adapted from data from Pew Research Center, 2019)

The Texas Tribune, 2018

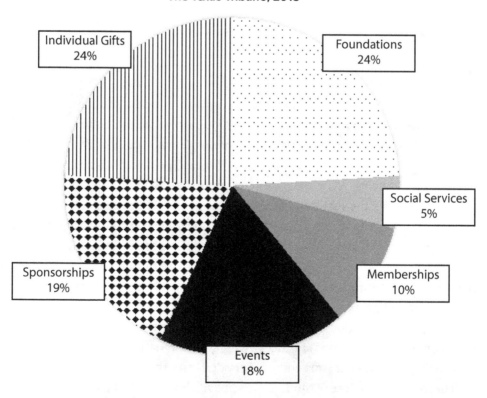

Individual Gifts
24%

Foundations
24%

Social Services
5%

Sponsorships
19%

Memberships
10%

Events
18%

FIGURE 10.4. The diversified revenue streams at *The Texas Tribune*

(Source: The Texas Tribune Annual Report, 2019)

2019, said the outlet was founded in 2009 in response to the dramatic reduction of coverage of state government and politics in the early 2000s. The ecosystem of Texas journalism was losing one of its most important components: reporting that held the state government accountable. In its first 10 years, the *Tribune* has grown its Capitol bureau to at least 20 reporters at any given time — the largest state bureau staff in the country. The result is what Ramshaw called "The Trib Effect: what happens when lawmakers and politicians know someone is watching."

FIGURE 10.5 Emily Ramshaw, left, was editor of *The Texas Tribune* and Amanda Zamora chief audience officer for several years until 2020.

(Photo by Paul Voakes.)

The *Tribune*'s nonprofit status makes a huge difference in its journalistic approach. Amanda Zamora, the chief audience officer until 2020, who had worked at both for-profit and nonprofit organizations before joining the *Tribune* in 2016, said "at a nonprofit, you become mission-driven, no longer profit-driven, so when the mission is news in the public interest, you do the journalism that will benefit the public good." Ramshaw added that none of the *Tribune*'s six revenue streams depend directly on page views, visits or clicks — often the driving force in for-profit business plans — so the newsroom can follow its basic news values in setting coverage priorities.

Nor does the *Tribune* erect a paywall to boost revenue, on the theory that paywalls can actually block the kind of reader engagement they seek. Terry Quinn, the outlet's chief development officer (head fund-raiser), said that one of her most successful pitches to prospective members and donors is that their gifts "enable our journalism to be free to all, and so avoid a news desert in Texas."

FIGURE 10.6 Terry Quinn is chief development officer at *The Texas Tribune*.

(Photo by Paul Voakes.)

Government Funding for Journalism

At some point the discussion about funding the news inevitably turns to this question: If a strong local news ecosystem is the lifeblood of a vibrant community and a responsive local democratic government, why not consider journalism to be a public good, rather than a niche within the economy's private sector? If journalism provides a public good to the citizenry, much like a museum, a park or snow removal, why could it not be part of the government's budget?

That notion has been anathema to the industry's leadership ever since the days of the penny press, when newspapers realized they could be more profitable with private advertising than with political party patronage. But with the disappearance of advertising from traditional media, what is the objection? Traditionalists argue that when the news media's role (among others) is to be a constant watchdog against governmental misbehavior, how could it, with governmental funding, be expected to bite the hand that feeds it?

Actually, governmental subsidies to news media have a long history in the United States. Ever since the early days of the republic, publishers have enjoyed postal-rate subsidies to help defray the costs of mailing their products. Newspapers have enjoyed various forms of income-tax and sales-tax breaks unavailable to other businesses. Governments have often been required to pay to "advertise" public notices in local newspapers. Governments, both federal and currently 36 states, have allocated funds to support public radio and public television. A 2014 study of public funding for media among 18 high-income democracies found that U.S. funding ranked lowest. Among the other 17 countries, the average level of public funding was about 28 times that of the United States (PEN America, 2019).

The objection based on the implied censorship of "biting the government hand that feeds you" seems to have been addressed satisfactorily by those 17 other democracies. Several creative, innovative suggestions have emerged in recent years. Chief among them is the proposal to tax the digital advertising revenue of the tech giants like Google and Facebook, whose appropriation of ad sales is in some ways responsible for the implosion of the 20th-century business model. The tax revenue could be earmarked for local news outlets, perhaps based on their financial distress and their commitment to community-building. Another idea is to levy a "link tax" on online news aggregators and search engines. This would be a fee levied whenever they link to reproduce content that was created by a news organization.

We're not about to advocate any specific solution, but this much seems clear: In order to win approval for any kind of funding, a bipartisan coalition of lawmakers would have to agree on a system that would keep political considerations far, far away from funding decisions. Still, the basic concept of governmental subsidies is not alien to American public policy, and other democracies do subsidize journalism. And as we've discovered in this chapter, a revenue-balanced news organization would not need to receive more than a modest percentage of its budget from the public coffers.

As it has in the past, journalism once again finds itself at a critical point in its evolution as a key contributor to the ongoing American experiment in democracy. We have no doubt that media managers and the journalists who work for them are anxious for the correct answer to the question of "Who will pay for the level of journalism that democracy demands?" We have no doubt that bright young minds will come together, as they are already doing, to arrive at workable solutions. But this pivoting is still in its early days. Jarvis (2014) likes to point out that 150 years elapsed between Gutenberg's invention of the printing press and the publication of the first newspaper. It's only been 25 years since the emergence of the World Wide Web and only 15 years since the introduction of social media. We're just getting started.

EXERCISES

1. Initiate a conversation with each of three people you know well from different generations — a grandparent or older community member, a parent or family friend of similar age and a friend or fellow student your own age.

    -   Explore a series of questions with them about their media use: Where do they get most of their news? How much do they pay for journalism today? Do they donate money to public radio or television? Do they subscribe to newspapers, magazines, digital or print? How much would they be willing to pay for access to news? What kinds of things might incentivize them to pay for journalism? What is important to them about the news they consume? Over their lifetime, how has their media use changed? What do they think the news will be like in the future?

    -   What observations can you make about the responses you heard? Based on what you learned, what ideas do you have for developing new ways to fund journalism in the future?

2. Write an assessment of your local (or campus) news ecosystem, as described in the first section of this chapter. Name the news outlets within each category: legacy media, ethnic media, digital media and nonmedia sources of current information. What gaps do you see in the ecosystem?

3. Imagine that you plan to create a community-focused news organization that will provide local information about climate change and the environment.

    -   Identify as many possible specific sources of revenue streams as you can (e.g., philanthropic donors, membership plans, sponsorships from private companies, specialized content you could charge for and special events) and explain how each would generate revenue.

- Point out any ethical challenges or other pitfalls in each of the revenue streams you identified.

4. In no more than 300 words, sketch out a system of U.S. government funding for journalism. Your proposal must include these elements:

- A means of keeping funding decisions as far away from politics as possible. Try to ensure that journalists would not be censored or influenced by those who hold political power (even to the point of not censoring themselves out of fear of losing funding later).

- What organizations would be eligible? Devise a means of ensuring that areas whose only local news outlets are struggling to stay alive, and especially areas already declared "news deserts," receive full consideration for government funds.

- A system for ensuring your government program has adequate resources to provide the funding. Would you use monies from a government's general budget? Would you levy a special tax or fees from certain groups (such as social-media giants)? How would that work?

CREDIT

Fig. 10.1: Jim Collins, from *Good to Great and the Social Sectors: A Monograph to Accompany Good to Great*, p. 21. Copyright © 2011 by Harper Business.

CHAPTER 11

A Challenge to Future Journalists

I MAGINE A WORLD WHERE JOURNALISTS:

- Listen carefully for a community's ever-changing information needs and declare themselves part of the communities they cover

- Help people identify the problems and issues that are most important to them

- Find the key facts people need as they struggle to find solutions to those important problems

- Look beyond credentialed experts, spokespersons and officials in sourcing their stories, and seek out the people most affected by the issue at hand

- Organize meetings and discussions, in partnership with other civic organizations

- Partner with citizens on various aspects of producing news and information

- Don't stop at investigative reports that detail how awful a problem is but go an extra mile to research possible solutions to the problem

- Collaborate on major, complex regional problems with colleagues at other news organizations — the same ones they used to distrust as "the competition"

- Commit to the sustainability of news production that is not based on a single revenue stream

- Turn away from "conflict" as the driving determinant of newsworthiness

- Adhere to the traditions of truth-seeking, fairness and independence but do so in innovative ways that get citizens more directly involved

- Recognize that they are skilled participants — but no longer the controllers — in a complex ecosystem of public information

In short, imagine a world where journalists have discarded the tradition of reporting that resembles extractive mining and replaced it with relational journalism. Its ultimate result is a nation of communities where citizens have regained confidence in their abilities to work together to improve their lives.

That's the world of journalism we envisioned when we set out to write this book. After speaking with journalists at 19 innovative news organizations, we remain convinced that the vision is no pipedream. Skilled, experienced journalists are experimenting with exactly the strategies and techniques listed above, and many more, to see whether community-building, citizen-centered journalism can be viable in a time when journalism struggles to redefine its role in American society. It's a daunting challenge, to be sure. But we believe that in the early 21st century, American journalism has entered one of its transitional phases, and that young journalists are imaginative enough, and prepared, to lead the way.

It's difficult to overstate the importance of this transition in journalism. As we've said more than once in these pages, American democracy flourishes when American journalism flourishes. But civic life has struggled just as journalism has in the early 21st century. Reforming the national political culture, where political polarization has increased and distrust of news content has likewise grown, is beyond the scope of this book. But the dispiriting national trends only serve to intensify our belief that reform will occur first at the local level — for government and politics as well as for journalism.

A growing body of research tells us just how important local news is to community health. At its most basic level, local news always has kept citizens educated, and therefore prepared and motivated to vote. It has kept a check on institutional power by monitoring it. It also serves as a building block for social cohesion — the bonds between and among citizens who can't meet face-to-face — which in turn serves as a building block for citizen engagement. One study found that local news and feature stories foster a sense of belonging and shared experience that prompted citizens to want to cooperate in working toward community health and prosperity (PEN America, 2019). Local news has also been shown to correlate with voters' knowledge and voter turnout.

In the 21st century, local news has been shrinking at an alarming rate, with one in every five newspapers that existed in 2003 having been shuttered by 2018. In fact, about 1,300 counties across the country lost their local news coverage between 2004 and 2018, according to a University of North Carolina study (Fulwood, 2018). Realistically, of course, the downsizing or loss of local news organizations is largely due to business factors beyond the control of any single group of journalists. The good news, as we discovered in Chapter 10, is that new models — many of which look nothing like a traditional newspaper — are emerging that offer hope for sustainability, both financially and journalistically.

Reversing the downward trend will be difficult, to say the least. Just the step of getting journalists to adopt a more citizen-centered approach, as we are advocating with this book, will in itself be difficult. But throughout this book, we've met journalists whose passion for this kind of journalism is instructive. For example, Jennifer Brandel, the founder of Hearken, whom we met in Chapter 7, found that local residents at first were skeptical when approached by journalists for their questions and ideas. By following through on people's curiosities, she found, journalists were able to convince them that their ideas and questions are important and deserve public communication.

Often the challenge lies in the deep-seated values of journalism's traditions. Sara Catania, the trainer for Solutions Journalism Network we met in Chapter 6, encountered resistance from old-school journalists who would dismiss solutions journalism as unethical "advocacy" journalism that took sides. The Solutions staff works hard to emphasize that the solutions that reporters write about are the result of rigorous investigative reporting, and that their purpose is to provide options for a community — not to support one particular proposal at the expense of others. Likewise, Ashley Alvarado, the community engagement director at KPCC in Pasadena, whom we met in Chapter 9, observed that "engagement journalism" is still being assigned "niche" status in many news organizations — a curiosity to be indulged as long as the publisher can afford it. She counters enthusiastically that in the future, every act of journalism will involve community engagement: "Just as all journalism is data journalism (once considered a niche for math-enabled reporters), all journalism is engagement journalism as well."

The most difficult challenges can be logistical: How does a news organization experiment with time-consuming projects like community listening when it barely has the personnel to cover the basics of local news? New Jersey News Commons, which we met in Chapter 6, is working hard to find solutions. As one example, it awards small grants to news organizations to participate in citizen meetings or discussions; the grant is used to pay a freelance reporter to cover that "basic" meeting, game or event that the local outlet is obligated to cover.

Sometimes the challenge is with the newest aspects of relational journalism. Facilitating discussions among citizens, particularly when they don't particularly like each other, is one such challenge. Creative journalists at AL.com, with the Reckon platform, and at *The Texas Tribune*, with "This Is Your Texas," are making tremendous strides. Eve Pearlman and Jeremy Hay, the co-founders of Spaceship Media, whom we met in Chapter 8, insist that "dialog across difference" is essential to democratic deliberation. Without succeeding in dialogue, societies and communities are condemned to polarized dysfunction. "Once people stop villainizing 'the other,'" Pearlman told us, "deliberation is more likely to yield results. People just need practice talking to each other."

The work of this new brand of journalism is challenging, but it is having impact, even in its early days. The most obvious impact is on the practice of journalism. In only a few years, Hearken has seen its innovative techniques for drawing out citizens' questions grow from one public radio station in Chicago (WBEZ's "Curious City" program) to more than 250 news organizations nationwide. The New Jersey News Commons, as part of its experimentation with collaboration among news outlets, has created a set of resources for members, whose numbers have grown to 260, to develop and diversify their revenue plans, thereby lowering the chance of news deserts emerging in New Jersey. And often the shift in journalistic focus has an impact on the community itself. As just one example, *The Seattle Times*, a pioneer in solutions journalism, organized meetings with dissatisfied parents that led to reforms in the Seattle public schools' policies on detention and on recruitment into the program for gifted and talented children.

Now Is the Time

Throughout its history, American journalism has been remarkably adaptable. It has repeatedly responded to changes in communications technology, media economics and the civic culture. All three of those forces have undergone profound changes in the early years of the 21st century. Already, journalism is responding. In the civic realm, for example, social media have also given citizens an ability to "speak" to one another, more efficiently, more thoughtfully, more frequently and more publicly than at any time in history. Historian Michael Schudson's "monitorial citizens" haven't checked out of the public life but rather scan the information environment and tune in to those issues they feel socially or politically impact them or those they care about (Schudson, 1998, p. 311). In these cases, they are willing to align with others and work to effect change.

As we learned in Chapter 10, the economics that have threatened the very existence of journalism's 20th-century business model are being replaced by models that rely on a number of revenue streams and often bypass Wall Street entirely for their sustainability.

Journalism has benefited from technological change. The 21st century has brought some of the best reporting, analysis and visual presentation in journalism history, thanks in large part to the technologies available (as well as the now-ingrained ethos of evidence-based investigative reporting). Much of the great journalism we see today has been produced by online startups.

Journalism's success in these times of major change will depend on journalists who are curious, creative and adaptable. These are more likely to be younger journalists not wedded to the traditions and techniques of the previous century. Just as the circumstances around journalism are undergoing major transitions, so too are the nation's demographics. In 2018, the group known as Generation Z — those born after 1996 — became the most populous generation in American society. With 28 percent of the nation's population in 2020, this group outnumbers its three famous predecessors, the Millennials, Generation X, and the Baby Boomers. And in 2020, the oldest members of this group were 23 years old.

We look to the next generations of journalists for future leadership. It just so happens, for example, that the characteristics of the next generation up, Generation Z, align nicely with the needs of relational journalism.

This is the nation's first-ever truly digital-native generation. Generation Z members have never known a world without the World Wide Web or mobile phones. Social media and smartphones became prevalent when the oldest of this group were nine years old. As young adults, they are expert at both private and public communication on mobile platforms, and they are comfortable learning and adapting to whatever new digital platforms become available (Seemiller & Grace, 2016). They are more efficient at finding information than any previous generation has been.

Equally important, Generation Z values community and public communication. Much of their communication is social, as it often includes more than one recipient per message sent. Yet, according to Seemiller and Grace's research, they still say their preferred form of communication is face-to-face. They went to school with more collaborative forms of learning than previous generations, and they quite naturally collaborate online as well as in person. This combination bodes well for the multi-faceted community-building a new kind of journalism will require.

Generation Z is confident that it will "make a difference," especially as agents of social change (Seemiller & Grace, 2016). Fitting nicely with Schudson's views of the modern citizen, these young people see activism as issue-specific. They are unlikely to stay vigilant on a broad array of themes constantly but will rise to action when they see a need. Similarly, a relational journalist organizes work around specifically named shared, wicked problems and issues.

As for the gloomy state of the news business, Generation Z's traits again offer hope. Many in this group grew up when their families were struggling with the effects of the 2008 recession. The concepts of budget cuts and reductions in institutional services have always been a part of their lives. Accordingly, Generation Z members are more aware of financial insecurity — and want to avoid that in their own lives. They show unprecedented entrepreneurship: Seemiller and Grace found (2016) that 60 percent would rather be an entrepreneur than work for an employer's paycheck, and 72 percent intend to start their own business at some point in their lives. Given the need to reimagine journalism's sustainability scenarios, these traits cannot help but benefit the news business. The career path that dominated in the 20th century, where the journalist would aspire to a large news organization and then build a career there, is rare today. Indeed, in the journalists we interviewed for this book, we see abundant entrepreneurial energy. Several of the innovators we interviewed in 2018 and 2019 will have moved on to new challenges, often in the form of startup enterprises, by the time the book is in readers' hands. In this dynamic, we see the future of journalism's workforce.

Generation Z tends to see dysfunction in the current political system, and fewer of this group identify as members of the Republican or Democratic parties than any previous generation. Again, given the recent polarization in the two-party system nationally, this distance from party politics may well serve as an asset to community-building journalism. Also, more than one-third of Generation Z see themselves as future community leaders (Seemiller & Grace, 2016).

Generation Z values diversity and inclusion — another vital component of relational journalism. This group itself consists of 47 percent ethnic minorities (Pew Research Center, 2019), by far the most diverse generation in American history.

Media scholar Paul Mihailidis has developed, through his studies of recent changes in communication technologies and the civic culture, a theory of the "emerging citizen," as we discussed in Chapter 1. His emerging citizen not only dovetails with Schudson's view of today's "monitorial citizen," but it aligns with what Seemiller and Grace have discovered about Generation Z. Media communications have evolved into an ecosystem where the consumers can be producers, where public and private communications can be blended and where a single person posting a meme that goes viral can reach a greater global audience than the most-read article published in *The New York Times*. And Mihailidis' emerging citizen is best equipped to navigate successfully through this new ecosystem.

In his research, however, Mihailidis discovered a disconnect that presents a challenge to expectations that young adults can embrace relational journalism. Studying college students in the early 2010s, he found that while they used social media efficiently and frequently, they seldom saw much use for social media beyond tracking

BOX 11.1 Community Engagement: "The Future of Journalism"

When Alex Samuels was majoring in journalism, she never thought that, in her first job, she'd be spending most of her time in conversation with Texas citizens.

That first job was "community reporter" at *The Texas Tribune*, and in that role, Samuels became the first manager of "This Is Your Texas," a Facebook group for *Tribune* readers established in 2018. Using a technique the *Tribune* learned from Hearken, Samuels asks the group's 3,500 members each month: "What topics do we want to discuss?" She receives their ideas for three days and then announces the top four for a final vote. The winning topic becomes the "topic of the month" for "This Is Your Texas."

As moderator of the group, Samuels ensures that the comments are on-topic and civil. When an issue seems confusing, Samuels writes a background piece called a "Texplainer." Every now and then, the discussions reveal a trend or situation that deserves coverage as a story, but mostly "This Is Your Texas" is a way for Texans interested in state politics and government to connect with each other.

Samuels' work embodies all five principles we've explored in Part II of this book. She said she still spends about 40 percent of her work week reporting stories as a traditional reporter would, but she loves the new dimension of community engagement. She said she values the way citizens are included in the early stages of reporting stories, which also enables reporters to include "ordinary" people in stories that otherwise would include just politicians and other officials. She also likes the way "This Is Your Texas" creates unusually strong bonds among the members — and between the members and *The Texas Tribune* itself.

Samuels, whose age puts her on the generational border between Millennials and Generation Z,

FIGURE 11.1   Alex Samuels is a community reporter at *The Texas Tribune*.

(Photo by Paul Voakes.)

didn't learn community engagement in J-school, she said, but now she feels her new skills in listening and drawing people into public-affairs discussions are tools she'll use in any journalistic capacity. In fact, she said, she's convinced that "Community engagement is the future of journalism."

their friends' activities, posting pictures of themselves and friends, watching amusing videos, and keeping up on celebrity news. Not many saw that social media could function as the kind of communicative glue that holds communities together (just as mass media had done in the 20th century). There are certainly examples of social media triumphs: The Arab Uprising of 2010–2011, powered largely by citizens using social media, touched off a series of pro-democracy reforms throughout the Middle East. Protesters used social media to stop an arbitrary monthly fee on debit cards by

Bank of America and a sudden monthly fee hike at Netflix; and social media emerged as one of the most powerful tools in the 2008 presidential campaign of Barack Obama (Mihailidis, 2014).

The challenge of convincing young citizens that their social-media skills can also "drive public discourse" (Mihailidis, 2014, p. 154) is an important goal for schools and colleges, he writes, but educators alone cannot imbue that elevated spirit of citizenship in young people. He calls for backup from other societal institutions and networks. We believe journalism to be one of those. No one is better suited than young digital-savvy, media-literate journalists to welcome other young citizens into the process of (as Mihailidis would put it) curating, critiquing, contributing, collaborating and creating, in a public setting.

A Skill Set and a Mindset

What will this new style of journalism require of its practitioners to be successful? The journalists we interviewed for this book had some suggestions about what they considered to be the key skills journalists doing citizen-centered journalism ought to acquire as they prepare for this kind of work. They described a number of techniques and practices, but in each response, they pivoted fairly quickly to what we would call a mindset: a set of attitudes and perspectives that speak to the deeper purposes of relational journalism. First, the skill set:

- *Multimedia Skills.* Today's journalists should feel equally at home recording and editing video and audio, as well as shooting and editing digital photos. They should be skilled at writing in a number of different styles and lengths, from summary blurbs and teasers to long-form feature stories and profiles.

- *Non-Narrative Delivery.* As we saw with Spaceship Media (Chapter 8) and KPCC's Human Voter Guide (Chapter 9), journalists can sometimes answer a community's information needs best not with polished articles, photo essays or video packages but with more basic forms like lists, charts, graphs and any other kind of fact sheets.

- *Social Media Skills.* Journalists should feel confident using any app in the constantly evolving array of social-media platforms — both for learning from a community and for producing their own journalistic content.

- *Promotional Skills.* Journalists should know, at the very least, how to promote their own work on social media, and how to achieve optimal visibility on search engines. Some (but not all) of our interviewees urged young journalists to learn the basics of fund-raising for nonprofit work and even how to write a business plan.

BOX 11.2 Hearken's Founder on What She Didn't Learn in School, and How It Shaped Her Work

In this July 2016 speech, Jennifer Brandel, founder of Hearken (featured in Chapter 7), reveals personal insights about the journalism journey that led her to found one of the most innovative news organizations in the United States. She is grateful not to have to "unlearn" some habits others learned in journalism schools.

Here is the text of the presentation she gave, at the Entrepreneurial Journalism Educators Summit at CUNY (July 15, 2016): https://medium.com/we-are-hearken/7-things-i-never-learned-in-journalism-school-db63078618bf

To whet your appetite, a summary:

1. I never learned: Journalists are the only people who have smart questions that make for great stories. In other words, I never thought the public's questions were not as good or worthy as a journalist's questions.

2. I never learned: The public does not have a right to be involved in deciding which stories are produced on their behalf. Which is why with Curious City, we gave the public the opportunity to decide which story WBEZ journalists reported out.

3. I never learned: Members of the public should not be allowed to participate in reporting. Which is why with Curious City, we invited members of the public to physically accompany reporters in the field. They weren't just bystanders either. These nonjournalists were allowed to ask sources questions. Turns out they often had different and better questions than reporters, and they provided valuable input on which angle of the story was most interesting and relevant to them.

4. I never learned: the public's role in journalism is pure consumption. Which is why we treated audience members as individuals with valid ideas and insights we could learn from, instead of as data composed of clicks, shares or time on site.

5. I never learned: News consumers or "the audience" is composed of ignorant, angry people. Which is why at Curious City we gave audiences so much agency and power. Perhaps because I believe human beings are fundamentally noble and good and their personalities are dynamic, I never bought the idea that angry people in the comments section were representative of the whole audience, or that they were angry and unproductive all the time. I saw the audience members just as I saw journalists around me: knowledgeable, fascinating, complex individuals yearning for ways to find purpose, feel effective and make sense of the world.

6. I never learned: the job of being a journalist had to be extremely self-serious and devoid of joy. Which is why I was hell-bent on infusing all the work we did at Curious City with some degree of delight and acknowledgment of humanity. With Curious City, reporters were encouraged to loosen their collars and be more like who they were off the clock. We encouraged everyone to be creative, take risks and use the word "I" in reporting. And the result: These stories have a really welcoming and accessible tone.

7. I never learned: the news should focus on the most morally suspect or the most successful people in society. Which is why we picked stories with no obvious villain or hero. We didn't require every story to be centered on conflict. Instead, we positioned reporters and the members of the public as curious explorers of a mysterious and interesting world they yearned to understand.

- *Skills for Listening, and Sometimes Leading.* As we saw with innovators like Your Voice Ohio (Chapter 6), City Bureau in Chicago (Chapter 7) and Alabama

Media (Chapter 8), journalists can be called upon not only to listen actively and empathetically to citizens' concerns but sometimes to lead discussions, to bring order to a cascade of authentic expressions of concerns.

- *Collaborative Skills.* As we saw in Chapter 7, citizens educated or trained as journalists are not the only producers of useful information in a community's media ecosystem. Tomorrow's journalists will know how to collaborate, that is, how to identify which strengths each partner — especially a non-journalist partner — brings to the project and how best to maximize each partner's contribution.

But our sources were more excited to talk about a new set of values that can change journalism in a more fundamental way. We call this the mindset: the perspectives and attitudes that propel what we've been calling relational journalism. Here are a few of their suggestions:

- *A Passion for Democratic Practice and the Power of Citizenship.* This is perhaps the most basic element of the mindset. This requires a deep and honest commitment to the idea that the First Amendment should embolden free expression for all citizens for the purpose of their empowerment, and that trained journalists are uniquely positioned — and legally protected — to be the key facilitators of that empowerment. This kind of journalism casts away the 20th-century adherence to detached, robotic objectivity and instead embraces certain democratic values. It accepts that a journalist must have the energy and passion of an advocate — not an advocate for a particular cause, party or policy, but an advocate for the empowerment of citizens and their communities.

- *Willingness to Get Out.* This type of journalism must counteract the tendency in today's journalism to do every aspect of reporting and writing from a desk, with all the tools the smartphone and laptop have to offer. Those may be efficient, but they don't build the relationships or make the connections that journalists should be investing in. This requires engagement (even if masked and distanced to support public health) taking place out in the community.

- *Cultural Competence.* Tomorrow's journalist will seek out sources and ideas that may not automatically appear on journalists' radar and will accord such voices appropriate respect in ways that bridge the "faultlines" discussed in Chapter 6.

- *Patience.* We've been describing a process that doesn't fit well with the extractive demands of the traditional news cycle, which is ever-quickening. Journalism's compulsion, especially over the last 50 years, to publish the story as quickly as possible has hindered reporters' ability to understand more accurately how to meet a community's information needs and then to help bring citizens together in common cause. In the meetings organized by Your Voice Ohio (Chapter 6), for example, the citizens' conversations with reporters didn't amount to much of value in terms of the upcoming news cycle. But they did provide an abundance of story ideas to develop over the following weeks — not to mention abundant public evidence of the news media's commitment to ongoing listening.

- *A Sense of Partnership.* This approach also rejects the aspect of professionalism whereby journalists seek access to elites in order to share elites' values with a mass audience — and the assumption that they alone are skilled enough to tell these stories. Instead, journalists are more likely to be contributors, among many others, in an informational ecosystem. As such, they seek to be partners with citizens and citizen groups.

- *Alternatives to Conflict.* This journalism recognizes that when journalists gravitate first and foremost to elements of conflict in a story, over time citizens will become dispirited, having learned through the media that politics and policy formation are beset with intractable differences among warring factions. That attitude has not engendered citizens' trust in the media, in their institutions or in each other. As we saw in Chapter 6, solutions journalism is providing one example of how much more interest a story attracts when it hasn't stopped at the "this problem is awful" stage.

- *The Constancy of Change.* Several of the journalists we spoke to encouraged young journalists to embrace the likelihood that change will occur, and in some domains at an ever-faster pace. No one media platform or business model will dominate the media environment for long. No single job in journalism will become "the career."

- *The Search for the Ties That Bind.* Michelle Holmes, an early leader at AL.com in Birmingham, and Ashley Alvarado, one of KPCC's editors in Pasadena, both speak passionately about journalists' ability to identify the themes or values that residents of a place share, regardless of political ideology, ethnic origins or class distinctions. AL.com elicited beautiful paeans to life in Alabama, with audience members' adaptations of "Song of Myself." KPCC invites Southern California residents to tell their stories of "Unheard LA," which brings a bit of cohesion to a region that can seem as disparate as any place in the world. Neither project looks like journalism as anyone in the 20th century would know it, but it speaks to a mindset that seeks a foundation for the community building that precedes grassroots democratic action.

A Matter of Trust

And yet, it's only fair to ask: Even with a relational-journalism mindset, can the digitally skilled "emerging citizen" make a difference in journalism if most members of the public no longer trust journalism? Americans' trust in the media was on the decline in the 2010s, just as it had been in the previous four decades. But our purpose of this book has never been to resolve the national or global, ideology-driven debates over the legitimacy of journalism. We acknowledge that American journalism is undergoing one of its periodic transitions (this one more seismic than most), and, given the polarized state of national politics in the early 2020s, that a clearer path to improvement exists at the level of local communities. Fortunately, there is good news regarding trust in local media.

A Gallup poll in 2019 found that while only about 45 percent of Americans trust news media nationally, strong majorities agreed that local journalism is better than national journalism in providing information they can use in their daily life, and that local media report news without bias to a greater degree than national news. They also saw local journalists as far more trustworthy, caring, accurate and unbiased than national journalists (Mayer & Walsh, 2019). About 60 percent said the newspaper in their community is an important symbol of civic pride. In 2018, the Poynter Media Trust Survey had similar findings, especially that citizens' trust in local media is higher than it is for national media (Guess et al., 2018).

A 2016 study at the Pew Research Center found that civic activity often occurs hand-in-hand with strong local journalism. Researchers found that the more people consume the local news, the more likely they are to vote, feel attached to their communities, get involved in local politics and rate the quality of their community as high (Barthel et al., 2016).

The American Press Institute teamed up in 2018 with NORC, a social-science research program at the University of Chicago, to learn American citizens' views of the civic duties of citizens and media. Roughly three-fourths agreed that the press's role of holding political leaders accountable was either very important or extremely important. About three-fourths also agreed that questioning leaders — whether political leaders or community leaders — was very important or extremely important. Far fewer citizens felt confident that they themselves could make a positive impact on their community (American Press Institute, 2019). This suggests an opportunity for a bond between citizens and journalism: Citizens believe it is their duty — and the news media's duty — to question leaders and hold them accountable, at every level of public life in America. Why not tap into that attitude of support and work out ways for journalists and citizens to join forces, especially in the ways we have described in this book?

So there seems to be plenty of opportunity, at least at the local level, for people to start believing in a journalism that can become so necessary, so empowering and so interesting that audience members will pay to sustain it financially. We're skeptical that local successes are "scalable" in the business sense, but they certainly can be replicable. Some local successes may end up being successfully applied at regional levels, and a few of the most successful practices at regional levels may work for national media organizations. It's not out of the question.

Going Forward

More than 100 years ago, John Dewey, the social philosopher we met in Part I who believed that citizens had the wherewithal to band together to solve seemingly intractable problems, wrote this about the value of communication: "People live in a community by virtue of the things they have in common, and communication is the way in which they come to possess things in common" (Dewey, 1916, p. 4). The dynamics of public communication have become much more complex than in Dewey's time, but his observation seems incredibly relevant to communication and community in the 21st century. Communication is still just as vital as ever to democratic practice. But disinformation, misinformation, gossip, rumor and naïve inaccuracy now compete too easily with reliable information. And a community's system of news and information is no longer the exclusive purview of the news company hiring professional journalists. The newsletters, social-media feeds and blogs of individual activists, neighborhoods, civic organizations and institutions comprise an ecology of news that professional journalists contribute to — yet no longer dominate.

These are the same people and groups who are responsible, in every community, for making public life go well. Is it possible that the missions of journalism and citizenship are closely aligned? We believe so. Every act of democratic deliberation, from naming and framing problems to archiving what a community has collectively learned about those problems, depends on responsibly sharing reliable information. That's what journalists do. We all need people who are trained and committed to monitor those in power for abuses; to sift through the data in our information-overloaded environment to help us make sense of current events; to verify or debunk claims that have people wondering; to provide a respected platform for diverse citizens' voices to be heard, and to persist as an independent force that facilitates citizens' efforts to improve their communities' well-being.

But clearly, the late-20th-century model of journalism that blended sensationalism with detached objectivity was not serving democracy well. Politics, and the people driving politics, became dangerously polarized. *New York Times* columnist David Brooks wrote in 2020:

Everywhere I go I see systems that are struggling — school systems, housing systems, family structures, neighborhoods trying to bridge diversity.
These problems aren't caused by some group of intentionally evil people.
They exist because living through a time of economic, technological,
demographic and cultural transition is hard. Creating social trust across
diversity is hard.

Everywhere I go I see a process that is the opposite of group vs. group war.
It is gathering. It is people becoming extra active on the local level to repair
the systems in their lives. I see a great yearning for solidarity, an eagerness
to come together and make practical change. (Brooks, 2020, p. A27)

We believe that journalism should be at the core of what Brooks calls "gathering."
This project set out to discover what journalists have been doing in recent years to
rebuild trust in the profession, but in ways that also rebuild citizens' trust in their
own power to effect change.

We learned about dozens of projects, experiments and attitude changes that
offer hope of moving the profession, and the citizens they serve, to a better place.
We found particular wisdom in this regard from the editors at Zócalo Public Square.
The highest calling in journalism, founder Gregory Rodriguez told us, is to build a
democratic culture — a persistent, shared sense that no matter what the situation,
citizens have the ability to figure out a solution, if they can agree to come together
to hear and discuss new ideas.

No single idea or project we've described has emerged as the panacea. The challenge is far too complex, and the news ecosystems much too diverse, for that to be
the case. But we've seen that journalists are already committing to deeper listening,
to relationships with communities, to honest transparency, to collaborations with
citizens that utilize their wisdom, and to enhancing the community conversations
that are already under way. When those things happen, journalism can indeed build
civic capacity. In doing so, journalism will play a major role in restoring the health
of American democracy — one community at a time.

References

Agora Journalism Center. (2019, April 1). Building engagement: A report on supporting the practice of relational journalism. *University of Oregon*. https://agora.uoregon.edu/2019/04/01/building-engagement-a-report-on-supporting-the-practice-of-relational-journalism/

AL.com. (2014, September 12). Shape Alabama prison reform by considering and choosing the possible approach you favor. https://www.al.com/opinion/2014/09/alabama_prison_reform_approaches.html#incart_special-report

AL.com. (2015, January 1). After hundreds joined in deep deliberation, here are eight things you told us about prison reform. https://www.al.com/opinion/2014/12/after_hundreds_joined_in_thoug.html#incart_related_stories

Amditis, J. (2016, March 29). We're launching another collaborative reporting project. Join us. Center for Cooperative Media. https://medium.com/centerforcooperativemedia/we-re-launching-another-collaborative-reporting-project-d289b7cd73f7

American Press Institute. (2019, December 18). How the press and public can find common purpose. https://www.americanpressinstitute.org/publications/reports/survey-research/how-the-press-and-public-can-find-common-purpose/?utm_source=API+Need+to+Know+newsletter&utm_campaign=110a8c5903-EMAIL_CAMPAIGN_2019_12_18_01_02&utm_medium=email&utm_term=0_e3bf78af04-110a8e5903-45799665

Armour-Jones, S. (2019, September 19). Journalism grantmaking: New funding, models and partnerships to sustain and grow the field. *Media Impact Funders*. https://mediaimpactfunders.org/wp-content/uploads/2019/09/Journalism-report-for-web-hyperlinks-1.pdf

Aviv, R. (2013, March 4). Local Story: A community newspaper covers a national tragedy. *The New Yorker*. https://www.newyorker.com/magazine/2013/03/04/local-story

Barber, B. R. (1984). *Strong democracy: Participatory politics for a new age*. University of California Press.

Barthel, M., Holcomb, J., Mahone, J., & Mitchell, A. (2016, November 3). Civic engagement strongly tied to local news habits. *Pew Research Center*. https://www.journalism.org/2016/11/03/civic-engagement-strongly-tied-to-local-news-habits/

Belair-Gagnon, V., & Anderson, C. W. (2015). Citizen media and journalism. In R. Mansell, *The International Encyclopedia of Digital Communication and Society*. https://conservancy.umn.edu/handle/11299/182984

Benkelman, S. (2019). Getting it right: Strategies for truth-telling in a time of misinformation and polarization. American Press Institute. https://www.americanpressinstitute.org/publications/reports/strategy-studies/truth-telling-in-a-time-of-misinformation-and-polarization/

Blau, M. (2019, January 24). How Chicago's 'J-School of the Streets' is reinventing local news. Politico. https://www.politico.com/magazine/story/2019/01/24/city-bureau-local-journalism-training-school-chicago-what-works-next-224114

Blumler, J. G., & Gurevitch, M. (1995). *The crisis of public communication*. Routledge, 1995.

Bornstein, D., Martin, C., & Rosenberg, T. (2015). *Solutions Journalism Network annual report*. https://s3.amazonaws.com/sjn-static/reports/2015annualreport.pdf

Boyte, H. C. (2017). "Back to the people" journalism: Journalists as public storytellers. In A. Garman & H. Wasserman (Eds.), *Media and citizenship: Between marginalisation and participation* (pp. 72–89). HSRC Press.

Boyte, H. C. (2019, November 2). *A "We the People" Green New Deal: Building a movement of climate citizens (Paper presentation)*. The Green New Deal and the Future of Work in America, Arizona State University, Tempe, AZ, United States.

Brandel, J. (2019, April 23). Newsrooms are focused on innovating the distribution of news. The process, not so much. *We Are Hearken*. https://medium.com/we-are-hearken/search?q=brandel%20newsrooms%20are%20focused

Briggs, M. (2012). *Entrepreneurial journalism: How to build what's next for news*. SAGE/CQ Press.

Brooks D. (2020, February 21). Why Sanders will probably win the nomination. *The New York Times*, A27. https://www.nytimes.com/2020/02/20/opinion/bernie-sanders-win-2020.html

Brown, F., & Society of Professional Journalists Ethics Committee. (2011). *Journalism ethics: A casebook of professional conduct for news media* (4th ed.). Marion Street Press.

Buchanan, M. (2002). *Nexus: Small worlds and the groundbreaking science of networks*. W. W. Norton & Co.

Bugeja, M. (2008). *Living Ethics: Across Media Platforms*. Oxford University Press.

Bui, P. K. (2019, June 18). Redistributing power in communities through involved journalism. *The Membership Puzzle Project*. https://membershippuzzle.org/articles-overview/redistributing-power

Carey, J. (1995). The press, public opinion, and public discourse. In T. Glasser & C. Salmon (Eds.), *Public opinion and the communication of consent* (pp. 373–402). Guilford.

Carpenter, C. (1995). Unpublished memo to staff of *The Charlotte Observer*.

Catania, S. (2018a, October 28). Why I teach solutions journalism in college and grad school classrooms: It's a powerful antidote to negative news — and students want it. *Solutions Journalism Network*. https://thewholestory.solutionsjournalism.org/why-i-teach-solutions-journalism-in-college-and-grad-school-classrooms-e29543eb3347

Catania, S. (2018b, November 25). "I'm on fire to teach solutions journalism": How reporting on responses to problems can combat news fatigue among students, both as consumers and producers of news. *Solutions Journalism Network*. https://thewholestory.solutionsjournalism.org/im-on-fire-to-teach-solutions-journalism-dd71321ebaf3

Center for New Democratic Processes. (2021). About us. https://www.cndp.us/about-us/

Chen, W., & Thorson, E. (2019, May 13). Perceived individual and societal values of news and paying for subscriptions. *Journalism*. https://doi.org/10.1177/1464884919847792

Christakis, N. A., & Fowler, J. H. (2009). *Connected: The surprising power of our social networks and how they shape our lives*. Little, Brown & Co.

Christian, S. E. (2012). *Overcoming bias: A journalist's guide to culture & context*. Holcomb Hathaway Publishers.

Christians, C. G., Glasser, T. L., McQuail, D., Nordenstreng, K., & White, R. A. (2009). *Normative theories of the media: Journalism in democratic societies*. University of Illinois Press.

City Bureau. (2020a). Our mission. https://www.citybureau.org/our-mission

City Bureau. (2020b). Community engagement guidelines. https://www.citybureau.org/community-engagement-guidelines

Clark, R. P. (2016, June 3). Can "public journalism" reform campaign coverage? The Poynter Institute. https://www.poynter.org/reporting-editing/2016/campaign-coverage-is-a-mess-to-fix-it-we-should-look-to-the-past/

Collins, J. (2011). *Good to great and the social sectors: A monograph to accompany good to great*. Harper Business.

Commission on Freedom of the Press. (1947). *A free and responsible press* (2nd ed.). University of Chicago Press.

Constitution of the United States. (1995). Applewood Books. (Original work published 1787)

Constructive Journalism Project. (2015, June 23). What is constructive journalism? https://www.constructivejournalism.org/about/

Daly, C. B. (2018). *Covering America: A narrative history of a nation's journalism* (2nd ed.). University of Massachusetts Press.

Dewey, J. (1916). *Democracy and education*. Simon & Brown.

Dewey, J. (1954). *The public and its problems*. Swallow Press. (Work originally published 1927)

Downie, L., Jr., & Kaiser, R. G. (2002). *The news about the news: American journalism in peril*. Alfred A. Knopf.

Dzur, A. W. (2018). *Rebuilding public institutions together: Professionals and citizens in a participatory democracy*. Cornell University Press.

Edmonds, R. (2019, November 4). As other local news outlets struggle, NPR affiliates are growing — and quickly. Poynter Institute. https://www.poynter.org/business-work/2019/as-other-local-news-outlets-struggle-npr-affiliates-are-growing-and-quickly/

Fording, R., & Schram, S. (2017). The cognitive and emotional sources of Trump support: The case of low-information voters. *New Political Science, 39*(4), 670–686.

Foreman, G. (2016). *The ethical journalist: Making responsible decisions in the digital age* (2nd ed.). Wiley Blackwell.

Fulwood, S., III. (2018, October 17). As "news deserts" widen across America, communities and civic engagement fray. *Think Progress*. https://thinkprogress.org/news-deserts-widen-across-america-new-study-037965b22dc6/

Gardner, H., Csikszentmihalyi, M., & Damon, W. (2001). *Good work: When excellence and ethics meet*. Basic Books.

Glaser, M. (2006, September 27). Your guide to citizen journalism. *MediaShift*. http://mediashift. org/2006/09/your-guide-to-citizen-journalism270/

Grieco, E. (2018, November 2). Newsroom employees are less diverse than U.S. workers overall. Pew Research Center. https://www.pewresearch.org/fact-tank/2018/11/02/ newsroom-employees-are-less-diverse-than-u-s-workers-overall/

Grieco, E. (2019, July 9). U.S. newsroom employment has dropped a quarter since 2008, with greatest decline at newspapers. *Editor & Publisher*. https://www.editorandpublisher.com/ stories/us-newsroom-employment-has-dropped-a-quarter-since-2008-with-greatest-de- cline-at-newspapers,3673?

Guess, A., Nyhan, B., & Reifler, J. (2018, August 10). All media trust is local? Findings from the 2018 Poynter Media Trust Survey. (Unpublished manuscript). Dartmouth University. http:// www.dartmouth.edu/~nyhan/media-trust-report-2018.pdf

Gutmann, A., & Thompson, D. (2004). *Why deliberative democracy?* Princeton University Press.

Haagerup, U. (2017). *Constructive news: How to save the media and democracy with journalism of tomorrow*. Aarhus University Press.

Habermas, J. (1991). *The structural transformation of the public sphere: An inquiry into a category of bourgeois society*. MIT Press.

Haeg, A. (2017). GroundSource CEO Andrew Haeg on the engagement cycle. https://www.wib- bitz.com/blog/groundsource-ceo-andrew-haeg-on-the-engagement-cycle/

Hansen, E., & Holcomb, J. (2020, January). Local news initiatives run into a capital shortage. *Nieman Lab*. https://www.niemanlab.org/2020/01/local-news-initiatives-run-into-a-capi- tal-shortage/?utm_source=Pew+Research+Center&utm_campaign=000f386a7e-EMAIL_ CAMPAIGN_2020_01_06_02_22&utm_medium=email&utm_term=0_3e953b9b70-000f 386a7e-399348541

Hauser, G. A., & Benoit-Barne, C. (2002). Reflections on rhetoric, deliberative democracy, civil society, and trust. *Rhetoric and Public Affairs* 5 (2), 261–275. https://doi.org/10.1353/ rap.2002.0029

Inc.com. (2020). Cooperatives. *The Inc.com encyclopedia*. https://www.inc.com/encyclopedia/ cooperatives.html

Ingram, M. (2011, December 15). Defining journalism is a lot easier said than done. *GigaOm*. https://gigaom.com/2011/12/15/defining-journalism-is-a-lot-easier-said-than-done/

International Fact-Checking Network. (2019). Fred Fact doesn't fall for fake news. Poynter Institute. https://factcheckingday.com/assets/files/hs2xhbfskr.pdf

Jackson, S. (2019, March 22). Journalism schools find new approaches to covering under- represented audiences. *Insight into Diversity*. https://www.insightintodiversity.com/ journalism-schools-find-new-approaches-to-covering-underrepresented-audiences/

Jarvis, J. (2014). *Geeks bearing gifts: Imagining new futures for news*. CUNY Journalism Press.

Kennedy, D. (2013). *The wired city: Reimagining journalism and civic life in the post-newspaper age*. University of Massachusetts Press.

Kennedy, Dan (2020, January 27). Can perennial hopes for local news co-ops ever turn into reality? *Nieman Lab*. https://www.niemanlab.org/2020/01/can-perennial-hopes-for-local-news-co-ops-

ever-turn-into-reality/?utm_source=Pew+Research+Center&utm_campaign
=840c90b76b-EMAIL_CAMPAIGN_2020_01_27_02_18&utm_medium=email&utm_term=0
_3e953b9b70-840c90b76b-399348541

Kettering Foundation. (2011). *Naming and framing difficult issues to make sound decisions.* Charles F. Kettering Foundation.

Knight Commission on Trust, Media and Democracy. (2019). *Crisis in democracy: Renewing trust in America.* Aspen Institute.

Kovach, B., & Rosenstiel, T. (2014). *The elements of journalism: What newspeople should know and the public should expect* (3rd ed.). Three Rivers Press.

Lambeth, E. B., Meyer, P. E., & Thorson, E. (1998). *Assessing public journalism.* University of Missouri Press.

Lehrman, S. (2019). Diversity toolbox: How to cross your "faultlines." Society of Professional Journalists. https://www.spj.org/dtb2.asp

Leslie, G. (2009, Fall). Who is a "journalist"? *The News Media and the Law, 4.*

Liebling, A. J. (1960, May 14). The wayward press. *The New Yorker, 109.*

Mansbridge, J. (2012). Everyday talk in the deliberative system. In D. Barker, N. McAfee, & D. McIvor, *Democratizing deliberation: a political theory anthology* (pp. 211–239). Kettering Foundation Press.

Mathews, D. (2002). *For communities to work.* Kettering Foundation Press.

Mathews, D. (2014). *The ecology of democracy: Finding ways to have a stronger hand in shaping our future.* Kettering Foundation Press.

Mayer, J., and Walsh, L. (2019). A collection of research. *Trusting News.* https://docs.google.com/presentation/d/16g86ZoMErxJfMVIMyXYoNIC6sveIocTtHBF4PLoonqI/edit#slide=id.g6cc4a8dfdf_0_0

McBride, K., & Rosenstiel, T. (2014). *The new ethics of journalism: Principles for the 21st century.* SAGE/CQ Press.

Merritt, D. (1995). *Public journalism and public life: Why telling the news is not enough.* Lawrence Erlbaum.

Merritt, D. (2005). *Knightfall: Knight Ridder and how the erosion of newspaper journalism is putting democracy at risk.* AMACOM (American Management Association).

Mihailidis, P. (2014). *Media literacy and the emerging citizen: Youth, engagement and participation in digital culture.* Peter Lang.

Mihailidis, P. (2018). *Civic media literacies: Re-imagining human connection in an age of digital abundance.* Routledge.

Miller, S. (2019). Citizen journalism. *The Oxford research encyclopedia of communication.* DOI: 10.1093/acrefore/9780190228613.013.786. https://oxfordre.com/communication/view/10.1093/acrefore/9780190228613.001.0001/acrefore-9780190228613-e-786

Morgan, F. (2019). A guide to assessing your local news ecosystem: A toolkit to inform grantmaking and collaboration. *Democracy Fund.* www.ecosystems.democracyfund.org

Murray, C., & Stroud, N. (2019). The keys to powerful solutions journalism. Center for Media Engagement, University of Texas at Austin. https://mediaengagement.org/research/powerful-solutions-journalism/?utm_source=API+Need+to+Know+newsletter&utm_

campaign=0a20798e90-EMAIL_CAMPAIGN_2019_08_22_12_20&utm_medium=email&utm_term=0_e3bf78af04-0a20798e90-45799665

Nesbitt, M., & Glaspie, R. (2004). A guide to the *New Readers* culture report. Readership Institute at Media Management Center, Northwestern University. https://www.yumpu.com/en/document/read/50112472/quick-guide-to-the-new-readers-culture-report-readership-institute

Nip, J. Y. M. (2010). Routinization of charisma: The institutionalization of public journalism online. In J. Rosenberry & B. St. John III (Eds.), *Public journalism 2.0: The promise and reality of a citizen-engaged press.* (pp. 135–148). Routledge.

Ober, J. (2008). The original meaning of "democracy": Capacity to do things, not majority rule. *Constellations* 15(1), 3–9.

Online News Association. (2016). Diversity. https://ethics.journalists.org/topics/diversity/

Owen, L. H. (2019, October 23). I've got a story idea for you: Storyful's new investigative reporting unit helps publishers dig into social media. *Nieman Lab.* https://www.niemanlab.org/2019/10/ive-got-a-story-idea-for-you-storyfuls-new-investigative-reporting-unit-helps-publishers-dig-into-social-media/?utm_source=Pew+Research+Center&utm_campaign=dc7bfe3fc5-EMAIL_CAMPAIGN_2019_10_24_01_36&utm_medium=email&utm_term=0_3e953b9b70-dc7b-fe3fc5-39934854

Oxford University Press. (2016). Relational communication. *Dictionary of media and communication.* Oxford University Press. https://www.oxfordreference.com/view/10.1093/oi/authority.20110803100412531

Park University. (2020). Peace journalism: An introduction. https://www.park.edu/wp-content/uploads/2018/01/PJ-An-Introduction-3.pdf

Peck, C. (1997, December). Cover letter accompanying The Spokesman-Review's "Soapbox: A guide to civic journalism."

PEN America. (2019). *Losing the news: The decimation of local journalism and the search for solutions.* https://pen.org/wp-content/uploads/2019/12/Losing-the-News-The-Decimation-of-Local-Journalism-and-the-Search-for-Solutions-Report.pdf

Pew Research Center. (2019, July 9). Newspapers fact sheet. https://www.journalism.org/fact-sheet/newspapers/

Rosen, J. (1999). *What are journalists for?* Yale University Press.

Rosenberry, J., & St. John, B., III. (2010). Introduction: Public journalism values in an age of media fragmentation. In J. Rosenberry & B. St. John III (Eds.), *Public journalism 2.0: The promise and reality of a citizen-engaged press* (pp. 1–8). Routledge.

ross, jesikah maria. (2020). *JMR's participatory journalism playbook: A field guide to listening and reporting with communities.* Listening Post Collective. https://internews.org/sites/default/files/2020-07/JMR_playbook_07-10-20_V3.pdf

Safford, S. (2009). *Why the garden club couldn't save Youngstown: The transformation of the Rust Belt.* Harvard University Press.

Saunders, H. H. (2005). *Politics is about relationship: A blueprint for the citizens' century.* Palgrave Macmillan.

Schaffer, J. (2015, December 21). Journalism as relationship building. *NiemanLab.* https://www.niemanlab.org/2015/12/journalism-as-relationship-building/

Schudson, M. (1998). *The good citizen: A history of American civic life.* The Free Press.

Seemiller, C., & Grace, M. (2016). *Generation Z goes to college*. Jossey-Bass.

Shapiro, I. (2014). Why democracies need a functional definition of journalism now more than ever. *Journalism Studies, 15*(5), 555–565.

Shirky, C. (2010, April 1). The collapse of complex business models. Blog post at Shirky.com (no longer available).

Silverman, C., & Tsubaki, R. (2019). Educator's guide: Types of online fakes. *Verification Handbook*. https://verificationhandbook.com/additionalmaterial/types-of-online-fakes.php

Society of Professional Journalists. (2020). Diversity Toolbox. https://www.spj.org/dtb.asp

Solutions Journalism. (2020). Who We Are. https://www.solutionsjournalism.org/who-we-are/mission

Stanford University, Center for the Study of Language and Information (CSLI). (2006). Citizenship. *Stanford encyclopedia of philosophy*. https://plato.stanford.edu/entries/citizenship/

Stark, K. (2019, March 2). How do you find out if your neighborhood is contaminated with lead pollution? WBEZ Chicago. https://www.wbez.org/stories/how-do-you-find-out-if-your-neighborhood-is-contaminated-with-lead-pollution/156e3042-56e4-425d-a6a8-a7345aed1c6e

Stearns, J. (2014, November 10). 5 kinds of listening for newsrooms and communities. *American Press Institute*. https://www.americanpressinstitute.org/need-to-know/try-this-at-home/5-kinds-listening-newsrooms-communities/

Stehle, V. (2020, March 26). In the Covid-19 crisis, philanthropy's investment in local news pays off. *The Chronicle of Philanthropy*. https://www.philanthropy.com/article/In-the-Covid-19-Crisis/248347?utm_source=Pew+Research+Center&utm_campaign=9d021092df-EMAIL_CAMPAIGN_2020_03_27_01_44&utm_medium=email&utm_term=0_3e953b9b70-9d021092df-399348541

Texas Tribune. (2019). *Annual report*. https://static.texastribune.org/media/files/27687dd795d6aa7c250e829bc3933a56/TT-2019-Annual-Report-021220.pdf?_ga=2.190014635.1487659769.1588002315-379715003.1584131918

Tocqueville, A. de. (2002). *Democracy in America* (H. C. Mansfield & D. Winthrop, Trans. & Eds.). University of Chicago Press. (Original work published 1835, 1840)

USLegal.com. (2020). Non profit corporation law and legal definition. *U.S. Legal.com*. https://definitions.uslegal.com/n/non-profit-corporation/

Ward, S. J. A. (2009). Truth and objectivity. In L. Wilkins & C. G. Christians (Eds.), *The handbook of mass media ethics* (pp. 71–83). Routledge.

Warren, A. (2017, October 16). The rise and fall of the citizen journalist. *MinuteHack*. https://minutehack.com/opinions/the-rise-and-fall-of-the-citizen-journalist

Weaver, D. H., Beam, R. A., Brownlee, B. J., Voakes, P. S., & Wilhoit, G. C. (2007). *The American journalist in the 21st century: U.S. news people at the dawn of a new millennium*. Lawrence Erlbaum.

Weaver, D. H., Willnat, L., & Wilhoit, G. C. (2018, July 4). The American journalist in the digital age: Another look at U.S. news people. *Journalism & Mass Communication Quarterly, 96*(1), 101–130. https://doi.org/10.1177/1077699018778242

West, S. R. (2014). Press exceptionalism. *Harvard Law Review 127*, 2434–2462.

Wihbey, J. P. (2019). *The social fact: News and knowledge in a networked world*. The MIT Press.

Wimmer, K. (2014, June 1). A poison pill for the federal shield law. *Huffington Post*. https://www.huffpost.com/entry/a-poison-pill-for-the-fed_b_5065174

Yankelovich, D. (1991). *Coming to public judgment: Making democracy work in a complex world*. 1991. Syracuse University Press.

Zahay, M. L., Jensen, K., Xia, Y., & Robinson, S. (2020, September 20). The labor of building trust: Traditional and engagement discourses for practicing journalism in a digital age. *Journalism & Mass Communication Quarterly*. DOI: 10.1177/1077699020954854

Zócalo Public Square. (2019). Mission Statement. https://www.zocalopublicsquare.org/mission/

Zuckerman, E. (2018, May 30). Protected: Six or seven things social media can do for democracy. www.ethanzuckerman.com/blog/2018/05/30/six-or-seven-things-social-media-can-do-for-democracy

Index

democratic practices, 29

democratic professionalism, 62, 63

democratic system journalism, 85

detached outsider, 72

Deuze, Mark, 21

developmental journalism, 56, 57

Dewey, J., 14, 24

The Devil Strip, 96

dialogue journalism, 55–57, 83, 124, 125

Dictionary of Media and Communication (Oxford University Press), 37

digital advertising, 158

digital communication, 2
  antidemocracy effects of, 21

digital communications, 20

diversity, 41–42

Downie Jr., Leonard, 48

Drag Queen Story Hour, 1

Dukes, Jesse, 109

Dzur, Albert, 62

E

economics of print news industry, 154

ecosystem of news and information, 69

The Economist, 65

Emergent Digital Media, 157

The Elements of Journalism, 139

emerging citizens, 2, 20–21, 178

engaged journalism, 56

entrepreneurial citizen, 20–21

Entrepreneurial Journalism Educators Summit at CUNY, 181

entrepreneurship, 11

Essential Partners, 132

Ethnic Media, 157

Everyday Democracy, 132

extractive journalism, 38, 63

extractive journalists, 73

extractive or transactional listening, 114

F

Facebook, 19, 163, 170

facilitative journalism, 34–36

fact-checking, tips for, 142–143

FactStacks, 125

fairness, 144–145

fake news, 112

falsehood, 143

faultlines, 99, 146

"Feeding the Conversation" community meetings, 138

Find Common Ground, 37

5Ws and H, 118

five-minute stories, 1

For Communities to Work (Mathews), 128

Foreman, Gene, 141, 149

for-profit news organizations, 158

Fourth Estate of government, 147

Fox News, 18

framing, 39

Franklin Pierce University's New England Center for Civic Life, 132

freedom of press, 31–32, 80

G

Ganz, Marshall, 16

gatekeeping function, 17

gateway questions, 128

Generation X, 177

Generation Z, 5, 103, 177–178

Glasser, Theodore, 30

good work, 15, 16, 25

Good Work: When Excellence and Ethics Meet (Gardner et al.), 15

Google, 163, 170

government funding for journalism, 170–171

GroundSource, 82

guided citizen reporting, 71–72, 81

Guide to Crafting Great Questions, 118

About the Authors

Paula Lynn Ellis

Paula Ellis, a former senior media executive, foundation executive and journalist, has long been a leader in journalism innovation, transformative change and community engagement.

Ellis has a bachelor's degree in government and politics from the University of Maryland, where she was editor of the student daily recognized as the nation's best by the Society of Professional Journalists. She has a master's degree in journalism from Northwestern University.

She began her career as a metropolitan newspaper journalist. In 1980, at the (Gary, Ind.) *Post-Tribune*, she joined Knight Ridder Inc., for decades one of the nation's largest, most respected news organizations. She worked for Knight Ridder for 26 years, as a reporter, editor, managing editor, publisher and eventually corporate vice president for operations, where she was responsible for 15 newspaper/internet operations when the company was sold in 2006. *The Sun News* in Myrtle Beach was Knight-Ridder's top performing news organization for five of the seven years she led it. As a news executive, Ellis was at the forefront of the coaching writers' movement, newsroom organizational redesign and the public journalism movement of the 1990s. A Harvard Business School case study in the mid-1990s explored her early work in transitioning *The State* newspaper in Columbia, South Carolina, to digital. As an editor at Knight Ridder's Washington Bureau, Ellis steered the coverage of such historic events as the end of the Cold War and the demise of Gary Hart's 1988 presidential bid.

In 2006 she became vice president for strategic initiatives at the Knight Foundation, where she led transformative change efforts in journalism and communities, national grantmaking and evaluation.

Throughout her career as a news, corporate and civic leader, Ellis developed deep experience in national and community issues. This work shaped ideas about community well-being that would evolve into the groundbreaking "Soul of the Community" research with Gallup at the Knight Foundation.

Ellis is a trustee of the Poynter Institute and a director of the National Conference on Citizenship. She is also a senior associate with the Kettering Foundation, where she works with the program team to research innovations in journalism, philanthropy and communities aimed at making democracy work as it should.

She is president of Paula Ellis and Associates, a consulting firm headquartered in Charleston, South Carolina, where she lives with her husband Gary Galloway, a retired journalist.

Paul S. Voakes

Paul Voakes is a professor emeritus at the College of Media, Communication and Information at the University of Colorado Boulder. He has a bachelor's degree in political science from the University of California at Davis; a master's in journalism from the University of California at Berkeley and a Ph.D. in mass communication from the University of Wisconsin-Madison. Voakes served on the faculty of the School of Journalism at Indiana University from 1994 to 2003, when he became dean of the University of Colorado's School of Journalism & Mass Communication. After the school was reorganized into the new college, Voakes served as founding chair of the Department of Journalism, until his retirement in 2018.

IMG 0.2

Voakes has held leadership roles in the Association for Education in Journalism and Mass Communication (AEJMC) since 1998, and he was elected president for the 2016–2017 term. As president he launched efforts to build bridges between media scholarship and the media professions. He is a co-author of *The American Journalist in the 21st Century: U.S. News People at the Dawn of a New Millennium*, which received the Sigma Delta Chi Book Award from the Society of Professional Journalists in 2007, and *Working with Numbers and Statistics: A Handbook for Journalists*. His research has appeared in numerous scholarly journals, including *Journalism & Mass Communication Quarterly*, *Journal of Mass Media Ethics*, *Newspaper Research Journal*, *Communication Law & Policy*, and *Journalism & Mass Communication Educator*. He is the recipient of the Harold L. Nelson Alumni Award for Achievement in Mass Communication Research (2010, University of Wisconsin) and AEJMC's Nafziger-White Dissertation Award (1996). Voakes has taught news writing, multimedia reporting, media law, media ethics, news editing, math and statistics for journalists, and journalism in film. He won numerous teaching awards at Indiana and Colorado.

Before entering academia in 1990, he was a journalist for 15 years at newspapers in the San Francisco Bay Area including the (San Jose) *Mercury News*. In 2012 he served as a Fulbright Specialist, teaching journalism and mentoring faculty at Makerere University in Kampala, Uganda.

He lives in Boulder, Colorado, with his wife, Barbara.

Lori Bergen

Lori Bergen is founding dean of the College of Media, Communication and Information at the University of Colorado Boulder, where she holds the James E. de Castro Chair in Global Media Studies. As leader of CU Boulder's first new college in more than 50 years, Bergen's focus is on the interdisciplinary approach to media, communication and information education.

Bergen came to Colorado from Marquette University, where she was dean of the J. William and Mary Diederich College of Communication and the William R. Burleigh and E.W. Scripps Professor. There she was instrumental in developing the O'Brien Fellowship in Public Service Journalism and the Milwaukee Neighborhood News Service, an online journalism project covering underreported urban neighborhoods. Bergen held faculty appointments at Texas State, Wichita State and Kansas State universities and worked as a journalist in Kansas, Indiana and California. She earned a bachelor's degree in history and political science and a master's degree in journalism and mass communication from Kansas State University and a PhD in mass communication with a minor in organizational behavior from Indiana University-Bloomington.

Bergen is a member of the Poynter Institute's Board of Trustees and was president of the Association for Education in Journalism and Mass Communication. Along with Kettering Foundation Senior Associate Paula Ellis, Bergen created an AEJMC Presidential Initiative to support research in relationships between journalism education and practice with citizenship, communities and democracy in the digital age. She is a member of Page, the professional association for corporate communications executives and educators, and served on the Accrediting Council on Education in Journalism and Mass Communication. Bergen received the Scripps Howard Foundation Journalism and Mass Communication Administrator of the Year in 2014.

Bergen is co-author of the book *Media Violence and Aggression: Science and Ideology*, published by SAGE in 2008. She was a contributor to *The American Journalist, A Portrait of U.S. News People and Their Work*, by D. Weaver and G. Wilhoit, and her research has appeared in *Newspaper Research Journal*, the *Journal of Advertising, American Behavioral Scientist*, and *Human Communication Research*.

Bergen and her husband, Charles Mangano, live in Boulder.

CPSIA information can be obtained
at www.ICGtesting.com
Printed in the USA
FSHW022104240921
85012FS